The *ESSENTIAL* Guide to

BLACK CAN

D1474605

of the GUNNISON
NATIONAL
PARK

Includes
Curecanti National
Recreation Area
and
Gunnison Gorge National
Conservation Area

John Jenkins

The Colorado Mountain Club Press
Golden, Colorado

Published by *The Colorado Mountain Club Press.* Founded in 1912, the *Colorado Mountain Club* is the largest outdoor recreation, education and conservation organization in the Rocky Mountains. Look for our books at your favorite book seller or contact us for a catalog at: 710 10th Street, Suite 200, Golden, CO 80401, (303) 996-2743, Email address: *cmcpress@cmc.org*, Website: *www.cmc.org*

Managing Editor for CMC Press: *Terry Root.*
Layout, Illustration and Maps: *Terry Root* and *Steve Meyers.*
Proofing: *Joyce Carson* and *Linda Grey.*
Front cover photo: by *John Jenkins.*
Front cover inset photo and title page photo: by *Mike Endres.*
Back cover photos: by (l to r) *Allen Russell/Index Stock Imagery, Terry Root, Mike Endres, Todd Caudle/Skyline Press.*
For a complete list of credits for photographs in this book, see page 238.
Special thanks to *Todd Caudle* at *www.skylinepress.com* for use of his photographs.
Additional contributors: *Michael Bateman* (chapter on mountain biking), *Monty McCord* (hiking description for the North Vista Trail), *Paul Zaenger* (Foreword) and *Dale Carter* (chapter on rock climbing.)
Copyright 2004 by Colorado Mountain Club Press.

The Essential Guide to Black Canyon of the Gunnison National Park
by John Jenkins
Library of Congress Control Number: 2004101991
ISBN # 0-9724413-4-4

We gratefully acknowledge the financial support of the people of Colorado through the Scientific and Cultural Facilities District of greater metropolitan Denver, for our publishing activities.

SCFD
Scientific & Cultural
Facilities District
Making It Possible

Curecanti National
Recreation Area

*Painted Wall from
near Chasm View*

ACKNOWLEDGEMENTS:

Special thanks to **Paul Zaenger**, Chief of Interpretation, Black Canyon of the Gunnison National Park, for his assistance with sections on climbing, hiking, camping, facilities, ranger programs, and more.

Thanks to **Greg Holden**, Geology Professor at the Colorado School of Mines, who for two days taught park personnel, and the author, the complicated geologic history of the Black Canyon.

Thanks to **Mike Schene**, of the National Park Service in Lakewood, Colorado, for his support and assistance with research and introductions to the people at the Black Canyon, who so admirably manage the park and Curecanti National Recreation Area. Also thanks to the staff of the Bureau of Land Management in Montrose, Colorado who offered so much assistance for information on the Gunnison Gorge National Conservation Area.

A special notice should be given to **Berle Clemensen** for consistent support and excellent advice in research and writing.

DEDICATED TO:

Laurie Stanton and Shirley and Harvey Doidge for ongoing support and motivation.

Special mention is made of **Abbott Fay**, a leading Colorado historian and history professor, who taught the author research and writing skills.

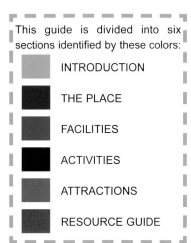

This guide is divided into six sections identified by these colors:

INTRODUCTION

THE PLACE

FACILITIES

ACTIVITIES

ATTRACTIONS

RESOURCE GUIDE

TABLE OF CONTENTS

INTRODUCTION

THE PLACE

FACILITIES

ACTIVITIES

THINGS TO DO (continued)

HIKING (continued)

ATTRACTIONS

RESOURCE GUIDE

MAP LEGEND

ELEVATION TINTS:

The maps in this guide are tinted by the colors shown below, to indicate the approximate elevation above sea level in feet. Tinted contour intervals are 500 feet apart and range from a low of 5,000' above sea level to a maximum of over 9,000'.

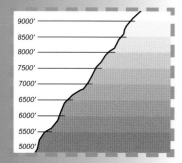

ABBREVIATIONS USED:

The maps in this guide use the following abbreviations:

CO (Colorado highway)
CR (County road)
FSR (Forest Service road)
FST (Forest Service trail)
Rd. (road)
Cr. (creek)
CG (campground)

USGS 7.5 MIN. QUADS:

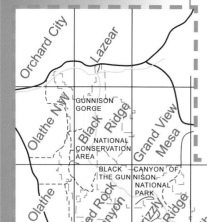

SYMBOLS USED ON MAPS IN THIS GUIDE:

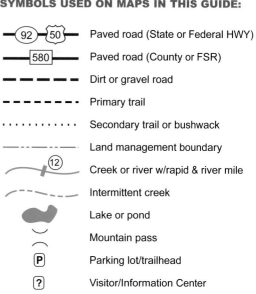

92 — 50	Paved road (State or Federal HWY)
580	Paved road (County or FSR)
— — —	Dirt or gravel road
- - - -	Primary trail
· · · ·	Secondary trail or bushwack
————	Land management boundary
(12)	Creek or river w/rapid & river mile
~ ~ ~	Intermittent creek
●	Lake or pond
◡	Mountain pass
P	Parking lot/trailhead
?	Visitor/Information Center
$	Entrance station
🛇	Picnic area
⚓	Marina
Boat launch ramp
X	River access site
△	Campground
△	Campsite (water access)
△	Campsite (land access)
📷	Point of interest
○	City or townsite
Piped water
WC	Restroom or outhouse
♿	Wheelchair accessible

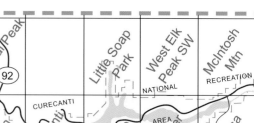

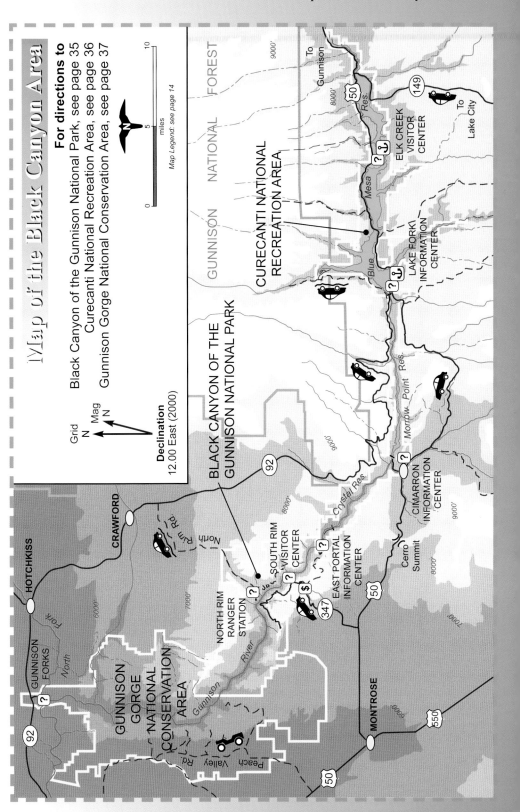

Map of the Black Canyon Area

For directions to

Black Canyon of the Gunnison National Park, see page 35
Curecanti National Recreation Area, see page 36
Gunnison Gorge National Conservation Area, see page 37

Map Legend: see page 14

Grid N   Mag N

Declination
12.00 East (2000)

GUNNISON   NATIONAL   FOREST

CURECANTI NATIONAL
RECREATION AREA

BLACK CANYON OF THE
GUNNISON NATIONAL PARK

GUNNISON GORGE
NATIONAL
CONSERVATION
AREA

HOTCHKISS

GUNNISON FORKS

CRAWFORD

North Rim Rd.

NORTH RIM RANGER STATION

SOUTH RIM VISITOR CENTER

EAST PORTAL INFORMATION CENTER

CIMARRON INFORMATION CENTER

LAKE FORK INFORMATION CENTER

ELK CREEK VISITOR CENTER

Cerro Summit

MONTROSE

To Gunnison

To Lake City

Peach Valley Rd.

Gunnison River

North Fork

Crystal Res.

Morrow Point Res.

Blue Mesa Res.

6000'
7000'
8000'
9000'

50
92
347
550
149
50

THE BIG WOW

by Paul L. Zaenger
Interpretive Ranger, National Park Service

Nothing can prepare you for the drama of the Black Canyon of the Gunnison. Upon first seeing it, people will sometimes drop their jaws as they gaze into its depths. Their hearts race, their eyes well up, and they are left speechless by the scene. Some rangers on the staff here at Black Canyon of the Gunnison National Park refer to such emotions as "The Big Wow."

The head of the Gunnison River is at Almont, Colorado where the Taylor and East Rivers come dancing out of the mountains, and are joined by a host of other streams and rivers bringing waters from the melting snows on high. In spring and early summer, the flooding Gunnison is a sight to behold, especially knowing that it was this force that wrought the canyon. When at the river, you can feel the power of this natural force. You can drive or hike to the river. Either way, experiencing this lifeblood of the canyon is an important part of understanding the wonder of this park.

Soaring eagles, dashing swifts, ambling deer, and slumbering marmots, along with many other species can be seen along the rims. The sea of Gambel oak and serviceberry covers most of the rims, adding a rich green of life in the summer, and painting the canyon with rich hues of amber, scarlet, crimson and ginger in the fall. At the western end of the park, the oaks give way to pinyon pine and juniper trees. Walking along trails here in the early morning brings out the rich aroma of the pine, and the incense of the juniper.

Look down into the canyon and you'll see Douglas fir trees dot the ledges and cliffs. And there among the pillars and columns, people can witness the muscle of the earth etched into the rocks. Blocks of rock under extreme pressure, pushed deep in the earth, were transformed in their nature. Bodies of magma, thrust up from below, created a revolution far below the surface. Here is rock that is nearly half as old as earth itself, exposed and revealed for us to study.

Rangers on staff patrol into the canyon, and are able to witness some of this muscle. It is a skidding, crumbly, boot snagging scramble into designated wilderness that makes up about half of the park. And for those that may have not stayed active through the winter, the first return hike to the rim can be a muscle stretching encounter with stiff reminders the next day.

Some of the more intrepid visitors do this, too, on one of the several routes that lead to the river. They do this to fish, to test themselves or just to sit next to the river and listen to it sing. The canyon is big enough for your imagination, but don't be fooled. This isn't *Disneyland* where everything is controlled by humans. Nature is the force to reckon with and such adventures can be at once beautiful and hazardous.

By spending time at the canyon, though, we are most able to gain a new understanding of the natural world around us. When doing so, we are able to gain strength for our daily struggles against schedules and deadlines.

Such is the case for the author and contributors to this book in your hands. They have each developed a special relationship with the canyon, and through their in-depth knowledge, you can learn more of the aspects of the gorge and further your own relationship with it. Here you will learn of the intimate beauty, and the rugged nature of the canyon. You can revel in the challenges that were met by early explorers, and you can delight in the wisdom of the aged trees along the rim.

If you are reading this at home, come back to the canyon. Come back to soak your feet in the bracing waters of the Gunnison. Come back to listen to the screech of a red-tailed hawk circling the skies. Come back to sit on the rim and feel the breeze as the sun goes down. Doing such things deepens your sense of life in this world; and this time, the canyon will have prepared you.

YO DOWN THERE! Watch your step; it's a long, long way down! Hey, I'm **Blackie** and I'm a Peregrine Falcon. Yep, that's right, the swiftest bird on earth. We almost disappeared forever, but I'm making a comeback here — one of the few wild places left for me. Because I'm so special, I've been picked as the *unofficial* symbol of this special place, the Black Canyon of the Gunnison. And I'm also your **official guide** for this book. Look for me to dive in every once in a while as you explore the pages of this guide, with tips, info and advice. As you might guess, I know this place pretty well, so folks often ask me a lot of questions. Hey, that's fine with me, that's what I'm here for! I'll share with you some of the most frequently asked ones:

Painted Wall at dawn.

Q: How did the canyon get here?

A: It's a long story — in fact, a two-million-year-old story. It seems that the river began cutting down through softer volcanic rock. Once firmly entrenched in its course, the river had no alternative but to continue cutting down through harder, crystalline rock of the dome-shaped Gunnison Uplift. Inexorably, the process of erosion — by scouring of the river, by occasional rockfalls and by the relentless creep of debris slides — deepened the canyon at a rate of perhaps 1 foot per 1000 years. It continues today, although lessened by upstream dams.

Q: Why "Black" canyon? How deep and narrow is the gorge?

A: The deepest spot is at **Warner Point Overlook**, at the west end of the South Rim Drive. There, you are looking down some 2,772 feet to the ribbon of river below. Its great depth and narrowness means that the dark walls are shrouded in shadow for most of the day — thus, the name. In most other places in the canyon, both rims average about 1,800 feet above the Gunnison River. The narrowest width between the rims is at **Chasm View**, where you're almost in shouting distance at only 1,100 feet apart.

Q: What is the Painted Wall? What can I see there?

A: The famous **Painted Wall** is the tallest cliff face in Colorado at nearly 2,400 feet. It's named for the swirling patterns of pink and white *pegmatite*, a rock-type that was injected into the dark walls under great pressure while still in a molten state. Several overlooks in the Park offer a *birds-eye* view (pardon the pun) of this spectacular wall. Bring your binoculars and look for me there! Peregrines find this sheer wall offers ideal nesting sites. It's also favored by rock climbers.

Q: How can I get down to the river? What can I do there?

A: The easiest way is to just drive down! You can access the Gunnison River by driving down the **East Portal Road**, from near the park entrance station on the South Rim Drive. The 6-mile road is quite steep (16% grade) and vehicles over 22 feet are prohibited. At the bottom, you can camp, hike, fish or just take in the immensity of the steep canyon walls. Hey, I'll meet you down there! (Let's see — if I dive at my customary 200 mph, I'll be there in like — *3 seconds!*)

Q: Can I hike down to the bottom of the gorge? Can I cross the river?

A: Well, that depends! Are you in excellent physical condition; can you navigate a trailless descent through steep, rocky terrain; can you carry a pack full of gear with plenty of water; are you deterred by poison ivy growing up to 5 feet tall; and can you scramble 2,000 feet back up to the rim? Discuss your intentions with the park rangers. They can advise you on routes, issue you the **required backcountry permit** and give you directions to primitive campsites along the river. Crossing the river to reach the other rim is extremely dangerous. People have lost their lives in the treacherous currents of this powerful river.

Q: What's so special about this place?

A: "No other canyon in North America combines the depth, narrowness, sheerness and somber countenance of the Black Canyon of the Gunnison," wrote geologist Wallace R. Hansen. This awesome gorge and its wild river remain a unique and untamed part of the American landscape, a home to diverse biological communities, a special place for mammals, insects, fish and birds, *like me,* that can live no where else, and a source of wonder and inspiration for all those who gaze into its depths.

INTRODUCTION

Dawn creeps over the rim at Black Canyon of the Gunnison National Park.

USING THIS GUIDE

Greetings from BLACK CANYON of the Gunnison

T he Gunnison River carves a deep and narrow gorge into the hard, ancient rocks of western Colorado — a roaring river, a wild canyon, a place like no other. The centerpiece of this stunning landscape is one of our nation's newest crown jewels, Black Canyon of the Gunnison National Park, created in 1999. Together with two other federally-protected units, Curecanti National Recreation Area and Gunnison Gorge National Conservation Area, a world-class ecosystem is united, preserving a priceless part of the nation's natural and cultural heritage. Despite sharing the common thread of a great canyon and its river, each of these units is unique, offering enough adventures in recreation, experiences in self-discovery, and opportunities for studying nature to last anyone a lifetime.

Along with the National Park Service and *Blackie, the Peregrine Falcon,* we wish to welcome you to the Black Canyon! Our goal with this guide has been to provide a definitive resource that *any* visitor to the Park can use. Whether you are a hiker, rock climber, backpacker, equestrian, mountain biker, camper, photographer, birdwatcher, fisherman or white-water enthusiast, you'll find the information you need in this guide to pursue your adventures at the Black Canyon. Even if you need to limit your explorations to just a stop at the Visitor Center, our chapters on the fascinating natural and human history of this unique place will help you understand why our nation has chosen to protect the Black Canyon.

Be sure to read the next section which explains how this guide is organized. It will help you to navigate all the resources in this book. We hope you like what you see here and enjoy the great places we lead you to. *Have fun and be safe!*

How This Book is Organized

The information in this guide is organized for your convenience into **color-coded sections**. Colored tabs in the upper corner of each page help you quickly turn to the section that you are interested in. Each section then is divided into **chapters**, with headings such as *natural history, local facilities* or *hiking*.

THE PLACE (pages 32-99)

This section provides essential information about how to get to the National Park, as well as basic climate data on this location in west-central Colorado. The map on page 33 shows the major roads leading to the area. **Federal highways**, indicated on all maps as "US" *(US 285)*, and **Colorado state highways**, shown as "CO" *(CO 19)*, are paved roads and open year-round. Local roads are indicated as **county roads**, "CR" *(CR 580)*, or as **Forest Service roads**, "FSR" *(FSR 119)*. These roads may be paved, but more likely are gravel or dirt. Many side roads may not be plowed on a regular basis; and some, like the road to the North Rim in the Park, may even be officially closed during the winter season. Some require 4WD to be passable and others may seasonally be too muddy for passenger vehicles. This is especially true for roads in the Gunnison Gorge NCA. (Jeeping on Colorado backroads is not for the unprepared. Always inquire locally with the proper land management agency if in doubt about driving on these roads.)

RATING THE ACCESS ROADS: These symbols indicate the normal condition of the roads on certain maps.

 Suitable for 2WD passenger cars

 Suitable for 2WD cars in normal conditions

 4WD required at all times

In this section, you'll also learn fascinating things about the unique geology of the Black Canyon and the story of how it was formed. The canyon and surrounding lands are also home to an astonishing variety of plants and animals, including some threatened or endangered. The Black Canyon encompasses such a wide range of habitats, from desert and scrub lands, to canyons and mesatops, to lakeshores and river bottoms, that visitors come away astonished at the natural diversity of species. Equally interesting is the long cultural history of the Black Canyon area. The brief history outlined in this section hardly does justice to the amazing capacity of native peoples, and later, white explorers, miners and railroaders, and finally, settlers, dam builders and townspeople to survive, and even thrive, in such a harsh and challenging land.

FACILITIES (pages 100-125)

Turn to this section for complete information about needed services and facilities within the National Park (including Curecanti NRA and Gunnison Gorge NCA) and in the nearby communities around the canyon. You'll find everything from campgrounds to hotels, basic groceries to fine dining. **Black Canyon of the Gunnison National Park** itself has much of what you would expect of basic facilities: a visitor center, a campground and several scenic picnic areas are located on each of the two rims of the canyon. **Curecanti National Recreation Area** has the most commercially developed facilities; including a visitor center, information centers, several picnic areas and campgrounds, marinas, and places to purchase basic groceries and gas. **Gunnison Gorge National Conservation Area**, on the other hand, offers only primitive facilities. For most modern conveniences, you'll want to visit the nearby communities of **Gunnison** (east of the Park), **Montrose** (west of the Park), **Crawford** (north of the Park) and **Delta** (northwest of the Park.) The towns of Gunnison and Montrose are the economic hearts of the Black Canyon area, with virtually everything you'll need and a warm, small-town feel. Maps on pages 119-124 locate most services and facilities in these towns.

We also indicate that some facilities may close entirely during certain slow times of the year. In a good sense, *slower* describes the way of life in these small communities — traveling against the fast pace of modern society. Hopefully, visitors will be relaxed and refreshed by a visit to this beautiful area.

MAKING CONTACT:
These symbols appear in descriptions for services and facilities:

▮▮ Mailing address

☎ Phone or fax

🖥 Email or website

You'll find **contact information** — mail addresses, phone numbers and email addresses — throughout this section. These things change often but are current as of 2004. We'll continue to update and refine these in future editions of this guide. If you find inaccuracies or omissions, please contact us at *cmcpress@cmc.org* or write us at 710 10th Street # 200, Golden, CO 80401.

ACTIVITIES (pages 126-209)

The range of interesting things to do at the Black Canyon is enormous; and this section is the largest in the book. It would be a shame if all that visitors to the Park did was get out of their vehicles to snap a few pictures. Check out this section for plenty of fun activities and you are sure to find something that matches your interests. For easier, less-taxing activities, there are **scenic drives**, **wildlife watching**, **fishing** and **boating** on the reservoirs. Looking for something a little wild and crazy? Grab your **kayak** and run a section of the Gunnison River (or better yet, check out one of the expert outfitters listed that offer guided trips on this very challenging river.) For those seeking solitude, the backcountry beckons with **hiking**, **backpacking** and **rock climbing**.

Gunnison Country was the birthplace of **mountain biking** in the 1970s and that tradition continues today. There are excellent rides at Gunnison Gorge NCA, with nearly year-round riding on easy backroads for the novice, as well as quite difficult trails for the expert rider. While biking opportunities are somewhat limited in the National Park and Curecanti NRA, we still have come up with some possible rides of varying difficulty. A few of these rides, notably the South Rim Drive, are equally enjoyable with road bikes. Each description of a ride includes an **information box** that lists the one-way or loop distance of the suggested ride and approximate elevation gain. Most of these rides can be shortened by altering the turn-around point. These rides are rated as *easy, moderate* and *difficult,* depending on the level of fitness required or needed expertise. A beginning rider can handle the easy rides, but for moderate or difficult rides, riders should be experienced in single-track riding on steep courses. All levels need safety equipment, including helmets. Note that none of these routes are signed or maintained specifically for bikers.

RATING THE BIKING TRAILS:
These symbols appear in information boxes next to each biking description and indicate the relative trail difficulty.

 Easy bike ride, short distance, easy grade, good riding surface

 Moderate bike ride, medium distance and grade, bumpy riding surface

 Difficult bike ride, long distance, steep grade, poor riding surface

We describe **23 hikes** within the National Park, Curecanti NRA and Gunnison Gorge NCA for hikers (as well as for backpackers and rock climbers.) Even if you have never walked a trail, you'll find nature walks and short, easy strolls to magnificent vista points that anyone can enjoy, including families with young children or seniors. There are even wheelchair accessible excursions.

RATING THE HIKING TRAILS: These symbols appear in information boxes next to each hike description and indicate the relative trail difficulty.

 Easy hike - short distance, minimal grade, good walking surface

 Moderate hike - medium distance and grade, rougher walking surface

 Difficult hike - long distance, steep grade, rough walking or off-trail

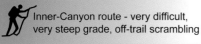 Inner-Canyon route - very difficult, very steep grade, off-trail scrambling

More experienced hikers will find only a few trails in the National Park that are more than a mile in length or that have significant elevation gain. Likewise, Curecanti NRA has several short hikes and nature trails. But there are also a couple of excellent foot trails in the NRA that descend into the canyon to river level that are especially attractive for overnight backpacks. Gunnison Gorge NCA has several good hikes down to the river that penetrate into the heart of that unit's rugged wilderness area. (A day-use fee is required for hikers upon entering Gunnison Gorge Wilderness Area.)

For those expert hikers wanting to experience the spectacular environment of the Inner-Canyon, we describe several established **Inner-Canyon Routes**. These routes in the National Park, descending from rim to river level and providing access for rock climbers, fisherman and canyoneers, have no maintained or marked trail — in fact, scrambling and route finding skills are as important as hiking skills. Physically and technically, these are much more difficult than mere hikes. Remember especially that it requires a lot more effort to make your way back up one of these steep ravines, then to descend. Also, note that it is dangerous and not advisable to attempt crossing of the river in order to reach the opposite canyon rim. A sign-in and a free permit, available at the Park visitor centers, is required for a hike into the Inner-Canyon.

Beside each hike or Inner-Canyon route description, you will find an **information box** with the one-way hiking distance and approximate elevation gain (or loss) to the furthest described destination. A few trails can be linked for a longer hike or to provide an alternate return route. Hikes are rated as *easy, moderate* or *difficult,* depending on the fitness level required or the amount of difficulty you may encounter. While even novice hikers will be able to handle any of the *easy* hikes described here, *moderate* or *difficult* hikes require experienced hikers who are properly equipped. Inner-Canyon routes are NOT individually rated — they are all *very difficult,* suitable only for very experienced and properly equipped adventurers. Included with each hike description is a **trail map**. Symbols used for all the maps in this book are shown on page 14.

Finally, for the hard-core, we include information about **rock climbing** within the National Park. For the very experienced, there are some of the finest big-wall challenges in North America here. This is extreme climbing, not for the faint of heart, with multi-pitch routes in very remote circumstances. We describe some of the main areas, conditions and the types of routes offered. For a less-daunting experience, we also describe a "bouldering" area in the Park. And for the *arm-chair* climber, we offer an historical perspective on this mecca that has drawn many of the country's best climbers. For any climb, you need training and experience — check in the **Resource Guide** in the back of the book for information about organizations that offer this (page 224.)

USEFUL MAPS

While the effort has been made to make the maps in this guide as informative and useful as possible, they should not serve as your sole guide in the field. You'll want to bring along more detailed maps such as **USGS 7.5 minute Quads** (listed on page 14). The USGS Quads are, in most cases, somewhat old and may not reliably show man-made features, like trails and roads; although they can be extremely useful for their topographic detail. USGS maps are available at Park Visitor Centers and at many of the area's outdoor retailers. There is an excellent commercial map from *Trails Illustrated* **(Map # 245)** that covers the National Park and Gunnison Gorge NCA, but lacks coverage of Curecanti NRA. Despite that omission, this map is more up-to-date than the USGS Quads and is waterproof and tear-resistant. *Trails Illustrated/National Geographic* also offers map coverage of the area on an interactive CD-ROM, **TOPO! COLORADO**. Purchase *TI/NG* products at outdoor retail outlets or visit their website at *www.nationalgeographic.com/maps*.

The Park Service and the BLM provide free **maps/park brochures** at park entrances, visitor centers, administrative offices and some trailheads and boat put-ins. Those maps are not detailed enough for most backcountry adventures.

OTHER ATTRACTIONS (pages 210-219)

Gazing into the awesome beauty and mystery of the Black Canyon will surely thrill you, but there are plenty of other interesting and fun things to do beyond the National Park. Explore the interesting culture and history of the Ute people at the **Ute Indian Museum** or herd some doggies while you stay at a 100,000-acre **working ranch** near Delta. Visit **Crawford State Park** for a relaxing summer day at the beach or bundle up to watch the human polar bear dive at the **Gunnison Winter Carnival** on the coldest day of the year. Or how about a fall drive along the **West Elk Loop Scenic Byway** through some of the Colorado Rockies' most spectacular aspen country?

All of the attractions in this section can be enjoyed in conjunction with a trip to the Black Canyon of the Gunnison National Park. Most are within 50 miles from the Park entrances. In the descriptions, we alert you that some attractions are only open seasonally. We also provide information listing annual festivals, events and special attractions that might interest you. These home-grown affairs are a great way to get a genuine taste of life in Gunnison Country.

RESOURCE GUIDE (pages 220-240)

The final section in this guide pulls together lots of supplemental information about the Park and surrounding area, plus provides you with recommended resources for discovering more. You'll find a **Check List** of birds found within Black Canyon of the Gunnison National Park and a **Glossary of Geologic Terms** that will help you understand the natural history of the area. We also include an extensive list of books and publications about the area and about related topics. An **Equipment List** for hikers and backpackers is provided by the experts, the *Colorado Mountain Club*, who lead thousands a trips a year into the Colorado backcountry. If you feel you need training or more experience for some of the activities in this books, such as hiking, climbing or backpacking, join one of the **organizations** listed in this section. And of course, you'll find a full and complete **index** to help you navigate this guide.

Safety Considerations

Visiting the Black Canyon of the Gunnison National Park can be an enriching and fun experience, but not without some potential hazards. Before setting out into the canyon or into the surrounding area, familiarize yourself with these hazards and be prepared with the best ways to avoid them.

HEAT

The unprepared Park visitor is potentially at risk from **heat exhaustion** or **heat stroke**. While normal summer temperatures generally hover around the mid-80° F readings, they can soar into the low 100s at times, especially in the depths of the Inner-Canyon. Be wise; wear a wide brimmed hat and drink plenty of water and other non-diuretic fluids.

DEHYDRATION

Your body consists of about two-thirds water. The effects of sun, wind and exercise in the Park's high-desert climate rob your body of its proper level of fluid. You will be dehydrated long before you become thirsty. Fluid losses of up to 5% are considered mild, up to 10% are considered moderate and up to 15% are considered severe. *Drink, drink, drink!* Water and sports drinks will help you recover your normal fluid and electrolyte level much faster than caffeine-based beverages like coffee, tea and colas. Coffee and colas act as diuretics and can cause you to lose fluid. Alcohol has an even greater negative effect on your body's fluid level.

Treat any water taken from unprotected sources before you drink it, and practice proper hygiene. You are at risk from **Giardia** contamination anytime you drink from untreated water sources in the Park. Giardia is a microscopic organism, that once it has inhabited the digestive system, can cause severe diarrhea. Giardia is mainly spread by the activity of animals in the watershed area of the water supply, or by the introduction of sewage into the water supply.

Giardia has become so common, even in wilderness areas, that water should always be treated chemically with pills which are specifically designed for water purification, by filtering the water with an approved water filter, or by boiling untreated water for several minutes before using. Adding a little flavored *Gatoraide* to boiled or treated water makes it taste so much better.

SUN

There are two types of **ultraviolet rays** (UVRs) radiating from the sun. They are UVB and UVA. If you desire *old* looking skin (or dismiss the risk of skin cancer), hang around out of doors without adequate sunscreen protection. Otherwise, apply sunscreen to all exposed skin areas one hour prior to sun exposure. This gives the sunscreen time to penetrate the deeper skin layers. Be aware that reapplying sunscreen does not extend the total amount of time that you can safely be exposed to the sun's rays. Sunscreen which is rated **SPF 30** is the suggested standard for extended outdoor exposure. Look for sunscreens that block both UVA and UVB rays.

Studies have shown that about 30% of the total daily UV flux hits the earth between 11 AM and 1 PM, so if possible, activities should be planned to avoid this peak exposure time. A useful rule of thumb is that if your shadow is shorter than you, the risk of sunburn is substantial.

At higher altitudes, like in the Colorado, UVRs are approximately 50% stronger than at sea level. Therefore, sunburn can occur more quickly and severely at altitude, especially in light-colored terrain where the sunlight is reflected back up by the rock, sand or snow. Also, UVRs can penetrate cloud cover, so that even on cool, overcast days, you can be at risk.

The sun's rays are damaging to your eyes, as well as your skin. Wear proper eyewear that protects against both UVA and UVB rays. Dark lenses with side shields are recommended.

LIGHTNING

Deadly lightning is always a threat when thunderstorms are present. Afternoon thunderstorms are fairly common during the summer; and the danger is real, especially in higher parts of the Park, such as along the rims of the canyon, and out on the open lakes at Curecanti NRA. These storms are quick moving and brief, but can be very violent. Lightning normally strikes the highest features in the vicinity — that could be YOU, if you are at a Park overlook or boating out on Blue Mesa Reservoir during thunderstorm activity! If out on the lakes, return to shore or a protected cove immediately when you see a thunderstorm starting to materialize. Observe this exciting phenomenon from the safety of the Park Visitor Center or your vehicle. *Live better electrically* is fine for your home, but not for your body!

ALTITUDE

You must recognize that you are at altitude when you visit the Park; your body recognizes it. The National Park Visitor Centers are located at an elevation of about 8,000 feet and much of the surrounding canyon rims are above 7,000 feet. **Acute Mountain Sickness** (AMS), a mild form of altitude sickness, is caused by a lack of oxygen when traveling to higher elevations. This usually occurs in individuals exposed to an altitude over 7,000 feet, who have not had a chance to acclimate to the altitude before engaging in physical activities. The symptoms of AMS include, but are not limited to, headache, nausea, vomiting and shortness of breath.

Drinking plenty of fluids and gradually moving up to higher altitudes over several days will help to offset the potential of being afflicted with AMS. If you do get AMS, the best advice is to descend immediately to a lower altitude.

EXERTION

Don't overdo it! A general rule of thumb, when hiking or climbing, is that if you can't talk to your hiking partner (or yourself), you're working too hard. If you can sing a song while you hike, you're not working hard enough.

Determining your **age-predicted maximum heart rate** will also help you from over-exerting yourself. It is generally accepted that you will derive the most benefit when you are exercising at 60-90% of your maximum exercise heart rate. Take into consideration your overall physical condition and past medical history when attempting physical exercise at elevation.

Calculate the **beats per minute** and write it down on your palm for monitoring your heart beat while hiking:
220 - (your age) = (age-predicted maximum heart rate) X .90 = (beats per minute)

FALLS AND FALLING ROCKS

When visiting the many scenic view points along the rims of the canyon, use extreme caution. Fatalities and serious injuries have occurred at Black Canyon from falls. Weathered, loose rock can make rim edges hazardous and many places have no guardrails. Closely supervise children and stay on established paths and trails. Also, please resist the urge to drop even just a small pebble into the abyss, that might endanger rock climbers, hikers and fisherman in the canyon.

If descending one of the Inner-Canyon routes, be cautious not to start any rockfall that might strike another party below your position. Either bunch very close together or spread out along the fall line so as to not knock rocks onto people in your own party.

WILDLIFE ENCOUNTERS

While most Park visitors don't perceive wildlife as a threat to them, bad encounters with wildlife are on the rise in Colorado. These can range from getting bitten by a chipmunk or ground squirrel (including the risk of transmitted rabies), to a rare encounter with a black bear or mountain lion. Most problems center around food. Don't feed wildlife; and hang your food out of reach when in the backcountry. Hiking at dawn or dusk may increase your chances of running into a bear or mountain lion. Use extra caution in places where hearing or visibility is limited: in brushy areas, near streams, where trails round a bend or on windy days. Avoid hiking alone and keep small children close and in sight. Hiking with your dog can sometimes precipitate an encounter.

Do not run from a bear or mountain lion. Running triggers a predatory response and they are more likely to attack. Back away slowly while facing a **black bear**. Avoid direct eye contact and give the bear plenty of room to escape. If on a trail, step off the trail on the downhill side and slowly leave the area. Use extra caution if you encounter a female bear with cubs. Avoid getting between cubs and their mother.

In the case of a threat from a **mountain lion**, stay calm and hold your ground or back away slowly. Stand upright facing the lion. Maintain direct eye contact and try to appear larger than you are by raising your arms. Don't crouch down. Mountain lions still have a healthy fear of humans in unpopulated areas, so aggressive behavior will often scare off the lion.

One poisonous snake, the **western rattlesnake**, is sometimes encountered in rocky and brushy country at lower elevations in Gunnison Gorge NCA. Wear high-top foot wear and long pants, watch where you place your footfalls and don't reach blindly under rocks or ledges. Snakes are not aggressive and only strike if surprised or cornered. If you hear the tell-tale rattle or see a snake, give it room to escape.

INSECTS BITES AND POISON IVY

Insects can be a less obvious, yet still potentially serious, hazard to visitors to the Black Canyon. The ubiquitous **mosquito** is never absent, even in this high-desert environment. They are active during cooler parts of the day, close to sources of standing water. Recently, *West Nile virus*, transmitted through that insect's bite, has shown up in Colorado, causing concern among health authorities. Wear long pants and long-sleeved shirts and apply a repellent that lists DEET as its active agent.

This strategy will also help deter **wood ticks** which can transmit the virus associated with *tick fever* (as well as the rarer, but more serious *Rocky Mountain spotted fever*.) In spring and early summer, in brushy areas in the Inner-Canyon, ticks can latch on to passing hikers. They take several hours to locate a suitable spot on your body to "lunch," so check for hitch-hiking ticks on your body and clothing a couple times during the day.

Another reason for covering any bare skin with clothing, including wearing light gloves, is the abundant presence of **poison ivy** in the Inner-Canyon, in brushy areas along the river and in ravines (especially cooler, north-facing ones, like those that descend from the south rim.) Learn to recognize the plant and avoid grasping it on your climb back out of the canyon.

BOATING AND WATER SAFETY

Federal boating safety regulations apply. Your safety equipment when boating on the lakes must include a Coast Guard-approved personal flotation device for each passenger, bailing bucket and paddle or oar, fire extinguisher, tools for minor repairs, anchor and an extra set of warm, dry clothing. The Park rangers at Curecanti NRA recommend that because of the potential of violent wind, it is best to travel west in the morning and east in the afternoon, especially if on Morrow Point or Crystal Lakes. Keep protective coves in sight and head for shore when strong winds arise. Know the rules of the road and navigational aids. Keep a safe distance from spillways, swimmers and smaller craft

Below Blue Mesa Dam, boating is limited to hand-carried craft. Fluctuating water levels and releases from the dams can cause boating hazards. Check on launch conditions at the visitor centers before starting your trip.

Swimming in the reservoirs is prohibited from docks, launch ramps and unanchored boats. In fact, with the cold water temperatures typical even for mid-summer, the Park Service does not recommend swimming in the lakes or in the river. Even wind-surfers are urged to wear a wet-suit, as prolonged exposure to the cold waters can bring on hypothermia. Don't swim or wade into the Gunnison River in Black Canyon. Cold water, strong currents, and slippery, hidden boulders combine to create dangerous conditions.

HYPOTHERMIA

Extended exposure to the cold waters of the reservoirs or the river can lower your body temperature to dangerous, even fatal levels. **Hypothermia** can be the result, with symptoms of uncontrolled shivering, impaired judgement, slurred speech, drowsiness and weakness. To treat hypothermia, as soon as possible, dress the victim in warm, dry clothing and place them in a sleeping bag. Give them warm liquids and high-energy food and seek medical help at once.

For ice fisherman, snowmobilers or cross-country skiers, winter at Curecanti NRA can be an especially dangerous time, with sub-zero temperatures worsened by bone-chilling winds. Adequate preparation is a must; including having clothing in multiple layers, as a check against hypothermia and frostbite. Boots should be big enough to allow good circulation. See the **Suggested Equipment List** in the *Resource Guide* on page 225 for more information on appropriate clothing.

Check with the Park rangers about the current ice thickness before venturing out onto Blue Mesa Reservoir in winter. **Four inches** of clear, hard ice are needed to support one adult afoot. **Seven inches** of clear, hard ice are needed to support snowmobiles.

STAYING FOUND

The ability to find your way in the backcountry is an essential skill to develop. First-timers should not travel alone, and even veteran adventurers should think twice about doing a difficult trip solo. Always let someone know your plans before hand — including your starting point, your destination and your date of return — and bring adequate gear, including map and compass. Global positioning devices, cell phones and so-called personal radios are doubtful, if not useless, in the deep confines of the canyon (although they may be useful tools for recreationalists on or around Blue Mesa Reservoir at Curecanti NRA.)

The State of Colorado assumes the cost of rescuing anyone with a valid Colorado fishing license, hunting license or **Colorado Outdoor Recreation Search and Rescue** (CORSAR) card. CORSAR cards are sold at sporting goods stores and outdoor retailers.

Self-rescue should be the first consideration in the event of an accident or illness. If it is deemed necessary to go for help, someone should stay behind with the injured person — or failing that, leave adequate food, water and warm clothing. Rescue is particularly difficult and dangerous for local agencies at Black Canyon, due to the extreme ruggedness of the terrain. *In cases where persons have acted irresponsibly, they may be held liable for all costs incurred if a rescue is necessary.*

Finally, consider joining an organization that offers classes and training in outdoor skills, including first aid and orienteering, such as those listed on page 224 in the **Resource Guide**.

Backcountry Ethics

Your visit to the Black Canyon of the Gunnison National Park, Curecanti National Recreation Area and Gunnison Gorge National Conservation Area should continue to protect and preserve these areas by following the rules and regulations that land management agencies have set up. Each of us needs to do our part and together we can preserve these natural treasures for everyone. Whenever applicable, we have noted current rules and regulations in this book. But things change over time. Before you engage in activities at the Park be sure to check in at the Visitor Center for the latest rules meant to ensure that your activity is compatible with protecting the environment.

As a general guideline for activities in the backcountry, you should follow the principles of **Leave No Trace** (LNT) which have been adopted by the National Park Service, the Bureau of Land Management and the National Forest Service. The LNT principles described below will help protect and preserve park resources for those visitors who will follow in your footsteps in the years to come. To learn more about the Leave No Trace movement, contact information is provided in the **Resource Guide**, page 224.

1. PLAN AHEAD AND PREPARE

It is important to know information about the Park, so that you will know what to expect. Find out about its ecology, climate, topography and rules and regulations. Be ready to modify your behavior and expectations accordingly.

2. TRAVEL AND CAMP ON DURABLE SURFACES

Stay on established trails. Don't take shortcuts that become unsightly and encourage erosion. When traveling cross-country, stay on durable surfaces. Camp only in established or sanctioned campsites. Check in with the Park personnel at the Visitor Center to obtain a backcountry permit and to ask about camping in the backcountry.

3. DISPOSE OF WASTE PROPERLY

Be prepared to pack out what you pack in. It doesn't take much effort to carry along a litterbag for those disposable items you are finished with. Pick up trash that you find along the trails. Pack out toilet paper and personal hygiene products. Please remove dog feces. Use small amounts of biodegradable soap in washing up and keep a clean camp.

4. LEAVE WHAT YOU FIND

It is not permitted within the Park to remove or deface plants, animals, rocks or archaeological artifacts. Leave them for others to enjoy.

5. MINIMIZE CAMPFIRE IMPACTS

Where fires are permitted, use established fire rings, fire pans or mound fires. Avoid the typical *white man's fire.* It's not necessary to have the flames jumping 20 feet into the sky to enjoy a campfire.

Wood gathering is not permitted within the Park; you'll need to bring your own firewood. Never abandon a campfire that is still burning or contains hot coals. Open fires are not permitted beyond the campgrounds in the National Park and Curecanti NRA, and wood fires are banned in the Gunnison Gorge Wilderness Area, including along the entire river corridor. If cooking in the backcountry, use a backpacker's stove.

6. RESPECT WILDLIFE

Do not attempt to feed, follow or approach wildlife. Be especially careful not to come between mothers and their young, such as a sow and cubs or a cow elk and fawn. Don't bury or throw unwanted food on the ground as it tempts wildlife and creates abnormal feeding habits. Store food legally and responsibly. Dogs must be on a leash at all times to prevent harassing of wildlife, and pets may not be taken into the Inner-Canyon or into wilderness areas.

7. BE CONSIDERATE OF OTHER VISITORS

Be courteous when on trails. Remember the rules of the road — everyone yields to horses; bicycles yield to pedestrians; pedestrians yield to each other where required. Consider the quality of your visit to the Park. Keep noise to a minimum. Respect the privacy of other visitors. Crowding causes conflict. Camp a reasonable distance from other groups.

Everyone, including the vehicle owner, is distressed when a car alarm goes off in the middle of the night. Consider turning yours off temporarily. With the exception of emergency personnel, cell phones do not have a place at ranger campfire programs. Leave them in your car or at camp.

THE PLACE

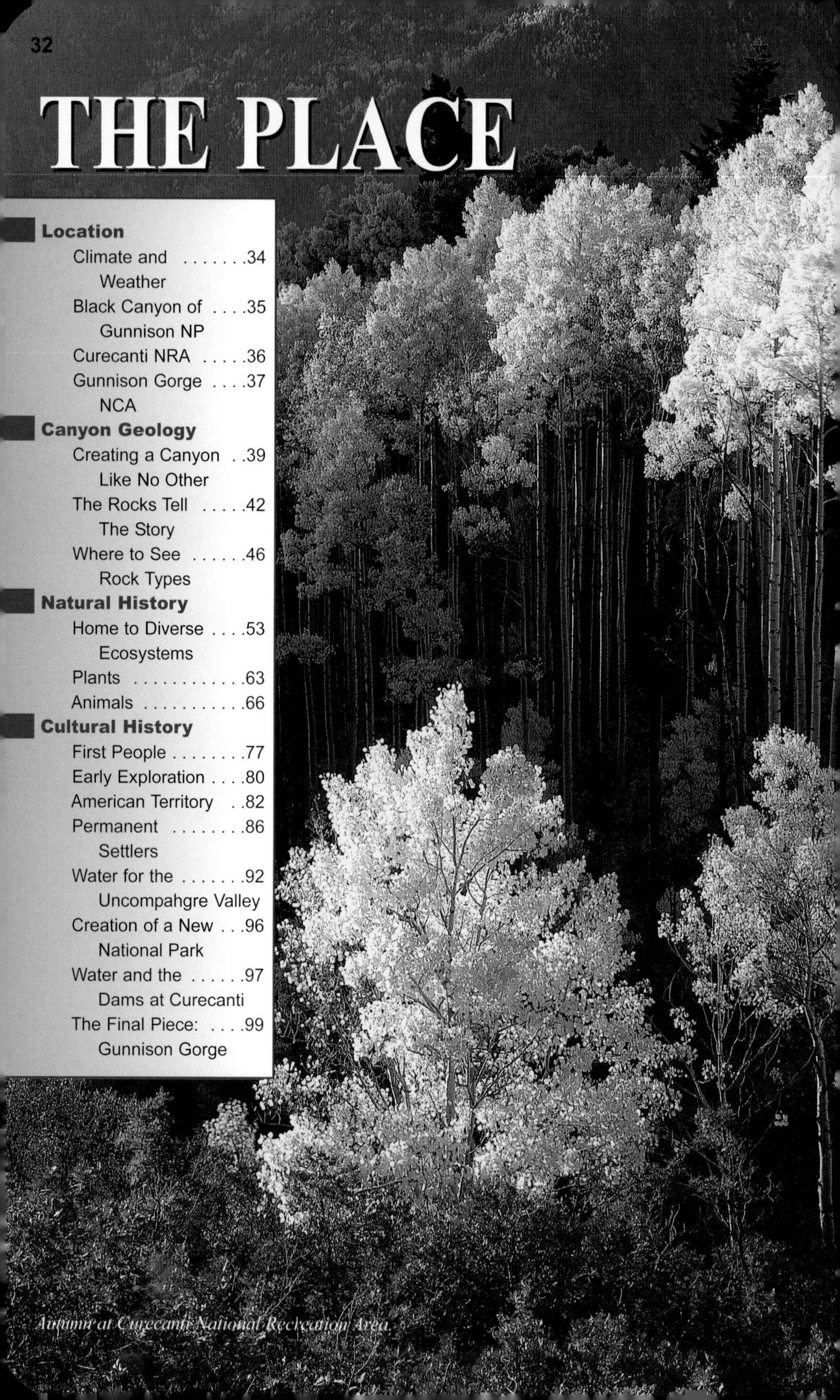

Autumn at Curecanti National Recreation Area

LOCATION

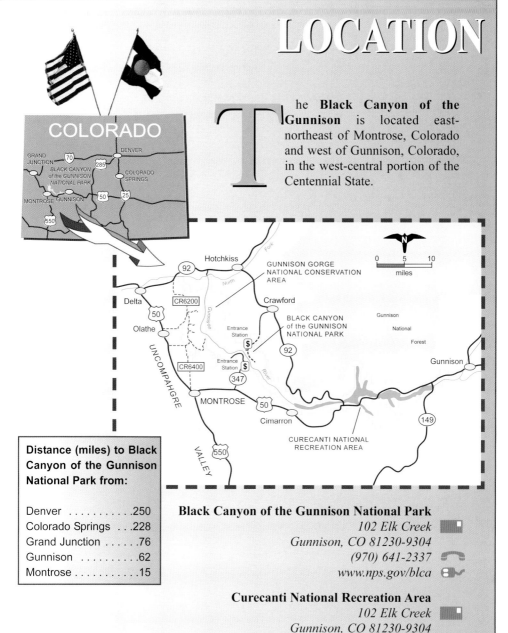

COLORADO

T he **Black Canyon of the Gunnison** is located east-northeast of Montrose, Colorado and west of Gunnison, Colorado, in the west-central portion of the Centennial State.

Distance (miles) to Black Canyon of the Gunnison National Park from:

Denver 250
Colorado Springs . . .228
Grand Junction 76
Gunnison 62
Montrose 15

Black Canyon of the Gunnison National Park
102 Elk Creek
Gunnison, CO 81230-9304
(970) 641-2337
www.nps.gov/blca

Curecanti National Recreation Area
102 Elk Creek
Gunnison, CO 81230-9304
(970) 641-2337
www.nps.gov/cure/home

Gunnison Gorge National Conservation Area
2505 South Townsend Avenue
Montrose, CO 81401
(970) 240-5300
www.co.blm.gov/ubra/gorgenca.htm

THREE JEWELS, ONE NATIONAL TREASURE

Black Canyon and the Gunnison River Basin are part of an integrated plan to manage the natural resources and public recreational opportunities of a national treasure made up of three major jewels. **Curecanti National Recreation Area** provides water-related recreation on Colorado's largest body of water, as well as additional recreation opportunities of hiking, cross country skiing, scenic drives and wildlife viewing. **Black Canyon of the Gunnison National Park** has spectacular scenery with hiking, climbing, cross-country skiing, and wildlife viewing. Downriver from the Park, **Gunnison Gorge National Conservation Area** provides scenic values, *Gold Medal* fishing, whitewater boating, hiking and wildlife viewing. These three units, while each unique, complement each other with shared values of conservation and preservation, creating one of the American West's largest, continuous protected ecosystems and providing recreational and wilderness experiences for over one million visitors a year.

Climate and Weather

Black Canyon lies in the transition zone between the hot, semi-desert of the Colorado Plateau and the cool, mountain environment of the Southern Rockies. The temperatures in this region can run the gamut from over 100°F in summer at Gunnison Gorge NCA to a brutal -35°F in winter at Curecanti NRA.

At the National Park's popular canyon rims (7,500 feet in elevation), late spring, summer and early fall months present visitors with ideal daytime temperatures ranging from **highs of 60° to 90°F** and nighttime **lows of 30° to 50°F**. When visiting the Park during October through April, visitors can expect daytime high temperatures to range from a pleasant 20° to 40°F, to occasionally a bone chilling 0°F, with nighttime lows of -10° to 20°F. At Gunnison, a few miles east of Curecanti NRA, frigid air slides down from the surrounding West Elk and San Juan Mountains to routinely produce some of the coldest winter temperatures recorded each year in the contiguous U.S.

Temperatures are typically about 5° to 15°F warmer in Gunnison Gorge NCA, which is lower in elevation than most of the Park. And the Inner-Canyon likewise can be considerably warmer than the rims. During the day, areas in the canyon that receive a lot of sunlight can be quite hot. The dark canyon walls soak up the sun, later releasing stored heat and tempering the evening's temperature drop.

The Gunnison Valley is usually a sunny and dry place, but visitors can expect occasional snow during the colder months and brief thundershowers during the warmer months. The average annual precipitation is less than 10 inches in the western part of Gunnison Gorge NCA and around 25 inches in the higher reaches of Curecanti NRA, which can fall as either rain or snow. The average for the Park is **less than 15 inches per year**. Southwestern Colorado experiences (what is commonly referred to as) the **monsoon season** during the months of July and August. Short but drenching thunderstorms, accompanied by severe lightning and hail, can occur at any time of the day or night during these months.

High winds can be a problem for recreationalists, especially on the reservoirs of Curecanti NRA. Sudden, violent wind events can whip up whitecaps in spring and summer. And the wind, combined with winter's frigid temperatures, can produce brutal windchill factors for ice fisherman and cross-country skiers.

Black Canyon of the Gunnison NP

Of all the spectacular canyons of The West, the **Black Canyon of the Gunnison** is unique. It is not as deep or wide a canyon; nor does it have the steepest gradient of all rivers in The West. But what makes the Black Canyon like no other is the nearly vertical walls of up to 2,700 feet — the highest cliffs in Colorado — and the extreme narrowness. At one point, it is just 1,100 feet from the south to the north rim; yet the canyon is nearly twice as deep as it is wide at this point. Through it all, the Gunnison River, unusually steep for a river its size, has carved a 53-mile gorge through the dark rock that is so deep and narrow that little sunlight can penetrate it; thus giving the canyon its name. The canyon walls are not really black, but primarily gray in color with intrusions that have a wide color range from cream to pink and from red to orange.

Upgraded from National Monument status in 1999 by act of Congress, **Black Canyon of the Gunnison National Park** protects some 30,300 acres of mesas, canyon rims and a 14-mile stretch of the most dramatic portion of the gorge. The **Inner-Canyon**, or park lands below the rim, have been further designated as a federally-protected Wilderness Area, free forever from development. The Black Canyon is truly unparalleled — with panoramic views of cliff tops and mesas, with soaring buttresses and colorful cliff faces, and the sounds of a roaring river, thousands of feet below the rim. In addition to the spectacular scenery accessed by road on both the south and north rims of the canyon, the Park offers camping, hiking, climbing, cross-country skiing, and wildlife viewing.

HOW TO GET THERE

From the south, the entrance to the Park is located 6 miles north of the junction of US-50 and CO-347. To reach this junction from Montrose, travel 9 miles east of town on US-50, or from Gunnison, drive 56 miles west of US-50. CO-347 turns into South Rim Drive and is the most popular access to the Park, reaching the **South Rim Visitor Center** and other attractions. The paved access road and the Visitor Center are open year-round (except for South Rim Drive, which normally is unplowed west of the Visitor Center in winter.)

The Park may be accessed **from the north** by traveling 4.0 mile south from Crawford on CO-92 and turning right (west) onto the North Rim Road, following the signs for 11 miles to the **North Rim Ranger Station** and the North Rim Drive. The first half of the road is paved; the second half is gravelled, but suitable for all vehicles. However, it and the North Rim Ranger Station are closed in the winter.

Note that there is no road that links the rims within the National Park.

CANYON FACTS

Greatest Depth (at Warner Point Overlook) . . . .*2,772 feet*
Depth at Chasm View . . . .*1,820 feet*
Depth at the Great Pillars (at Gunnison Point) . . . .*1,840 feet*
Narrowest Width at the Rim (at Chasm View) . . . .*1,100 feet*
Narrowest width at River Level (at The Narrows) . . . .   *40 feet*
Length of Canyon (from the Blue Mesa Dam to the Confluence
   with the North Fork of the Gunnison River) . . . . *53 miles*
Average Gradient of River in the Park . . . .*96 feet/mile*
Greatest Gradient in the Park (beneath Chasm View)   . . . .*480 feet/mile*

Curecanti NRA

Stretching between the eastern edge of Black Canyon of the Gunnison National Park to just west of the town of Gunnison, the 42,000-acre **Curecanti National Recreation Area** is part of the Upper Colorado River Storage Project (UPRSP). Known as the Wayne N. Aspinall Unit (for the congressman who pushed through legislation establishing the project), it encompasses three dams on the Gunnison River completed between 1965 and 1976: the **Blue Mesa**, **Morrow Point** and **Crystal Dams**. Blue Mesa Dam, with its large reservoir sporting a fishery of kokanee salmon and other lake-type fish, is the largest of the project's dams. Morrow Point Dam is further west from Blue Mesa Dam, at the beginning of the sheer canyon walls typical of Black Canyon. Crystal Dam is near the site of the Gunnison Diversion Tunnel, bringing water to the Uncompahgre Valley. Below Crystal Dam, the Gunnison River runs free to its junction with the Colorado River to the west.

Curecanti NRA is by far the most heavily visited of the three federal units, seeing over **800,000 visitors** a year. Most come in summer for boating, fishing and camping, but winter ice-fishing in sub-zero weather is also popular. *Burr!*

The entire UPRSP created water storage for irrigation, hydroelectric power and recreation. The main resource at Curecanti NRA is water, so most of the recreation opportunities are related to boating, water sports and fishing on the area's three reservoirs, most notably **Blue Mesa Reservoir**, the largest lake in Colorado. But there are also many trails in the NRA for hiking, wildlife viewing and camping, including some that provide access north into the West Elks Wilderness Area of the Gunnison National Forest. The NRA includes uplands and mesas, especially around the large "arms" of Blue Mesa Reservoir, that provide important wildlife habitat.

The National Park Service manages the area by an agreement with the Bureau of Reclamation (which built the dams and manages them and the water resource.) Curecanti NRA has the most commercially developed services of the three federally-protected units along the river. Marinas, a grocery store, boat tours and other services are offered by concessioners at Elk Creek and Lake Fork. US-50 and C0-92 run through Curecanti NRA, making access convenient. The Visitor Center at Elk Creek serves as park headquarters, with additional information stations at Lake Fork, Cimarron and East Portal.

HOW TO GET THERE

To get to the Elk Creek Visitor Center **from the east**, drive west on US-50 for 16 miles from Gunnison and turn left, following the signs for less than a mile. The **Elk Creek Visitor Center** is open mid-May to late-September, and intermittently afterwards. The turnoffs for the Lake Fork and Cimarron Information Centers are at 25 and 35 miles respectively from Gunnison. To reach the remote **East Portal Road**, travel west on US-50 for 56 miles and turn right (north) on CO-347 (the entrance road to the National Park.) After 6 miles, turn right unto the paved road for a steep, winding descent of 5.9 miles to the river. This road prohibits vehicles longer that 22 feet and is closed in winter.

From the west, travel on US-50 for 49 miles from Montrose and turn right (south) on the short road to the Elk Creek Visitor Center. The turnoffs (all on the north side of the highway) for the East Portal Road and the Information Centers at Cimarron and Lake Fork are at 9 miles, 30 miles and 40 miles respectively.

Gunnison Gorge NCA

Just downstream from the Black Canyon of the Gunnison National Park is the third, and largest and least developed, of the federal units protecting the Black Canyon. **Gunnison Gorge National Conservation Area** encompasses some 57,725 acres of public lands in Delta and Montrose counties, covering lands on either side of the river from the border with the National Park north to CO-92. NCAs have multi-use regulations, allowing activities not permitted in the National Park. For instance, some of the NCA, especially the plateaus on each side of the gorge, has leased land for grazing. There may be some oil, gas and mineral rights, which may be withdrawn in the future with wild river designation. Recreation use includes white water rafting, hiking, geology viewing, horseback riding, mountain biking, camping and limited climbing. Off-road vehicles such as motorcycles and ATVs are allowed in designated areas. There is no visitor center in the NCA, which has only limited facilities.

Within the heart of the NCA is the **Gunnison Gorge Wilderness Area**, holding about 17,700 acres, including about 14 miles of the river and its gorge as it exits from the National Park. Vehicles aren't permitted into the Wilderness Area and users (about 20,000 per year) must pay a fee and observe special use restrictions. Fees are payable at self-serve kiosks at wilderness trailheads. Currently, a **new management plan** (due out in 2004) is being created for the entire NCA to address conflicts that have arisen between different recreational users and to prevent damage to the environment and archaeological sites.

HOW TO GET THERE

From the southwest, in the city of Montrose, drive north on US-50 for about 10 miles and turn east on Falcon Road. Follow it to its end and turn north on unpaved, Peach Valley Road. Peach Valley Road going north intersects in succession the Chukar Road, the Bobcat Road, the Duncan Road and the Ute Road. Turn right (east) on any of these to reach the boundary with the Wilderness Area, where trailheads descend into the canyon. The Chukar Trail is the most popular trailhead, especially for boaters carrying their gear into the canyon. All trails into the wilderness are for foot or horse travel only. A four-wheel drive, high clearance vehicle is recommended for this access route.

From the northwest, in the city of Delta, go east on CO-92 for about 10 miles to the town of Austin and turn right (south) onto CR-2200. Follow the signs to Peach Valley Road. Follow Peach Valley Road south to meet any of the four access roads mentioned above. Four-wheel drive is recommended for this access route.

The NCA can also be reached **from the north** on CO-92, 13 miles east of Delta. Turn right on paved CR-28.10 and follow the signs south for a couple miles to the Gunnison Forks Day Use Area at the confluence of the Gunnison River and the North Fork.

Access roads into the NCA (except the north access on CR-28.10) can be pretty rough; and four-wheel drive, high clearance vehicles are recommended. (The Chukar Road is the easiest access, although the longest. When completely dry, it may not require a four-wheel drive vehicle.) When wet, these roads can be at times impassable with *any* vehicle. The bedrock of *Mancos shale* and other formations become very slick, with the consistency of soap. Tow trucks drivers out of Montrose can easily charge over $100 to get folks out of this mess.

CANYON GEOLOGY

> *"Several western canyons exceed the Black Canyon in overall size. Some are longer; some are deeper; some are narrower; and a few have walls as steep. But no other canyon in North America combines the depth, narrowness, sheerness, and somber countenance of the Black Canyon."*
>
> — geologist Wallace R. Hansen

The Ute people recognized the essential geology of the **Black Canyon** region by their name for the Gunnison River, **Tomichi**, which means *"land of high cliffs and plenty water."* They could see the results, but could not perceive the long geologic history of their home, a landscape indeed carved and shaped by "plenty water." The Black Canyon itself, when placed in the long geologic timescale, is just a newborn — younger than two million years old — yet in the canyon's depths are rocks nearly *two billion* years old, some of the most ancient in Colorado. The vast periods of geologic time between the creation of those rocks and the mighty gorge that we see today is an endless story of repeated **uplift**, **erosion** and **deposition**; with clear evidence of these slow, inexorable and powerful processes along the rims and in the canyon.

Creating a Canyon Like No Other

When a visitor first sees the **Black Canyon of the Gunnison**, they can not help but wonder, "*Why is the canyon so deep and vertical; and how old is it?*" Two main factors created the scenic canyon that we marvel at today — extreme resistance of the hard "basement rock" of the **Gunnison Uplift** and the highly efficient, erosive power of the **Gunnison River**.

A river tends to follow the easiest course possible, attempting to cut an even gradient throughout its length. If cutting through soft materials, a broad gradual gradient is created. The Uncompahgre River, flowing west of the Black Canyon through soft shale, has eroded the Uncompahgre Valley — as deep as the Black Canyon, but very broad. The Gunnison River faced very different conditions as it flowed west from the present site of the town of Gunnison. Volcanic activity from the San Juan Mountains south of the river and West Elk Mountains to the north laid down easily eroded *breccias* and *tuffs*. As the river flowed over these formations of little resistance, the river became entrenched about two million years ago. As the river eroded ever deeper through the soft volcanic material, it then encountered the harder and older crystalline rock that had been thrust up earlier in a formation known as the **Gunnison Uplift**. Unable to find its way to an easier course, the river was forced to cut into this once-buried, resistant core of rock. Melt waters and debris load increased during the **Ice Age**, accelerating the scouring of the canyon, until very recent times.

Upstream at Curecanti, the down-cutting was slower and a wider valley resulted; while downstream in the Gunnison Gorge, softer sedimentary rock allowed the river to cut a broader gorge. To achieve an equilibrium of grade, the river had to cut much faster through the resistant basement rock at Black Canyon then in either area, above or below the canyon. The river attempts an even gradient by falling at a much faster rate through the canyon then most rivers in The West. In Black Canyon, the river drops an average of 95 feet-per-mile (including its greatest drop of 480 feet-per-mile below Chasm View.) Throughout the 50-mile length of the canyon, the average fall is 42 feet-per-mile, a drop of 2,100 feet from the Lake Fork at Sapinero to the North Fork near Delta. (By comparison, the **Green River** in Dinosaur National Monument, a river of similar size to the Gunnison and in a canyon about as deep, averages only about a 12 feet-per-mile drop.)

This steep gradient gave the river more energy to cut faster. Side streams, with much lower energy, could not erode the side canyons fast enough to meet the river at its own level. Thus, the canyon has few streams entering it — those that do are usually waterfalls, or dry gulches, or have enough volume to keep pace, such as **Cimarron Creek**. Other streams, that at one time entered the canyon in its early formation, have been "beheaded" and flow away from the canyon.

In its short geologic life, the Gunnison River has removed some 25 cubic miles of rock, and the excavation process is still going on, although slowed because of the upstream dams.

Before the dams were built, **flood stage** reached 12,000 cubic-feet-per-second (at times up to 19,000 cubic-feet-per-second.) This energy equals 2 3/4-million horsepower; enough to produce two million kilowatts of electricity. The dams produce only a fraction of this power, with the river dissipating energy through turbulent flow, friction over the rapids, scouring of the riverbed, and in transporting debris.

THREE LANDSCAPES

Three distinctive **physiographic zones** (or surface landscapes) define Curecanti National Recreation Area, Black Canyon of the Gunnison National Park, and Gunnison Gorge National Conservation Area; but taken together, the three units form a complete geologic story of the canyon. Elevations range from over 8,000 feet in Curecanti NRA and along the South Rim in the National Park, to just above 5,000 feet in the lowest reaches of the Gunnison Gorge.

Beginning at the inlet to Blue Mesa Reservoir, until Blue Mesa Dam at Sapinero, **Curecanti's landscape** is of a broad valley, framed by skyline cliffs along both sides. The valley floor is of water-borne sediments from 245-65 million years ago (mya), while ancient rocks of late Precambrian age (2,500-544 mya) are seen at the shoreline at Elk Creek Campground; and at Cebolla Creek, Kezar Basin, Lake Fork and at the head of the reservoir. Much younger, volcanic rocks are seen along the skyline, plus atop the mesas on either side of the valley. These rocks also form the cores of the West Elks Mountains to the north and the San Juan Mountains to the south.

The **Black Canyon**, which begins at the Lake Fork near Blue Mesa Dam, is in a transition zone between the mountainous Rockies to the east, and the Colorado Plateau region on the west. The canyon could belong to either group and has attributes of both. From the rim, an observer can view the intense relief of the straight-walled canyon, to the narrow river course some 2,000 feet below. The canyon appears black

Sharp cliffs of younger rocks of volcanic origin rim Curecanti's broad valley.

The walls of Black Canyon are actually varicolored.

because of lack of sunlight reaching the depths; although the walls are actually varicolored, ranging from dark *schists* and *gneisses*, to colorful red and pink *pegmatite* dikes that intrude into the canyon. Most of the canyon rock is of very ancient age, up to two billion years old. Sedimentary rocks, that are clearly visible in the Gunnison Gorge, are rarely seen in the Park.

Farther downstream, the **Gunnison Gorge** is located on the eastern edge of the Colorado Plateau, an area that spreads west and north for 150,000 square miles. The difference between the Park and the Gorge is that the river cuts through much younger, sedimentary rocks in the gorge, characterized by gently

dipping sedimentary formations, cut by deep drainages. While of high relief, the Gorge is not a single sheer wall as in the Park, but is stair-stepped in topography with a unique **double canyon** system of hard, crystalline rock in the lower gorge, capped by sedimentary layers.

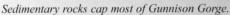

Sedimentary rocks cap most of Gunnison Gorge.

The Rocks Tell The Story

The very long chain of events that led to the actual creation of the Black Canyon has its roots in the dim past, nearly 2 billion years ago. For someone interested in understanding the complete and fascinating story, the evidence is found in the surrounding rocks.

The rocks of the **Inner-Canyon** of the Black Canyon, often called the "basement rocks," all exceed one billion years of age, with some close to two billion years old. Two main classifications of rocks are represented here — **metamorphic** and **igneous** — which formed during a period of great tectonic activity in Colorado, when continents collided and mountain ranges were raised up. By far the largest portion of today's Inner-Canyon is made up of metamorphic rocks from this period, dark-colored **gneiss** and **schist** that were altered from the original granites and other rocks by tremendous heat and pressure from tectonic forces. Great columns of igneous rock, as molten lava, also rose through cracks and faults and erupted on the surface. Lava not reaching the surface formed **pegmatite dikes**, some of which were miles long and hundreds of feet wide; and within them formed large crystals, some of them as much as 10 feet across. Containing light-colored quartz and mica with traces of gold and silver, these rocks are of a much smaller volume than the metamorphic rock in the Inner-Canyon walls; but they are responsible for the impressive and very colorful features seen today at places like the **Painted Wall**.

Don't know your *gneiss* from your *schist*? See the **Glossary of Geologic Terms** on page 230.

THE ANCESTRAL ROCKIES FORM

Over great periods of time, the mountain ranges eroded away leaving the area near sea level as a nearly flat plain, during which time thick-deposits of sedimentary rocks, primarily sandstones, formed over Colorado. About 350 million years ago, another **orogeny** (*mountain building phase*) occurred, formed from the core of the earlier range. These **Ancestral Rockies** comprised two parallel mountain ranges, running north to south, and roughly corresponding to today's Front and Sawatch Ranges. Also at this time, the **Uncompahgre Highland** formed, an ancestral version of today's Uncompahgre Plateau, lying west of the Black Canyon. The uplifted mountain mass eventually eroded away again, leaving only the roots of the ranges. Erosion of this uplift created thick deposits of sandstone to the northeast and southwest, forming the reddish-colored beds seen near Aspen in the famous Maroon Bells and in the canyon walls at present-day Ouray, south of the Black Canyon. The ancestral Uncompahgre Highland is obvious around the Black Canyon, as erosion has stripped away the deposits laid down after the highland subsided. It forms the summit of **Vernal Mesa** on the southwest rim and the top of **Mesa Inclinado** to the northeast.

By about 230 million years ago, the remains of the Ancestral Rockies had eroded to low relief; and seas invaded the western interior of Colorado, receding and reinvading four times. Deposits of sandstones and vari-colored shales formed on the Colorado Plateau and in western Colorado, including three distinct formations — the **Entrada sandstone**, the **Wanakah Formation**, and the

Morrison Formation. The latter is most interesting because it is in the Morrison that great, and small, dinosaurs left their skeletons. At about 80 million years ago, a shallow sea inundated much of the interior of North America, including western Colorado, depositing clay that became the **Mancos shale**, which comprises much of the Uncompahgre Valley west of Black Canyon. During these epochs, the **Burro Canyon Formation**, **Dakota sandstone** and the Mancos were deposited over the Morrison Formation. However, these have been eroded away in many areas of the canyon, as a result of a later orogeny, resulting in an **unconformity** (or a place where a particular sequence of rocks is missing.) An excellent example of this is at the rims of the canyon in the National Park, where these formations are missing entirely and a much younger set of rocks sits directly on the ancient basement rock. During this period, the seas advanced and retreated numerous time, until crustal uplift of the region drained off the sea for the last time. The scene was now set for events that would lead directly to the creation of the Black Canyon.

FINAL STAGE OF MOUNTAIN BUILDING

What is called the **Laramide Orogeny** began about 72 million years ago and resulted in the present mountain ranges of Colorado. As part of this great uplift of the Rockies, the **Gunnison Uplift,** into which the Black Canyon is cut, raised up along old fault lines. Erosion from streams with their sources high in the Sawatch Range to the east reduced the uplift to a nearly flat plain and the river flowed unhindered over the truncated top of the Uplift. Sequences of sedimentary rocks on the surface of the Gunnison Uplift were worn away, creating the unconformity mentioned above.

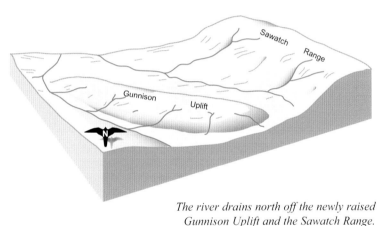

The river drains north off the newly raised Gunnison Uplift and the Sawatch Range.

Erosion strips off the top of the Gunnison Uplift and the rivers flow unimpeded across a plain.

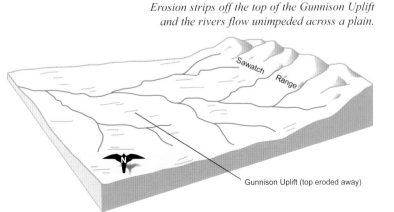

Gunnison Uplift (top eroded away)

SETTING THE COURSE OF A RIVER

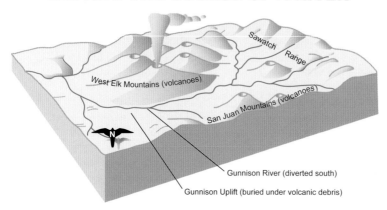

Gunnison River (diverted south)

Gunnison Uplift (buried under volcanic debris)

West Elk Mountains (volcanoes)

San Juan Mountains (volcanoes)

Sawatch Range

N

Volcanic activity north in the West Elk Mountains and south in the San Juan Mountains alter and define the course of the river.

Then about 40 million years ago, in the **West Elk Mountains** and the **San Juan Mountains**, north and south respectively of the nascent Gunnison River, volcanic activity broke out that had the far-reaching consequence of overhauling the entire drainage of the river. Over millions of years, volcanoes erupted, sending ash and fragmented material covering large areas. These eruptions took several forms. Some, such as the many cubic miles of ash that blew from the **La Garita Caldera**, largest in the world, formed deposits over the region called **tuffs**. These are seen as bright orange on cliffs in and along the rim of the canyon. Others, composed of fragmental rock, formed the **West Elk breccia** that today is seen in the dramatic pinnacles north of US-50 in Curecanti NRA. As the ash and volcanic rock accumulated, drainage patterns became confined and then blocked, only to restore themselves between eruptive periods. As thick ash flows covered the Gunnison Uplift, downward warping occurred that determined the course of the Gunnison River. If the downward warping had not occurred, the Gunnison could have flowed more to the north or the south into softer formations, creating a broad valley like the Uncompahgre. Instead, the river became increasing confined in a course around the southern edge of the West Elk Mountains until the last of the volcanic eruptions, about 18.5 million years ago.

CUTTING A GREAT GORGE

A period of erosion began as the river eroded through the softer, volcanic rock. About 2 million years ago, down cutting of the canyon began. Entrenched in its **syncline** (downward warped structure), and confined by the volcanic debris, the Gunnison cut into the hard gneiss and schist of the basement rocks. The softer formations of the Gunnison Basin above the Black Canyon, and below in the Gunnison Gorge, allowed the river to cut a broader plain. But forced into the hard crystalline rock in between, the river had no choice but to cut steeper and faster to maintain the river's natural proclivity to maintain a constant gradient. For the past 2 million years, the Gunnison River has continued to cut deeply into this basement rock, barely keeping up with the rate of erosion needed to achieve a stable gradient. So fast was the down cutting, which is still going on, that side streams could not keep pace. With exceptions such as **Cimarron Creek**, **Cebolla Creek**, **Soap Creek**, **Lake Fork**, **Blue Creek** and **Smith Fork** (all of which have cut their beds fast enough to match the down-cutting of the Gunnison), many side streams, with much lower energy, could not keep pace with the down cutting of the Gunnison. As a result, the canyon has few streams entering it; and those that do are usually waterfalls and dry gulches Other streams, that at one time entered the canyon in an earlier formation, have been "beheaded" and today flow away from the canyon.

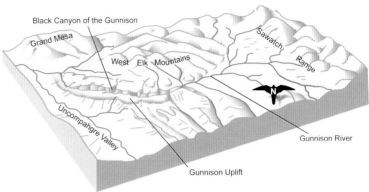

The Black Canyon forms as the Gunnison River becomes entrenched in the harder, older crystalline rocks of the Gunnison Uplift.

Massive glaciation during the **Ice Age**, lasting until some 10,000 years ago, effected the erosion of the Black Canyon. While glaciers never reached down into the canyon itself, extensive glaciation occurred in the higher ranges of Colorado, including the West Elk Mountains to the northeast and Sawatch Range to the east. Glaciers flowed far down alpine valleys, depositing sediments at the glaciers' termini. Increased flow of streams and rivers during spring and summer carried high volumes of this erosive material through the canyon, increasing the scouring action on the valley floor.

THE PROCESS CONTINUES TODAY

Other forces aid in erosion of the canyon including gullying, rill wash, frost action, atmospheric weathering, and rock fall that widen the canyon walls. Water and other agents act on the tributaries, joints, and faults, undermining the stability of the canyon walls. Huge blocks drop off into the canyon floor and talus slopes relentlessly creep down the slopes, carrying large and small rocks slowly into the gorge. Occasional cloudbursts lubricate the walls and gullies, accelerating the process; but none of these forces can match the pace of the Gunnison River, cutting ever downward. The Black Canyon continues to erode today at the rate of about **one foot per thousand years**. Although the upstream dams now control seasonal flooding, about the same volume of water still moves through the canyon each year. But early visitors, who had the chance to view the river before construction of the dams, described the unleashed power and fury of floodstage in early summer as *"absolutely frightening."* Management plans have posed the possibility of future controlled releases from the dams that could partially simulate seasonal flow, motivated not by any wish to speed up down-cutting of the canyon, but rather, to restore habitat conditions. In any case, the dams may have muted the flow, but they've not eliminated the continued down-cutting of the Black Canyon.

Perhaps in another two million years, when the dams are long gone and the river's headward erosion of the canyon has proceeded inexorably upstream, visitors and residents in the town of Gunnison may find the new entrance to Black Canyon of the Gunnison National Park at their very doorstep.

Where to See Rock Types

For geologists or amatuer rock hounds, the Black Canyon is an endlessly fascinating place where the geologic record goes back nearly 1.7 billion years. This record manifests itself in dozens of formations and rock types from all epochs exposed by erosion of the canyon, although because of several **unconformities**, some rock sequences are missing at several locations.

What follows is a list of major rock types and where they can be readily seen in and around the Black Canyon. It is assumed that the user has some familiarity with the physical characteristics of common rock types. An excellent reference for understanding the complex geology of the canyon is *The Black Canyon of the Gunnison: Today and Yesterday* by Wallace R. Hansen (see **Additional Reading**, page 222.) For more information about some of the terms used here, refer to the **Glossary of Geologic Terms** on page 230. Please remember that it is illegal to collect rock specimens in the National Park.

METAMORPHIC ROCKS

The metamorphic rocks in Black Canyon are overwhelmingly of two types, **gneiss** and **schist**. Metamorphic rocks of up to 1.7 billion years of age form much of the dark inner walls of Black Canyon in the Park, and are also found in the uplands away from the rim at Vernal Mesa, Poverty Mesa, Coffee Pot Hill, Fitzpatrick Mesa, Blue Creek and along the shore of Blue Mesa Reservoir at the Lake Fork and Cebolla Creek.

Colorado's highest cliff, Painted Wall, owes its beauty and structure to a matrix of **feldspar-enriched gneiss**, approaching granite in composition, intruded by light-colored pegmatite dikes. At The Narrows, gneiss, again intruded by pegmatite, comprises the highly resistant rock at that location.

Vertical dikes of pegmatite intruded into gneiss "basement rocks" of the Park's Inner-Canyon.

Migmatite gneiss, formed by the injection of magma into a pre-existing gneiss, is more deformed than other gneiss formations in the canyon. It is coarse-grained and also called *injection gneiss.* These rocks can be found at Morrow Point Dam and Pioneer Lookout along CO-92.

Schists are also widely distributed in the Black Canyon

These are mostly **micaceous schist** and **amphibolite**. Both become gneiss by the addition of feldspar. At Morrow Point Dam, micaceous schist contains *sillimanite* (aluminum silicate) formed under high heat and pressure. These schists were probably originally siliceous shale. It is also found with the Pitts Meadow granodiorite near Smith Fork. Micaceous schists can be seen near the South Rim Campground and up the canyon for more than three miles. Some of these schists contain garnets.

Amphibolite, or *hornblende schist*, is not as common; but with its black and shiny luster, it is easily recognized at a distance. Amphibolite was probably originally a basaltic lava or tuff. Amphibolite can be seen at Red Canyon, Crystal Creek in Delta County, Chukar Canyon, Black Canyon upstream from Red Rock Canyon and Crystal Reservoir two miles downstream from Cimarron Creek.

Muscovite schist contains quartz veins and is disjointed by fracturing into shapes that look like sausages called *"boudinage."* A lustrous muscovite schist can be seen at Chukar Canyon and Pleasant Park.

SEDIMENTARY ROCKS

Brightly colored Entrada sandstone along the Chukar Trail.

The **Entrada sandstone** was deposited about 140 million years ago along the margins of a shallow sea as dunes, but may also have been partly deposited by ancient streams. It has mostly a reddish color, but can be pink or yellow, and is characterized by cross-bedding and planar-bedded. Massive sand dunes covered the region, leaving deposits that form a cap of sandstone that is thin at the Park (but thick at nearby Colorado National Monument.) The Entrada weathered from the remnants of the Uncompahgre Highland and contains pegmatite, gneiss, and quartz angular fragments. The Entrada is best seen at Red Rock Canyon, continuously to the Smith Fork in Gunnison Gorge. It is well exposed along the northeast rim, where its pink or yellow band is just above the inner-canyon wall. The North Vista Trail brings the hiker close to the formation. It can also be viewed along CO-92 in Curecanti. In the Gunnison Gorge at the top of the formation, there is a pale-green, chrome-bearing layer that is widespread and may be associated with *vanadium*.

The **Wanakah Formation** consists of varicolored shale, mudstone, gypsum, friable gray sandstone and gray limestone laid down in an arid landlocked seaway or lake that flooded parts of New Mexico and Colorado. It thins eastward, as does the Entrada. It is seen as a drab-gray color separating the colorful Entrada below it, from the lighter Morrison above. The best locations to view the Wanakah is in the outer walls of the Gunnison Gorge, in the lower part of Smith Fork and at Chukar Canyon. In the Park, it is mostly covered by soil and brush.

There are two members associated with the Wanakah Formation — the **Pony Express limestone** and the **Junction Creek sandstone**. The Pony Express limestone is at the base of the Wanakah formation. It was identified and named in the San Juan Mountains near Ouray, where it is an ore carrier. The Pony Express is *oolitic,* or looks like fish roe. It is fragmental and broken up by the dissolution of interlayered gypsum. The Pony Express was deposited in a lake or arm of an inland sea, whose shoreline followed a line south-southeast through the Black Canyon, from Red Canyon of Crystal Creek in Delta County, to the south end of Dead Horse Mesa in Montrose County. The Pony Express can be viewed along the North Rim Drive near The Narrows, but it disappears to the east.

Another member of the Wanakah Formation is the Junction Creek sandstone, similar to the Entrada. It is coarser grained, cross-bedded, and lighter in color than the reddish Entrada sandstone. The cross-bedding indicates that winds deposited and rearranged the sand dunes on the floor of a dried up sea. It is easily seen at the mouth of Smith Fork in the Gunnison Gorge area. At Blue Mesa Dam, it surfaces and continues east beneath the reservoir to near Gunnison. It can also be seen along CO- 92 at Soap Mesa and on the slopes of Black Mesa.

Every child's delight, dinosaurs, dominated the landscape when the **Morrison Formation** was being deposited. Broad leaf plants grew abundantly. Sandstones and conglomerates accumulated on a broad alluvial plain in channels of meandering streams. Overflow from the rivers deposited shales in shallow lakes. The Morrison is one of the most widespread and recognized formations in The West. In the Gunnison Gorge, parts of a *Sauropod* dinosaur have been found and fragments of vertebrae and limbs have been uncovered in the Salt Wash member of the Morrison Formation, first discovered by Uranium prospectors in the early 1950's. The Morrison has two members in the Black Canyon — the **Salt Wash member** overlaid by the **Brushy Basin member**.

The Brushy Basin member is light gray shale with some red shale and a little gray sandstone and a bed of red and green chert known as the *"Christmas Tree conglomerate."* The Brushy Basin contains dinosaur bones, fossilized tree trunks, and plant debris.

The Salt Wash member has alternating mudstones and claystones. It was deposited in fluvial and flood plain environments. The Salt Wash is variegated green, red, purple, and gray bentonitic mudstones, interbedded with conglomerate sandstones, and limestone beds. Fragments of dinosaur bones have been found The clay in this formation may be volcanic in origin. The Morrison is well exposed in the Gunnison Gorge and caps the dark rocks of the Inner Canyon in the Park, but is mostly covered by soil and brush. It is in evidence along the shore of Blue Mesa Reservoir.

The **Burro Canyon Formation** lies directly on top of the Morrison. Above it are the Dakota sandstone and Mancos shale. It is composed of a pebbly conglomerate and coarse-grained sandstone. The pebbles are mostly a light-gray chert and quartzite, that may have had their source in western Utah or eastern Nevada. The Burro Canyon Formation can be viewed along the north shore of

Rock Types of Black Canyon (composite section)

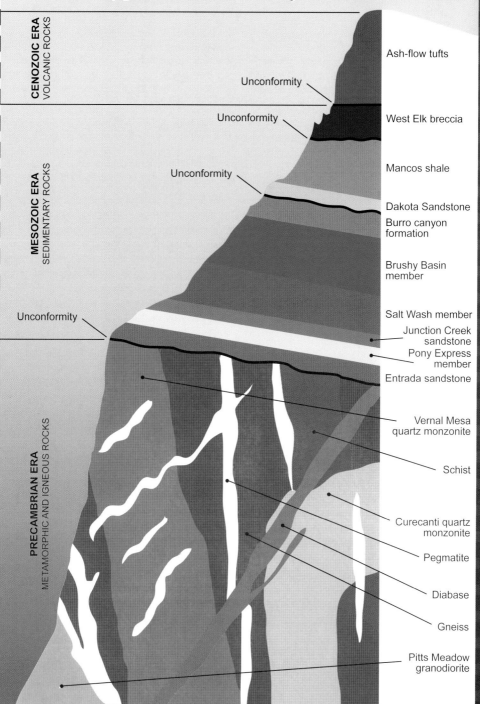

CENOZOIC ERA
VOLCANIC ROCKS

Ash-flow tufts

Unconformity

Unconformity

West Elk breccia

MESOZOIC ERA
SEDIMENTARY ROCKS

Mancos shale

Unconformity

Dakota Sandstone

Burro canyon formation

Brushy Basin member

Salt Wash member

Unconformity

Junction Creek sandstone

Pony Express member

Entrada sandstone

PRECAMBRIAN ERA
METAMORPHIC AND IGNEOUS ROCKS

Vernal Mesa quartz monzonite

Schist

Curecanti quartz monzonite

Pegmatite

Diabase

Gneiss

Pitts Meadow granodiorite

Blue Mesa and in Gunnison Gorge, plus 100 to 200 feet below the rims at Fruitland Mesa and Grizzly Ridge. The road into the Park climbs onto the Burro Canyon Formation.

The **Dakota sandstone** formed in a shallow sea where fine sand and mud were deposited. It is composed of pebbly conglomerate, shale, and coal, and has fossil ripples, worm trails and burrows. It also contains petrified wood and carbonized plant matter, indicating deposition in shallow water. The upper part of the Dakota mixes with the lower part of the Mancos shale. Since the Mancos is a marine-deposited formation, the upper part of the Dakota indicates the transition from land to inundation by a sea. Like the Morrison, the Dakota is widespread throughout the west and is known for the trapping of groundwater and petroleum. It caps the hills of the North Rim. The Dakota sandstone is best seen along the upper wall of the Black Canyon, north of Chasm View, and in the uppermost walls of the Gunnison Gorge. It forms hogbacks, rim rocks and dipping slopes that cap Fruitland Mesa, Grizzly Ridge, Poison Spring Hill, Dead Horse Mesa and Pine Ridge.

Mancos shale formed away from the shore of an inland sea, where black mud accumulated in deeper water marine. This deposit is very thick, soft, and dull gray in color. The Mancos shale forms some of the slopes and rounded hills seen in the Uncompahgre Valley and upstream from the Black Canyon. When wet, it becomes glue-like and slippery. Soap Creek in Curecanti is named for this property. Mancos Shale is associated with landslides that can be seen along the highway between Blue Creek Canyon and Montrose. The Mancos shale is viewed at Soap Creek, north of Blue Mesa Reservoir, and comprises most of the Uncompahgre Valley and that valley's badlands.

IGNEOUS ROCKS

There are three main types of igneous rocks found in the Black Canyon — **quartz monzonite**, **granodiorite** and **pegmatite**. All of these are similar to granite in mineral content. (Much less common igneous rocks that show up in the canyon are diorite, aplite and lamprophyres.)

Quartz monzonite forms large, homogenous rock masses that are distinctive in the inner walls of the Black Canyon in the Park, as well as upstream. Two types express themselves. **Vernal Mesa quartz monzonite** is the dark, coarse grained rock that forms the sheer walls of the canyon from Rock Point, downstream past Chasm View to Cedar Point, Dragon Point, Sunset View and High Point. **Curecanti quartz monzonite** is light colored and finer grained, and is widely exposed in the upper canyon, most remarkably at the famous Curecanti Needle. Small garnets are often seen in outcrops of this monzonite.

Vernal Mesa quartz monzonite forms a highly resistant basement rock in parts of the gorge in the Park.

Pitts Meadow granodiorite is the dominant rock of the inner-canyon of the Gunnison Gorge. Similar to granite, it differs chemically and in certain minerals, making it darker in appearance.

Pegmatite applies to a variety of intrusive igneous rocks of coarse grain that are very common and form striking patterns on the dark walls of Black Canyon's Inner-Canyon. Famous Painted Wall is known for its system of pegmatite dikes, but other striking examples are evident at Pulpit Rock, Chasm View and Cedar Point. Very large bodies of this rock, hundreds of feet across, can be seen at several locations around the upper canyon. Coffee Pot Hill has a very large block of pegmatite that forms the top and eastern slope.

Volcanism in the San Juan Mountains and the West Elk Mountains formed tuffs and breccias, among the youngest of rock formations in the Black Canyon area. In the San Juan Mountains, magma formed deep and rose violently, erupting like a shaken pop bottle. Super-heated water spewed into the air, spraying out and flowing over the side. From these, the **Fish Canyon tuff** formed. Out of the **La Garita Caldera**, largest in the world, ash blew out covering large areas and creating additional tuffs. These are seen as bright orange on cliffs in and along the rim of the canyon.

The **Hinsdale Formation** forms the thick, basaltic cap of Cannibal Plateau and Alpine Mesa, south of Blue Mesa Reservoir. Some remnants remain on Pine Creek and Carpenter Ridge. The Hinsdale Formation once covered much of the area from Blue Mesa Reservoir to Cannibal Plateau, but it never reached the Black Canyon.

Flows of magma from the West Elks Mountains created the **West Elk breccia**. The main eruptive center was near the head of Elk Creek. It can be viewed at the head of Black Canyon, along the north shore of Blue Mesa Reservoir, and especially along Curecanti Creek, Soap Creek, West Elk Creek, Dillon Mesa, Red Creek, and East Elk Creek. The **Dillon Pinnacles** are composed entirely of West Elk breccia and are reached by a two-mile trail starting at the Middle Bridge on US-50. Another place to view the spires created by this formation is southeast of the town of Crawford at Castle Peak and Cathedral Peak.

West Elk breccia deposits around Blue Mesa Reservoir.

NATURAL HISTORY

A "pygmy forest" caps the rims of the Black Canyon.

The Black Canyon of the Gunnison has gone through a century of unprecedented development by man; as tunnels, dams, railroads, highways and cattle herds intruded into the once wild and remote canyon. With the creation of a new National Park in 1999, the pendulum has swung and the nation's highest level of protection has been extended over the canyon, with the hope of preserving its unique plants and animals (some of which are still threatened or endangered) for all time.

Home to Diverse Ecosystems

The Black Canyon of the Gunnison and its surrounding lands are home to a very diverse group of plants and animals. There are three factors that have shaped the fascinating natural history of the Black Canyon region.

Lying in a ecological **transition zone** between the great uplift of the southern Rocky Mountains in central Colorado and the vast Colorado Plateau stretching west through Utah, the Gunnison Valley shares plants and animals common to both. The diversity is tremendous — in a few square miles, you may find cactus and columbine, tall pine and pygmy oak, or rattlesnake and elk.

Secondly, the leap in **altitude** — between river and rim, as well as between the lowest reaches of the Gunnison Gorge and the highest mesas above Curecanti's reservoirs — is enormous. For instance, in only a few dozen miles, rainfall varies from less than 10 inches in the low semi-desert of the western part of Gunnison Gorge to 25 inches on the high rims of the canyon in Curecanti NRA. The variety of natural environments, each with unique plants and animals, created by differences in elevation in such a short distance is quite amazing.

Finally, the steep gradient of the Gunnison River, and the great depth and narrowness of the canyon it has created, has imposed a **physical barrier** or limit to the migration of plants, animals and fish. Plants and animals on the North Rim are the same as species on the South Rim, but some have developed unique characteristics. The depth and steepness of the canyon has also created *microclimates* for plant and animal life. Some areas rarely receive sunlight, while others are nearly always bathed in light. Such extremes of dark and light, and cold and warmth, play a large part in the Inner-Canyon in determining the distribution of plants and animals.

Actually, a fourth factor is shaping the environment around Black Canyon as well (but so recently, as to be difficult to fully appreciate) — the hand of man. With the construction of the dams and reservoirs in Curecanti NRA, habitats were destroyed or altered, and new ones were created. Migration routes for mule deer, winter range for elk, mineral licks for bighorn sheep, spawning beds for fish, and breeding sites for birds were lost. But new species of birds moved in and non-native fish were introduced by man to fill new niches in the environment.

THE ROCK BREAKERS

Coating the rocks and canyon walls in a multitude of subtle colors is a hardy mat-like vegetation, composed of moss and fungus growing together to form **lichen**. Lichen slowly decomposes rock by chemical action, creating cracks allowing larger plants to gain a foothold. This is an important erosive process providing a mechanism for the creation of soils. Cracks allow water to intrude; and where ice forms and expands, it further breaks apart rocks.

AUTUMN AT CURECANTI

The upland mesas surrounding the sparkling reservoirs of Curecanti National Recreation Area have a varied range of landscapes; and in autumn, contribute to a stunningly beautiful display of fall colors draping the hillsides at the NRA. Mid-September to early October is the peak time to view this popular pageant — when the days are still warm, the nights are crisp and the first dusting of snow has covered the distant San Juan Mountains, framed against a cobalt

blue Colorado sky.

Small, but exquisite, stands of **quaking aspen** in the NRA, with fluttering leaves of gold, orange or red, only hint at the glories hidden in the nearby West Elk Mountains; where reputedly, the largest *continuous* aspen forest in North America lies on its western slope near Kebler Pass (see **West Elk Loop** on page 215.) At Curecanti, the groves are smaller, mostly made up of clones spread from underground shoots of a single tree. Thus, each tree in a grove is genetically identical. All trees in a stand usually turn color at the same time; although groves next to each other, created from a different parent, will turn at different times. Elk may move down into the meadows between the groves in September; when their ringing bugles, as bulls collect their harems, may be heard echoing in the valley.

Gnarled, stiffly branched and unpenetrable stands of **scrub oak** *(Gambel oak)* add the other startling splash of color, bathing whole hillsides with scarlet. Further down slope, **rabbit brush**, which retain colorful flowers well into September, may add bright yellow to the scene and **cottonwoods, alders, wild rose, raspberry** and **serviceberry** bushes bring fall colors — ranging from yellowish-green, to gold, to bright red — to nature's annual feast for the eyes.

Looking across colorful displays of aspen and scrub oak to the snow-capped San Juan Mountains.

WINTER AT BLACK CANYON

With the first big snowfall in November, the North Rim closes for the season and the South Rim Drive remains unplowed until spring from the Visitor Center to High Point. While snow accumulation is not heavy during most winters at Black Canyon of the Gunnison National Park, temperatures do routinely drop below zero at night, even to -30°F. Of over 100 species of birds seen at the canyon, only about two dozen are year-round residents. Critters such as

bats, yellow-bellied marmots and black bears spend the season in hibernation. But to venture here during the winter season is to find a very active natural world made more beautiful by the stark contrast of white snow against dark cliffs.

In fact, some animals are much easier to spot at the canyon in winter time. Small herds of **mule deer** forage more widely during daylight hours in order to find enough food to get them through this brutal season; and **elk**, normally on their high-country summer range outside the Park, are driven down to where they can paw through the light snow cover and forage on rabbit brush, sage and other browse. A ski or snowshoe tour along either rim drive reveals that many animals are active all winter along the rims of the Black Canyon. A record of their comings and goings shows up in tracks left in fresh snow on the abandoned road.

A **mountain cottontail** appears to have been in a desperate hurry. The dog-like tracks of a **coyote** join the rabbit's and the pair dodge and weave, until the rabbit dives into the thick oak cover to the side of the road.

A wallowed-out trough in the snow leads to the base of a sturdy pinyon pine. Looking high up the tree trunk, large patches of bark have been gnawed off by a **porcupine**. At the base of the trunk, tracks recognized as those of an impossibly large cat are at first puzzling, until one realizes with a thrill that a **mountain lion** has passed by here, curious also about the *porky*.

At the next overlook, dry pellets and guano reveal a **golden eagle** had perched here, surveying its realm.

Light snowfall on scrub oak.

SPRING AT GUNNISON GORGE

For most of the year, the sagebrush flats, buff-colored hills and deeply dissected canyons of the Gunnison Gorge are a very dry place. Fewer than 10 inches of moisture falls in the low, semi-desert portions of the National Conservation Area; and snow that falls on the higher pinyon/juniper-studded ridges quickly melts without accumulating a reservoir of moisture for plants. Daytime temperatures in the summer can approach 100°F in all but the highest reaches of the NCA. Virtually all of the gulches are dry during the better part of the year; with only major waterways like the Gunnison, and its tributary canyons of the Smith Fork and the North Fork in the northern part of the NCA, having large areas of lush, green riparian vegetation year-round along their banks. One would think that this is a tough place for a plant to make a living.

Of course species have adapted with strategies to cope very successfully in this semi-desert. They develop deep tap roots to seek out underground moisture, or horde water in their cells; or their seeds lie patiently dormant, waiting for that uncertain event, a spring shower. And during a brief period each year, the Gorge comes to life.

In begins as early as February, when on south-facing slopes a tiny introduced geranium, called **filaree**, pops up. Filaree germinates in the fall; so that as soon as soil temperature warms up in sheltered spots, the tiny pink flowers bloom. It is so small as to be practically unnoticed; but in years of ample moisture, entire hillsides can appear to take on a faint pink tinge.

By March and early April, larger, more obvious plants begin their big show. The beautiful blue cups of **pasqueflowers** appear in damper meadows and under shade on hillsides, and bright white **sand lilies** spread in the sandy soils between sagebrush. The peak of the display in Gunnison Gorge is reached in May. With spiny leaves plump with stored water, colorful cactus bloom in seemingly the most inhospitable locations. Perhaps the most beautiful is the **claretcup cactus**; its large cup-like flowers are a deep, wine-red. Also common out on the sagebrush flats, **yucca** send up huge stalks of large greenish-white flowers.

As the season progresses, plants flower further up on the sage, scrub and pinyon/juniper clad hills. If it has been a wetter year, these displays can be quite stunning. Lovely **Indian paintbrush,** bright orange **wallflowers**, and tall **mules ears** bloom just as the first sage grouse chicks appear. Hummingbirds migrating up the canyon toward their summer nesting areas in the mountains, refuel themselves from the red trumpets of **scarlet gilia**. And by the time that bighorn sheep drop their lambs on secluded ledges in the canyon, **arrowleaf balsamroot** often have colored the dry hillsides a golden yellow.

With the arrival of the intense heat of summer, the hillsides and canyon walls of Gunnison Gorge take on a dull brown to gray-green color, relieved by the pastels of the sandstones and thin ribbons of green along the watercourses.   But there is one final burst being saved up. In September, the flowering of thousands of acres of **big sagebrush** and **rabbit brush** (the former with inconspicuous silver-green heads and the latter with showy golden blooms) heralds the end of summer.

Sage and arrowleaf balsamroot.

SUMMER IN THE INNER-CANYON

At mid-summer, a trip into the sanctum of the Inner-Canyon of the Black Canyon reveals an ancient world seemingly all its own — away from camera-toting tourists, begging chipmunks, and exhaust-belching camper trailers. From the start of the steep descent, the smells and sounds of civilization are quickly replaced by the sweet scent of pines and the haunting music of **canyon wrens**. These uninhibited songsters, synonymous with canyon country to veteran canyoneers, are more often heard than seen, as they poke along rock ledges searching for food.

Descending in hot sun one moment, then in cool shade the next, differences in temperature and soil moisture create *microclimates* where hanging forests of **ponderosa pine**, **Douglas fir** and **quaking aspen**, with their communities of plants and animals, thrive in small pockets. A dull background murmur is ever present, steadily increasing in volume to a roar at the bottom of the gorge — the sound of water crashing against rock.

Despite the impression that the world of the Inner-Canyon is one that has escaped the hand of man, in fact, developments upstream have had a profound effect on the ecology of the Inner-Canyon. Dams have curtailed the annual scouring of the canyon, allowing silt, soil and vegetation to build up along quieter stretches of the river. These backwater spots provide good habitat for wildlife, especially songbirds like the **yellow warbler**. These tiny bundles of bright-colored energy build a nest — a deep, felted cup — amongst the willows and small cottonwoods, and harvest the bounty of summer insects. Grasshoppers and other recently hatched bugs fall into the water and the river overturns rocks releasing larvae of caddis flies to the surface. From deep in pools, 20-inch **brown trout** rise to the feast, sometimes leaping completely out of the water.

With a lot of luck, perhaps even a **beaver** or **river otter** may be spotted, although you'll have more of a chance noticing sign of their activities. Beavers are occasionally on the river, active mostly at night; and gnawed remains of willows and small tree stumps mark their passage. To see a pair of river otters is a special treat because of their great playfulness and curiosity. Recently reintroduced, no one really knows how many of these delightful creatures are in the canyon; but scat and other sign can be found. Look for a "rolling area" of flattened grass next to a muddy "slide" leading down a bank into the river — their version of *Water World*.

Perhaps no other animal seems so at home in the chaos of the river than the plump, wren-like **dipper**, or *water ouzel*. Dippers are so small, drab looking and shy as to escape notice by some visitors, until one notices it resting, on a boulder mid-stream in the foaming torrent. Bobbing incessantly up and down, it then surprisingly dives right into the fast-moving water to feed on aquatic insects and even small fish. Its wings unfolded, it seemingly *flies* underwater in the strong current, then pops back up on a rock, with a juicy larvae in its thin bill. Then it's off down the river, skimming low on wing over the water, its skittering call nearly drowned out by the sound of the cascades.

Riffles and rapids on the Gunnison River.

The Gunnison River flowing through the Inner-Canyon.

FIVE MAJOR ENVIRONMENTS

The Black Canyon of the Gunnison NP, Curecanti NRA, and Gunnison Gorge NCA have **5 major environments** that overlap, supporting a great variety of plants and animals.

The **riparian environment** exists in a thin, non-continuous band of lush vegetation along the Gunnison River and its tributaries in all three units of the canyon. At lower elevations, cottonwoods, box-elder, alder, mountain maple and red-osier dogwood grow in this zone. In places, the cottonwoods and box-elder give way to shrubs, dominated by willows. Riparian environments, dense with vegetation and wildlife, have actually increased considerably with the advent of the dams, which control spring flooding.

The **sagebrush environment** is a cold, semi-desert, found from lower altitudes on much of the Gunnison Gorge NCA, to moderate altitudes around Blue Mesa Reservoir. Sagebrush lands are dry and wildlife must have mechanisms to cope with the scarcity of water and shade. In summer, daytime conditions can be very hot, while nighttime can approach freezing. In winter, there can be deep snow and sub-zero temperatures. Everything from cactus, to grasses, to rabbit brush add diversity to these slopes.

The **scrub oak and pinyon-juniper woodland** is found at moderate elevations in the Rockies; and sometimes, can be so dense as to be impenetrable. This plant community drapes virtually all of both the south and north rims in the National Park, and extends up to the volcanic-capped rims in Curecanti NRA. Scrub oak and pinyon-juniper woodlands provide excellent cover and browse for many animals. Since it is a dryland ecosystem, devastating fires are common. Be careful with campfires while in these forests.

Ponderosa pine forests are the lowest elevation timber tree. They tend to be the first trees cut for lumber and fuel, so old-growth ponderosa pine forests are rare. Individual trees are spaced far apart and grasses and small shrubs grow in between. Curecanti NRA has good stands of ponderosa pine; with only small communities existing in the National Park, including in south facing gulleys of the Inner-Canyon.

Douglas fir grows in moist cool sites, occurring normally at higher elevations than ponderosa pine forests. But they also grow in *microclimate* sites at lower elevations in the sun-shaded Inner-Canyon zone of the Black Canyon, where moisture and temperature are right for growth. Douglas fir tend to grow close together with very little ground cover.

Two other unique environments cover small areas. Lovely **aspen woodlands** grow on higher, moister slopes around Curecanti NRA. The open understories of these forests are resplendent with wildflowers in summer. A **shoreline environment** around the reservoirs in Curecanti NRA is varied; in places identical to the riparian environment; but in other areas, it also encompasses marshes and even sagebrush meadows.

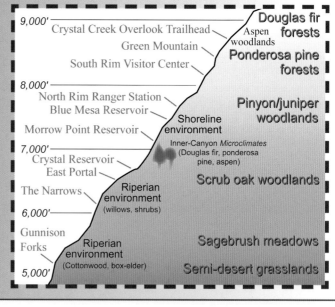

9,000'
Crystal Creek Overlook Trailhead
Green Mountain
South Rim Visitor Center

Douglas fir forests
Aspen woodlands
Ponderosa pine forests

8,000'
North Rim Ranger Station
Blue Mesa Reservoir
Morrow Point Reservoir

Pinyon/juniper woodlands
Shoreline environment

7,000'
Crystal Reservoir
East Portal

Inner-Canyon *Microclimates*
(Douglas fir, ponderosa pine, aspen)

The Narrows

Riperian environment
(willows, shrubs)

Scrub oak woodlands

6,000'

Gunnison Forks

Riperian environment
(Cottonwood, box-elder)

Sagebrush meadows

5,000'

Semi-desert grasslands

Plants

Because of the incredible range in habitats from river to rim, there are hundreds of flowering plants found in the region. Pick up a *Common Flower List* at the South Rim Visitor Center.

Cottonwood

A lush ribbon of vegetation takes hold in the bottom of the canyon where soil and seed can escape from the scouring power of the river. In this riparian environment, animals, especially songbirds and small rodents, find food and cover. The **narrowleaf cottonwood** is the most common tree along rivers and streams in The West. The cottonwood grows up to 40 feet tall, has numerous, narrow branches, and has narrow leaves resembling willow leaves. It's common to all the streams and rivers of Curecanti NRA, Black Canyon of the Gunnison NP, and Gunnison Gorge NCA.

The **box elder** is another tall tree growing streamside up to 50 feet in height. It can be identified by leaves that grow along stems of 3 to 5 leaflets. In fall, they are associated with little black-and-red bugs in great numbers. They appear mostly along the Gunnison River at lower elevations in Gunnison Gorge NCA.

Fringed sage

Mountain maple is a tall shrub or small tree, occasionally growing to 30-feet high, with gray bark and dull red winter twigs. The leaves look like a typical maple. Mountain maples occur streamside along the river and some tributaries up to elevations of 7,000'.

Willows are the most common of several shrubs that grow near water along the river, all of its side streams, and some intermittent streams. Leaves are long and slender. Twigs are narrow and the bark is smooth. Flowers are in the shape of a spike.

Rabbit brush

The ubiquitous **sagebrush** covers thousands of acres in Gunnison Gorge NCA and extends into the lower elevations of the National Park and Curecanti NRA, especially around Blue Mesa Reservoir. Found in habitats throughout The West, it is recognized by its silver-gray leaves and pleasant aroma. Leaves alternate along the stem and may have up to three clefts. Flowers are small and yellow to yellow-white. Rather than one, there are 27 species of sagebrush, each one characteristic of a different altitude and habitat.

Prickly pear cactus

The uninformed often mistake **rabbit brush** for sage, as this low shrub sometimes covers large expanses in the sagebrush environment. Its large clusters of yellow flowers bloom well into September, adding striking color to the fall scene. Rabbit brush is winter browse for elk that migrate down into Curecanti NRA and the National Park.

Sand lily

Wild buckwheat

Utah juniper

Serviceberry

Pasqueflower

Quaking aspen

The dry patches of soil between sagebrush come alive briefly in the spring with the blooming of cactus and several dozen species of wildflowers. The **prickly pear cactus** is well known for it edible properties. The fruit can be peeled and eaten raw, boiled, fried, stewed, or dried. Easily recognized, the prickly pear has flat, fleshy, spiny pads with reddish fruit growing on the tops of the ridges. Hummingbirds passing through Gunnison Gorge NCA in the spring are attracted to the bright red flowers of **scarlet gilia**. Others to look for during this brief, but showy time, are **Indian paintbrush**, **claretcup cactus**, **evening primrose**, **mules ears**, **sand lily** and **wild buckwheat**. Once in a great while, in a year of ample moisture, the flats and hillsides put on a breathtaking display.

The mesa tops and uplands of the Gunnison Uplift are blanketed by a so-called *pygmy forest*, a trio of small trees characteristic of the Colorado Plateau. **Gambel oak** (also called *scrub oak*) is common in the uplands of Curecanti NRA and along the rims of Black Canyon and the Gunnison Gorge. While generally not much taller than a man, the tree can grow up to 60 feet. Gambel oak provides cover for deer, small mammals and their carnivores. The leaves and acorns are recognizable to anyone who has ever seen a true oak. Gambel oak put on a spectacular show of red color each fall.

Utah juniper (also called *cedar*) is often found in *pygmy forests* alongside pinyon pine. The plant ranges from low shrubs with needle-like leaves, to a much taller tree with scaled leaves. The bark is soft and shredded. Utes used the bark for baby diapers. The tree has a distinctive aromatic odor, and the blue-green berries are cone-shaped.

Colorado pinyon pine is widespread along the rims of the canyon. It can grow up to 40 feet, but generally is under 20 feet. Needles grow in clusters of two along the twigs. Pine cones are short and round, and produce edible seeds, useful to both man and wildlife. Pinyon is currently under attack over large parts of Colorado from the *ips beetle*.

Driving west along the South Rim Road, you'll notice that gambel oak is replaced by a juniper-pinyon forest as you gain altitude toward High Point. Several berry-producing shrubs occur in this scrub oak and pinon-juniper woodland, especially **serviceberry**. Serviceberry was important to the native Utes who used it as part of the recipe for *pemmican*; and as an edible berry, it provides food for a variety of animals. (*Remember:* Picking edible plants in the National Park is prohibited.) The plant varies from a shrub to a small tree. The leaves can be serrated, with the flowers being large and white. The fruit is blueish to purple. Find it in clearings among the pinyon-juniper forest, but also in the draws of the Inner-Canyon where moisture is available and along the banks of the river.

Above the scrub woodlands, a Montane forest takes over, chiefly in the uplands in the eastern part of the National Park and on into Curecanti NRA, but also in pockets *(microclimates)* within the Inner-Canyon. **Ponderosa pine** occur first, especially on south facing slopes. The ponderosa pine can grow to a great height of up to 130 feet. The three-sided needles are long and grow together from sleeves in clusters of two or three. The scaled cones have sharp barbs.

Ponderosa pine forests are open and airy, with trees spaced well-apart. Thus an understory of grasses, herbs and shrubs spring up. In spring, lovely cup-shaped **pasqueflowers** bloom. The blue blossoms appear very early in Gunnison Gorge NCA; then by late April, appear in the Park in places where snow has melted away. In draws and gulches, look for the **wild rose**, easily identified by pink flowers having a distinctive, pleasant aroma of the domestic rose. The wild rose has a red edible fruit, high in Vitamin C. In sunny, rockier areas, you'll find **wild raspberry**. The raspberry grows as a bush and is generally 3 to 6 feet in height. Sharp barbs are along the the stems and branches. It is at the ends of stems that the fruit grows, appearing in late summer.

At higher elevations than the ponderosa pine, a cool **Douglas fir** forest takes over. The Douglas fir is a tall slender tree growing up to 250 feet in height. One of the characteristics of the tree is the noticeable moss that grows on the trunk and branches. Needles are flat — for identification, associate the "f" in fir to flat needles. Needles grow individually along the stem. Cones are long and have three-pointed bracts between the scales. In fir forests, the trees grow very close together, not allowing much light to reach the forest floor, and the understory is typically thin. The Douglas fir has a mutual relationship with a fungus that grows on the forest floor. Botanists call it *mycorrhizal,* which is efficient in absorbing water, protecting the tree in times of drought. In return, the fungus draws nutrients from the tree. The fungus may also provide an antibiotic for the tree, to protect it from parasitic fungi. Fir forests exist above 8,000' in Curecanti NRA, but you'll also, somewhat surprisingly, find Douglas fir in protected *microclimates* at lower altitudes within the Inner-Canyon of the National Park.

Quaking aspen forests also form a small but unique ecosystem around the canyon, primarily in small groves in higher locations in Curecanti NRA. But here and there, individual stands crop up along side streams and in protected microclimates in Black Canyon. These slender, graceful trees have whitish bark, with broadly heart-shaped leaves that turn to yellow or red in the fall in one of The West's most cherished seasonal displays. Aspen reproduce mainly by suckers, producing clones of themselves in a single grove. Aspen forests are open, full of light, and summer wildflowers are typically in abundance. Look for **Colorado columbine**, **larkspur**, and **heart-leaved arnica** among dozens of other species.

MICROCLIMATES

The depth and steepness of the canyon has created **microclimates** for plants in the Inner-Canyon, where uneven patterns of extreme shade and sunlight exist. Along the lowest parts of the canyon or in areas receiving little sunlight, evaporation is less. Snow lingers in shaded areas until late spring, providing moisture for plants normally found at much higher elevations. Thus on craggy slopes, **aspen**, **Douglas fir** and rock gardens of beautiful **wildflowers** thrive wherever soil, temperature and water conditions are favorable. In contrast, the rims are a semi-desert environment, supporting scrub oak, pinon-juniper forests and other plants that grow in a very dry climate.

Animals

With so many different environments in such a small area, animal species are well represented in this part of the Gunnison Valley. Over three dozen species of mammals, hundreds of bird species, about a dozen reptiles and an equal number of fish species populate the rivers, landforms and the air above Black Canyon. Some of these are listed as endangered or threatened, often because of the activities of man. But a few stories are encouraging, like the return of the river otter, peregrine falcon and bald eagle to the canyon area. For the most part, wildlife still thrives here, affording the visitor with exceptional chances to view and appreciate the natural world. You'll find tips for **viewing wildlife** within the Park and in the surrounding areas on page 166 in the *Activities* section of this guide.

MAMMALS

With distinctive long ears, a coarse covering of hair and a mule-like tail, everyone will instantly recognize the **mule deer**. On any given day, visitors are likely to spot small herds along the South Rim Drive, unfazed by camera-toting tourists and seemingly aware of their protected status in this National Park. The range of mule deer in summer is sagebrush meadows, aspen woodlands, oak thickets, montane forests and pinon-juniper woodlands — in fact, nearly every habitat within Black Canyon of the Gunnison NP, Curecanti NRA and Gunnison Gorge NCA, including deep in the Inner-Canyon. But they are most common in shrublands and in rough and broken terrain, where browse is abundant and cover easily obtained. In winter, they'll congregate in larger herds at lower elevations. The mule deer in summer is yellowish-brown to reddish in color, but in winter it becomes grayish. It has a white patch on its rear, the underbelly is white, and the tail has a black tip. Peak activity is usually early and late in the day.

The mule deer's larger cousin, the **elk** (also known as *wapiti*) is usually only seen be visitors to the Black Canyon area in late fall or winter, when they have migrated down from their summer range high in the West Elk Mountains. Elk are seen in Curecanti, along the Black Canyon rims, and on the uplands of the Gunnison Gorge, in areas of sagebrush and pinon-juniper forests. It's the largest animal to be encountered in the area and has three colors — the head and neck are chocolate brown, while the body is tan, with a light-tan patch on the rump. The neck sags a little in front, so there appears to be a hump on the shoulders. Males are larger than females, with antlers that grow to a huge size, length, and weight. They favor steep slopes or ridgetops for bedding down. You'll often note proximity to elk by their distinctive odor or by heavily trampled vegetation.

The third, and most elusive, of the big *ungulates* (hoofed mammals) to frequent the Black Canyon is Colorado's *State Animal*, the **Rocky Mountain bighorn sheep**. The bighorn has been reintroduced in the Black Canyon and Gunnison Gorge; and small groups also descend out of the West Elk Mountains to winter near Blue Mesa Reservoir. Excellent climbers, and a match for the rugged, rocky terrain of the canyon, bighorn are rarely seen except by canyon enthusiasts willing to tackle the backcountry. Floaters in Gunnison Gorge sometimes spot them patrolling the cliffs above the river. Visitors who have the opportunity to see the animal are impressed by the male's large curving horns. Males are stocky with dense coarse hair; gray to brown on top, with a dark brown area on the chest and a dark stripe from halfway down the back. The females are smaller, with a slender body, and horns that curve but are not curled.

Mule deer

Pronghorn antelope are not a common visitor to the National Park, but these speedy denizens of semi-desert grasslands are seen on the western and southern reaches of the Gunnison Gorge NCA and on into the Uncompahgre Valley. Pronghorn are a light reddish with a white rump, with white underneath and on bands around the neck. Both males and females have the horn, mostly straight with a short "prong" pointing forward.

Elk

The largest of the carnivores/omnivores that roam the Black Canyon area is the **black bear**. Not commonly seen, yet bears inhabit nearly any habitat providing food, water and cover, especially shrublands and forests in mountainous areas around Curecanti NRA; but they also find a living in the canyon country. Colors can range from black to brown to blondish, and change seasonally from bleaching by increased exposure to sunlight.   Bears are shy, seek areas with rough topography, dense vegetation and cover for escape, and are rarely encountered (see **Wildlife Encounters** on page 28 for more information.) Your best chance of spotting a bear is in early spring when bears may range over a large area in search of food after hibernation, and in the fall, when they gorge on serviceberries in Curecanti NRA in preparation for their long sleep. Also, you may find evidence of their presence by claw marks on aspen trees in the NRA.

Bighorn sheep

Anywhere that you camp in the Black Canyon area, your peaceful slumbers may be disturbed by the eerie yips and howls of **coyotes**. They rival mule deer for number of habitats that they occupy around and in the canyon, aided by their omnivorous tastes and high intelligence. The animal is slender with a bushy tail, erect and pointed ears, and color that varies with season and elevation. Generally it is gray, with face, forelegs, and ears a reddish-to-brownish buff. The tail has a black tip. Coyotes are active anytime, but mostly in the evening. They are difficult to spot in broken canyon country, with the best chances occurring where they are forced to cross open areas, like access roads in the Park or along the shores of the reservoirs in Curecanti NRA.

Pronghorn antelope

There are several members of the weasel family in the Black Canyon area, including the **long-tailed weasel** and

Coyote

Yellow-bellied marmot

Porcupine

Golden-mantled squirrel

Whitetailed jackrabbit

the **mink**; but surely, the most fascinating has to be the **river otter**, which is in the midst of an encouraging recovery after nearly disappearing from Colorado in the early part of the 20th Century. Pairs of otters were reintroduced into the Black Canyon in the 1980s and signs indicated that they have recolonized the river from Blue Mesa Dam, downstream to the Gunnison Gorge, and beyond. The river otter has a long body and a thick tail, with a head that is small for the body and a short muzzle. Feet are short and webbed. The otter's colors are dark brown, with pale brown or silvery color underneath. Obviously, you'll have to be at river level to have a chance to spot them, but as they are active during the day — and curious to a fault — floaters through the Gunnison Gorge occasionally report sightings. They are still listed as an endangered species.

Your chances of spotting a **mountain lion** (also called *puma* and *cougar*) are quite low, but they are common in the rough canyon country, montane forests, shrublands and pinon-juniper woodlands of the Black Canyon — in fact anywhere that mule deer, their favorite prey, inhabit. Their stealth and mostly nocturnal habits make them a rare sighting (see **Wildlife Encounters** on page 28 for more information.) Color is brown to reddish brown, paler underneath, with a long, cylindrical tail with a black tip. You'll have more luck spotting sign of its passing, then actually sighting the big cat. Sign of mountain lion presence is seen by markers of scraped dirt and debris, marked with urine and feces, generally at the margin of home ranges, as well as tracks. If you do sight a mountain lion in Black Canyon of the Gunnison NP, report it to the rangers so that they can monitor the situation.

Another common cat in the canyon, and equally difficult to spot, is the **bobcat**. Much smaller than a mountain lion, with short tails, long legs, and short fur, bobcats are brown, with a lower area that is white with blackish spots. Bobcats inhabit brushy areas in the canyons, draws, washes and rough areas of Gunnison Gorge NCA and in the Park. But sometimes they are seen in the forests and meadows of higher areas, such as in Curecanti NRA. Bobcats avoid open areas and people, usually restricting their activities to dawn or dusk.

The lower elevations of Gunnison Gorge NCA are good habitat for the **ringtail**, a small and slender animal, related to raccoons, with a distinctive long tail. The upper region of the ringtail is yellow-buff with black-tipped guard hairs, while the underside is white. The tail has a black tip, and seven or eight alternating, dark and light bands. The muzzle is pointed, and the face has contrasting white areas around the eyes and below the ears. The ringtail is found in canyon country, foothills, pinon-juniper woodlands, montane shrublands, and conifer-oakbrush habitats up to about 8,000 feet. Nocturnal, they aren't observed too often; but they are fascinating creatures to watch because of their wonderful agility, climbing trees and rock faces with ease.

In all, nearly two dozen species of rodents burrow, gnaw and swim their way through every habitat in the Black Canyon area, from the pinyon-juniper uplands, to right in the river. One of the easiest for visitors to spot is the **rock squirrel**, common almost anywhere in the Gunnison Basin below 8,000 feet. The largest squirrel in Colorado, it is gray to blackish gray in color on the upper body and back, and is mottled on the flanks, with brown feet. On the underside of the body, it is lighter in color. The tail is nearly as long as the body and quite bushy. They dig burrows under bushes and rocks, and can climb quickly, often scrambling up trees and bushes. Mostly diurnal, they are active anytime of the year when the weather is warm.

Gunnison's prairie dog is the smallest of Colorado's prairie dogs and is identified by its yellow to cinnamon colored back and sides, with black hairs interspersed. The underside is paler and the top of the head, cheeks, and a line above the eyes are darker. It is found along the Gunnison River drainage, especially around Curecanti NRA. When alarmed, the prairie dog makes its distinctive sounds to warn others of the danger. Active during the day, these animals are easy to observe; except during winter hibernation. **Whitetail prairie dogs** hybridize with Gunnison's in areas where their habitats overlap, mainly on the north slope of the Gunnison Uplift around Crawford and Hotchkiss.

Another easy-to-spot critter is the **yellow-bellied marmot**, often seen sunning itself on boulders along either the north and south rim of the canyon, as well as on talus slides or rock piles in Curecanti NRA. Looking a lot like a woodchuck, with a bushy tail as long as its body, marmots have brown fur on top, with a yellowish color underneath. You'll likely hear them before you see them, as they have a distinctive, high-pitched whistle that warns the colony of your approach. They hibernate during the winter.

Two other rodents are the largest found in Colorado, but they occupy very different habitats. **Porcupines** are familiar to anyone, famous for their defensive quills. The porcupine is robust in build, stout with short legs and thick heavy tail. The tail aids in climbing trees and perching. Coniferous forests are the porcupines main habitat, but it can also be found in pinyon-juniper woodlands, cottonwood-willow forests, along river bottoms, aspen groves and semi-desert shrublands — in short, nearly anywhere within Black Canyon of the Gunnison NP, Curecanti NRA and Gunnison Gorge NCA. Porcupines are active year around and seen anytime of the day, but they are usually most active at night.

Beavers are even larger than porcupines, but couldn't occupy a more different niche in the environment. Despite man-made dams, many thousands of times larger than their own constructions, beavers are still found along the entire length of the river and in the reservoirs. The power of the river makes it nearly impossible for them to built dams, so instead they excavate dens in soft banks along quieter stretches or build lodges among talus boulders. A large, bulky animal with a big flat tail, small rounded ears and webbed hindfeet, beavers are excellent swimmers. Usually only the head shows above the waterline, unlike a muskrat where both head and back are seen. Best times to spot them are dawn and dusk.

Other mammals found in the Black Canyon area include four species of **bats**, **gray fox**, **striped skunk**, **badger**, **golden-mantled ground squirrel**, **Fremont's chickaree**, **least chipmunk**, **Colorado chipmunk**, **northern pocket gopher**, **deer mouse**, **pinyon mouse**, **canyon mouse**, **brush mouse**, **bushytailed woodrat**, **muskrat**, **longtailed vole**, **mountain cottontail**, and **whitetailed jackrabbit**.

Probably no other group of animals benefited more than **birds** by the radical changes in the environment that took place because of the construction of the dams on the Gunnison River at Curecanti NRA.. Despite the altering of some habitats, the number of species increased dramatically as new habitats were created.

The reservoirs have attracted lots of waterfowl and shorebirds, both as summer residents and migrants. Downstream from the dams, riparian habitat has taken hold as the dams have all but eliminated the spring floods that once scoured soil and vegetation from the canyon floor. The number of songbirds who thrive in that habitat has increased.

Losers are upland birds, including perhaps the endangered *Gunnison sage grouse*, that utilized the sagebrush plains covered now by huge Blue Mesa Reservoir and its accompanying roads and development.

BIRDS

In a vertical environment such as the Black Canyon, it is no wonder that those masters of the air, the birds, should be so well represented. Foraging on sagebrush flats, sheltering under a canopy of Gamble oak, nesting on cliffside ledges, wading along shorelines, flitting through stream-side willows, perched in cool spruce forests, and of course, soaring in the sky — a wide range of species have found diverse habitats to exploit in and around the canyon. You can pick up a **Checklist of Birds for Black Canyon of the Gunnison National Park** at the South Rim Visitor Center which lists 122 species (also see page 229), including permanent residents, summer residents and migrants. And there are perhaps twice that many species for the surrounding area. The following brief descriptions of birds are only a sample of the large numbers of species found from river level to montane environments in the Black Canyon of the Gunnison NP, Curecanti NRA, and Gunnison Gorge NCA.

Swifts and swallows are often mistaken for each other by novice birdwatchers, as these little speedsters zip through the canyon sky like miniature fighter pilots in search of a kill — in this case, insects. Several swifts and swallows dart through the skies around Black Canyon (including the rare **black swift**, which may migrate through the area.) The fast **white-throated swift** can be heard *swooshing* over the canyon rim, calling a shrill *jejejejejeje,* descending in scale. Six to seven inches in length, it has scythe-like wings, a short tail and a flat skull. Its colors are white underneath, with black side patches. Its habitat is open sky, cruising widely over the canyon.

Similar, but belonging to a different family, is the slim, streamlined form of the **violet-green swallow**. It is smaller and slower than the swift, growing to about five inches. This swallow is dark with glossy green on top, and purple and white underneath. The voice is a *chit* or c*hit chit.* While primarily canyon dwellers, both the swift and swallow will hunt over the reservoirs in Curecanti NRA as well.

The plump, stubby-tailed **American dipper**, or *water ouzel,* is commonly seen skimming over the surface of the river, then diving into the water for insects or small fish. It's about 7 to 8 inches long, and slate gray in color, with pale legs and white eyelids, and shaped like a large wren Note the almost continuous bobbing up and down behavior when resting on a rock in the foaming torrent. It makes a sharp *zeet* sound, singly or repetitiously. It's a year-round resident in the entire canyon, moving to lower elevations on the river during winter weather.

COMMON BIRDS OF BLACK CANYON

(permanent or seasonal residents)

IN THE SKY

Golden eagle, peregrine falcon, American kestrel, red-tailed hawk, sharp-shinned hawk, turkey vulture, common raven, great horned owl.

ON RIM OR IN THE CANYON

White-throated swift, rock dove, violet-green swallow, dusky flycatcher, common nighthawk, canyon wren, black-billed magpie.

IN STREAMSIDE WOODLANDS

American dipper, yellow warbler, white-breasted nuthatch, blue-gray gnatcatcher, black-capped chickadee, plumbeous vireo, hairy woodpecker.

IN BRUSH OR OPEN AREAS

Sage grouse, chukar, mourning dove, rock dove, chipping sparrow, mountain bluebird, bushtit, vesper sparrow, green-tailed towhee, rock wren, broad-tailed hummingbird.

IN UPLAND FOREST/SCRUB

Western scrub jay, pinyon jay, Stellar's jay, Clark's nutcracker, Virginia's warbler, western tanager, mountain chickadee, dark-eyed junco, northern flicker, blue grouse, turkey.

AROUND THE RESERVOIRS

Canada goose, mallard, common merganser, killdeer, spotted sandpiper, bald eagle, great blue heron.

American dipper

Turkey vulture

Blue grouse

Broad-tailed hummingbird

The spunky little **canyon wren** is a favorite of canyoneers. It has a white bib, with a dark reddish-brown belly, and a large curved bill. Its voice is characterized by a rush of clear gushing notes down the scale, picking up at the end. A year-round resident, listen in the sunlight-dappled depths of the canyon for its sweet song: *te-you, te-you te-you, tew tew tew tew* or *tee tee tee tee tew tew tew tew.*

The **yellow warbler** is a small bird about 4 ½ to 5 ¼ inches in length and mostly yellow in color. (The yellow warbler has yellow spots on its tail, in contrast to other species of warbler that have white spots.) The song is a cheerful *tsee-tsee-tsee-tsee-titi-wee* or a *weet-weet-weet-weet-tsee-tsee* in a rapid series. This species prefers riparian environments, so look for them in willows and poplars along the banks of the river.

Peregrine falcons are making a comeback in Colorado from the very brink of extinction. The Black Canyon is breeding territory for this amazing flier; with certain cliffs, including Painted Wall, closed off to rock climbers in the spring so as to not to disturb nesting pairs. Peregrines are 15 to 21 inches in length, with a wingspan of 3 to 3 1/2 feet. Wings are pointed, built for great speed, as the birds dive on their prey of small birds on the wing. They have black "mustaches" around and below their eyes, and are recognized by their pointed wings, a narrow tail and quick wingbeats. Adult are slate gray on the back, pale underneath with bars and spots. From the overlooks along both rim drives, you may be fortunate enough to spot a peregrine.

While gazing down from the rim, take a moment to look up instead and perhaps sight another formidable hunter, the **golden eagle**. Unlike peregrines, golden eagles are year-round residents of the canyon, generally searching for rabbits and large rodents. They range from 30 to 41 inches in length, soaring on four to six foot wings above the canyon, taking advantage of uplifts over the high cliffs. Adults are uniformly dark underneath with a slightly lighter color at the base of the tail. On the neck may be seen the golden color identifying this eagle from its cousin, the **bald eagle**. Balds are occasionally seen, usually as migrants in winter along the reservoirs in Curecanti NRA.

Another common soarer, high above the cliffs of the canyon, is the **turkey vulture**. Turkey vultures are dark colored, almost black, and are seen soaring on their six-foot wings in high wide circles, searching for carrion. Their heads are smaller than hawks and eagles. To identify them in the field, look for the two-toned blackish wings, with flight feathers lighter than the wing linings. Close up, the red head of the adult can be seen. Turkey vultures hunt everywhere within the National Park, Curecanti NRA and Gunnison Gorge NCA. Look for them perched on dead trees or posts along the rims of the canyon.

With their mournful call of *ooah, cooo, cooo, coo*, **mourning doves** are readily found from Curecanti NRA to the Gunnison Gorge. In fact, it's the most common dove in The West. The mourning dove is brown (slimmer and smaller than the domestic pigeon) with a pointed tail, bordered with large white spots. Look for them in the uplands beyond the rims; in open woods, grasslands and desert areas.

Inhabiting similar terrain, yet not as common, is the **chukar**, a sandy-colored quail with bright red legs and bill. The throat is light, bordered by a black necklace, and the sides are barred with a rufous tail. The voice is a a series of "chuck's" or a sharp *wheet-u*. Gunnison Gorge NCA is the best place to spot chukars, with a few in the western part of the Park as well.

Several members of the grouse family make their homes in the diverse habitats around the canyon. **Blue grouse** are quite common along both rims and in the coniferous forests of Curecanti NRA. They are dark gray and have a light band at the tip of the black tail. Males have a yellow or orange "comb" above the eyes. Females tend to be gray-brown, with black bars. Sagebrush areas hold habitat for two species of grouse, including the endangered **Gunnison sage grouse**. Grayish brown and whitish underneath, this rare bird puts on a spectacular mating display in spring that draws bird watching enthusiasts from around the country. Look for them in lower areas of Curecanti NRA.

The **green-tailed towhee** has a rusty-colored cap and a white throat. Slightly larger than a house sparrow, the green-tailed has an olive-green back and gray breast. It makes a mewing *weet-chur-cheeeeeeee-churr*. Habitat is on brushy mountain slopes, chapparal, pines, and sage throughout the Gunnison Valley.

Another common upland bird is the striking **mountain bluebird**, with a dark pointed bill, distinctive skyblue head, back and tail with a light blue chest, and a narrow white band from lower chest to tail. Females are dull brown, with some blue on the rump, tail and wings. Sound is a low *chur* or *phew*. The mountain bluebird's habitat is open terrain among scattered trees.

The strikingly beautiful, four-foot tall **great blue heron** stands motionless along the shore of Blue Mesa Reservoir, hunting for small critters to spear with its sharp bill. It is the largest long-legged bird in The West, except for the sandhill crane. It has a six-foot wingspan, and in flight, the head is tucked back in an "S" shape. The great blue is blue-gray in color and whitish around the head. There is a rookery near the Neversink Trail at the east end of the reservoir.

Another wading bird, the much smaller **killdeer** is built compactly, with a thick neck. It belongs to the family of plovers, who run along the shore in short stops and starts. In flight, it shows a golden-red rump, a long tail and a white stripe on the wing. Killdeer make a loud *kill-deer* sound repeated several times, or a *dee-e, dee de-dee*. They are common along the reservoirs in Curecanti NRA and very occasionally along the river.

The tiny **broad-tailed hummingbird** is the most abundant hummer to be found in the Gunnison Country. The male has a green back and bright red throat. The female is larger, with a black chin and sides tinged buff. The broad-tailed makes a *trill* sound from its rapidly beating wings. Hummers follow the flowers, appearing first in spring in the Gunnison Gorge, then migrating upstream as the season of flowering plants unfolds. Some will nest in the uplands of Curecanti NRA, but most will move into the mountains for the summer.

To find out more about birdlife of the canyon, the **Black Canyon Audubon Society** conducts field trips in the area year-round that are free and open to all nature lovers. They also have a monthly radio show on local KVNF.

P.O. Box 1371
Paonia, CO 81428
(970) 835-8867
www.western.edu/audubon/

AMPHIBIANS AND REPTILES

In such a dry environment, where water is limited, it's understandable that only a few species of amphibians are present, and they are seldom seen. But two of them, the **northern leopard frog** and the **tiger salamander**, can be found in all three units of the Black Canyon wherever water is present.

Reptiles on the other hand are in greater numbers and fairly easy to spot. Most of the half-dozen of so snakes found in the area are non-poisonous. But the venomous **western rattlesnake** does appear in Gunnison Gorge NCA in bushy, rocky country at lower elevations (see **Wildlife Encounters** on page 28 for more information.) The diamond shaped head, pits under the eyes and rattle identify it.

Other snakes are the **Great Basin gopher snake**, **wandering garter snake**, **western smooth green snake** and the **milk snake**. The smooth green snake can be found in Curecanti NRA, the National Park, and Gunnison Gorge NCA, nearly anywhere there is thick vegetation. While mostly around riparian environments, it can also be found away from water sources, including along the rims of the canyon. Smooth green snakes may climb up on low-lying vegetation.

The Gunnison Gorge NCA is home to the milk snake, where it ranges to altitudes under 6,000 feet. It is distinctive, 18 to 36 inches in length, with alternating bands of white, yellow, black, and red or orange. If disturbed, they can rear up, make a movement like a strike, vibrate the tail like a rattler, and emit an odorous secretion. But they are not poisonous and are quite harmless. All of these snakes hibernate under rocks, wood or rotting logs during the colder months.

Lizards are numerous and easy to spot almost anywhere, including in the depths of the canyon. The **sagebrush lizard** is just under 6 inches in length, including the tail. Color is a mottled brown-gray with lighter stripes along the back and a blueish throat. It is found throughout the area below 7,000 feet in pygmy forests, semi-desert environments, and woodlands of ponderosa pine and Douglas fir. Especially, look for this lizard along the base of ledges and in shrubby areas. The best time to see them is during the warmest part of the day.

One of the most beautiful reptiles, and one commonly seen in the Gunnison Gorge NCA and western parts of the National Park, is the **collared lizard**. Colors range from green to tan, and there may be green or yellow bars across the back. What makes this lizard distinguishable is the collar around the neck, a black band with lighter bands on either side. The head is large for a reptile, with total length at about 3 feet. The animal ranges up to altitudes of 7,000 feet. Collared lizard habitat is usually in rocky canyons and slopes where there are large rocks scattered across the ground. Visitors are likely to sight the collared lizard, since it sits on these rocks waiting for prey to pass by.

Collared lizard.

The **prairie lizard** is found in all three units of the canyon. Total length of the animal, including tail, is little more than 7 inches. Color varies from brown to gray. Another small lizard, the **tree lizard** is found in the Gunnison Gorge NCA and possibly in the National Park. While called the tree lizard, the animal's habitat is mostly in rocky areas.

Short-horned lizards may be seen in the National Park and Gunnison Gorge NCA up to elevations of 8,000 feet. It's brownish to grayish and has dark spots on its back. There are indeed short horns on its head. To defend itself, it hisses while puffing up its body to appear larger. When handled, it can squirt blood from the edge of its eye — gross, but harmless.

FISH

Man and human activities have had a profound effect on the waterways of the Gunnison Basin. Starting as early as the 1870s, non-native species of trout were introduced into the Gunnison River system to benefit sportsman. These aggressive species tended to outcompete the native cutthroat trout. In addition, habitat destruction and increased sediment and pollution from upstream agriculture and mining helped pushed some fish species towards extinction. But it was the construction of the dams in Curecanti that most profoundly changed the waterway; altering flow, temperature and silt levels. Ironically, while native fish suffered, introduced species flourished in both the river and the reservoirs. Today, the Gunnison River, with water temperatures ideal for trout growth, is designated a **Gold Medal** fishing resource. And lunker fish patrol the rocky depths of the submerged canyon at the three reservoirs. A huge re-stocking program involving millions of hatchery-raised fish per year keeps it all going.

For info about **fishing** in the river or reservoirs see page 134 in the **Activities** section.

The only trout native to Colorado, **cutthroat trout** were once common and widespread. The cutthroat has been downgraded from endangered to threatened in Colorado because of aggressive restocking and habitat improvement programs. The name refers to the circle of red behind the gills. *Cuts* can be found in upper reaches of the reservoirs and in the river. They are not well adapted to warm or silty and turbid waters. All other trout have been introduced.

Brown trout have a pattern of black spots and red-orange spots inside blue circles. They range in size from 10 to 40 inches. Browns can survive in muddy and more turbid waters that tend to kill more sensitive trout species. Find them in slower-moving, colder water in large, deep holes.

To identify a **rainbow trout**, look for black spots on a lightly colored body, with a red stripe running along the side (giving the fish its name.) Fisherman like the rainbow because it can be scrappy when caught. Rainbows are best found in lower and warmer water. The rainbow can be from 10 to 40 inches in length.

Many consider the **brook trout** to be the most beautiful of the trouts. Identify the *brookie* by its pectoral, pelvic and anal fins of orange, lined with a black and white edge. Its body is darker than the rainbow, with white spots and red spots inside blue circles. They tend to be small and are usually 6 to 18 inches in length. Brookies prefer smaller streams with gravelly bottoms, but when in the river, they grow larger. They favor the reservoir's tributary streams.

The biggest fish in Blue Mesa Reservoir is the **lake trout** or *Mackinaw*. To identify the Mackinaw, look for an irregular white spotting pattern on a dark body and the unique, deeply indented tail fin, not seen in other trout. The Mackinaw is long-lived, with 20 years or more a common age. They can grow from 12 to 48 inches, depending on conditions, and can weigh up to 60 pounds (although 35-40 pounds seems to be the limit in Blue Mesa.) Mackinaw tend to spend most of the year in deep, cold water at 60 feet or more.

Kokanee salmon are the landlocked version of the migratory sockeye salmon, introduced into Blue Mesa Reservoir. They hang out in schools and feed on plankton in deep water. At the end of three summers, the females develops a red-gray-white pattern. Males develop a hook jaw and turn brick-red.

There are other species, mostly natives and some threatened, that are found in the waterways of the Gunnison Basin, including **roundtail chub**, **flannelmouth sucker**, **bluehead sucker**, **razorback sucker**, **Colorado squawfish**, and **bonytail chub**.

CULTURAL HISTORY

An abandoned, century-old ranch house in the snowy Cimarron Valley.

The dramatic geography and geology of the Black Canyon have both impeded and guided settlement and development since humans first entered the Gunnison Basin, perhaps 12,000 years ago. The canyon has been a seemingly impossible barrier, with the inner gorge devoid of any history of occupation for millennium; yet beyond the rims of the foreboding abyss are rich ecosystems where humans learned to survive, and even thrive. From groups of **Paleo-Indians** hunting and gathering in Gunnison Country, to expeditions of **Spanish explorers** searching for fabled gold and silver, to **Americans** bent on pushing routes through a new land, to **mining men** seeking fortune in the surrounding Rockies, to **railroaders** battling nature to lay ribbons of steel, to **settlers** bringing life-giving water to the Uncompahgre Valley, to today's **recreationalists** enjoying a national treasure — the history of the Black Canyon area is a long and fascinating story.

Cultural artifacts in Black Canyon of the Gunnison National Park, Curecanti National Recreation Area and Gunnison Gorge National Conservation Area (as well as in the surrounding National Forests) are a shared heritage of the people of the United States. It is against the law to remove or disturb cultural or archaeological resources. Sadly, modern visitors include some who "collect" artifacts, such as arrowheads, bone fragments or pottery shards, or cause damage to old structures. This magical region's rich heritage deserves to be preserved for future generations to observe and ponder.

First People

PALEO-INDIANS

The earliest people to inhabit the Gunnison region were probably **Folsom people**, a **Paleo-Indian** culture that thrived from 12,000 to 7500 years ago (10,000-5,500 B.C.) Evidence of **Folsom points** has been found near Montrose, in northern New Mexico; and recently, a hill overlooking the town of Gunnison has yielded Folsom-attributed tools in such numbers as to suggest a major presence in the Gunnison Basin over a long period. Only tools made of imperishable materials such as stone or flint have survived from this period. Tools made for hunting and processing of game have also been found in the Uncompahgre area. Evidence shows that the Paleo-Indian groups hunted mega fauna, including *mammoth* and *giant bison*, with a diet that also probably included plants. Paleo-Indian culture was nomadic, following herds and building no permanent shelters that have survived. The Folsom people either died out or were absorbed into other cultures.

ARCHAIC STAGE

Around 6,000 years ago the climate of Colorado became warmer and drier. Archaeological evidence shows that on the Western Slope, a drier climate lead to a more settled lifestyle in areas where plant life thrived. A period characterized by hunting and gathering ensued, although the giant game of the Paleo-Indian period had become extinct and given way to deer, elk, bison and smaller game. Perishable artifacts and evidence of habitations have survived due to the warmer and drier climate. Archaeology has revealed sandals, wooden dart throwers, sewing tools made of bone and other tools and clothing. **Wickiups**, a type of simple, often temporary shelter made of brush, have been discovered along the Gunnison River. The people of the **Archaic Stage** (5500 B.C - 500 A.D) were short, stocky and dark skinned; and related to the Shoshoni in language. Any incursions by other groups were met with aggressive and fierce opposition. During the period, a larger population existed in West-Central Colorado then in the Paleo-Indian Stage or after the end of the Archaic age.

A discovery on a mesa top above the town of Gunnison could change long-held beliefs about Folsom hunters. Western State College archaeologist **Mark Stiger** and his students have been excavating a site on **Tenderfoot Mountain** (the one with the "W") since 2001 that contains what may be the oldest human dwelling discovered in North America. The substantial, circular rock-ring structure has yielded a treasure-trove of **Folsom artifacts**, including spear-points, scrapers and knives, as to suggest a more sedentary lifestyle than the nomadic one usually identified with Folsom people. The site, dubbed "Mountaineer" after the WSC mascot, could rewrite the books on this enigmatic culture.

Paleo-Indians arrive.	Start of the Archaic Stage of Indian Culture.	Change to a warmer/drier climate in Colorado.
Folsom	Period	Archaic Stage

| 10000 B.C. | 5500 B.C.   4000 B.C. |

FORMATIVE STAGE

The **Formative Stage** (550 A.D.-1450 A.D.) is characterized by a semi-sedentary or settled lifestyle. More permanent structures of masonry appear at the beginning of the first millennium. Use of ceramics, which are not easily moved, came into use and further indicate a settled lifestyle. The cultures dominating the region at the time are the **Anasazi** in southwest Colorado and the **Fremont people** of Utah and northwestern Colorado. Gunnison Gorge shows evidence of agriculture from this period.

The first people to build permanent, settled communities in south-western Colorado were the Anasazi around 550 A.D. The term *anasazi* is a Navajo word meaning *"enemies of our ancestors."* The development of the Anasazi tradition can be broken into several periods. During the **Basket Maker Period**, the Anasazi migrated north from the Rio Grande in central New Mexico to the Four Corners region. Here they built pit houses, especially on and around Mesa Verde. Later, during the **Development Period** (from 750-1100 A.D.) and then the **Classic Period** (from 1100-1300 A.D.), these peoples developed their distinctive pottery of intricate black designs on a white background, their elaborate irrigation and water storage networks, and a collective architecture of extensive pueblos built above ground, and later, cliff overhangs and caverns below the rims of mesa. While there is no strong evidence of the Anasazi culture in the Gunnison Basin, the area was undoubtedly within the sphere of influence of this powerful culture, centered in the nearby Four Corners area. Around 1300, the Four Corners region was suddenly abandoned for unknown reasons. The present tribal groups of the Zuni, Acoma, Taos, Sandia and other Pueblo peoples may be the descendants of the Anasazi.

HISTORIC PERIOD

When the Formative Period neared its end, an Archaic lifestyle returned to the Western Slope, comprised of hunter-gatherer peoples, beginning around 1200 A.D. From that time, to arrival of the white man, a **Ute-Shoshonean tradition** developed in the mountain regions. They guarded the eastern mountain passes from plains-dwelling tribes and roamed throughout the Western Slope area. The **Utes** may have arrived in the region as early as 1200, based on linguistic and archeological evidence. Firm evidence of the Ute tradition has been discovered in Curecanti National Recreation Area, dating to around 1490.

The Ute people made powerful six-foot long bows from juniper. *Flint* was mined from quarries near Montrose to tip arrow shafts made of *mountain mahogany.* To preserve meat, they used the red *serviceberry*, pressed into juice and forced into the meat, creating a form of pemmican. The Utes never fully developed the tepee tradition, but mostly used wickiups for shelter, consisting of branches placed in the ground to form an arch covered by brush. This style of shelter remained in use through almost the entire 19th century.

No single event in the development of the American Indian had greater impact for the Ute people than the introduction of the horse. The Utes probably

Start of **Formative Stage** of Indian culture.
Anasazi build permanent settlements in southwest Colorado.
Basket   Maker   Period   Development

550 A.D.   750

HUNTING TRAPS

Ute **hunting traps** can be found across the top of **Painted Wall**, and at **Serpent Point**. Serpent Point is nearly an island, connected by a narrow neck to Fruitland Mesa. Artifacts, arrowheads and evidence of large pits and traps have been found on Serpent Point. Hunters drove herds onto the point and into traps and pits where hidden hunters could rise up and kill the prey. Escape for the game was either over the 2,000-foot high cliff or back across the narrow neck where hunters blocked their escape — either route meaning death.

The narrow neck of land known as Serpent Point caps the top of Painted Wall's sheer cliffs..

first encountered the horse around 1540, when Spanish explorers entered the region of northern New Mexico and southern Colorado. Some of the horses escaped and became the mustangs and paints highly prized by the Utes. Raiding parties ranged into neighboring territory to steal horses from other tribes. The horse greatly increased the ability of the Utes to range over greater distances and bring back larger quantities of meat. The Utes hunted along both rims of the Black Canyon, but probably never entered the inner canyon. Superstition abounded that no man could enter the canyon and return alive. (So convincing were these legends that even whites believed the stories and avoided entering the inner canyon for many years.) At the time of the arrival of whites, two tribes of the several bands of the Utes, dominated the Gunnison, Black Canyon and Uncompahgre regions — the **Tabeguache** and the **Uncompahgre**. The first recorded contact between Utes and whites occurred during the **Dominguez-Escalante Expedition** of 1776, sent out by Spain to discover a trail that could be used for supplying their possessions in California. While the expedition never saw the Black Canyon, they did pass just west of the **Gunnison Gorge** and on up the **North Fork Valley**, encountering a sizable band of Utes near the site of present-day Paonia.

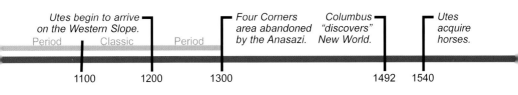

Utes begin to arrive on the Western Slope.

Period   Classic   Period

Four Corners area abandoned by the Anasazi.

Columbus "discovers" New World.

Utes acquire horses.

1100   1200   1300   1492   1540

Early Exploration

The first explorers in Colorado were the **Spanish**, whose first explorations largely went east of the Rockies, rarely approaching the plateaus and mesas of the Western Slope. The Spanish motivation to explore the northern reaches of their American empire was to punish the Indians who raided their settlements, to return fugitives from the law, to check on French incursions on Spanish territory, and to search for silver and gold. The Spanish followed three routes to enter Colorado, all originating from Santa Fe. One route went east to the Sangre de Cristo Mountains and the Purgatoire River, and onto the eastern plains. Another went almost directly north to the San Luis Valley. A third route went northward to the La Plata Mountains to search for minerals; and sometimes ventured as far as the Gunnison Basin and to the edge of the Great Basin near the present state line with Utah. The French and Spanish claims in America overlapped so a struggle between the powers existed for many decades. The Spanish had a clearer claim to the region west of the Continental Divide and the Southwest then France. France claimed the **Territory of Louisiana**, up to the crest of the mountains on the east. It is in this region along the Rockies that claims overlapped, with the Spanish sending explorers northward to explore the regions of present day Colorado and the French moving west into the mountain areas to explore and trap.

The first Spanish explorer to enter Colorado was **Francisco Vasquez de Coronado** who came searching for the famous seven cities of gold in 1541. He found mud huts and pueblos, but no gold. After Spain received the territory of Louisiana as part of the treaty between France and England that ended the French and Indian War in 1763, Spanish interest in exploring the southwest intensified. Governor Tomas Velez Cachupin of New Mexico believed minerals existed in the northern regions of the provinces. In 1765, he sent **Juan Maria de Rivera** to explore the San Juan and Gunnison country. Rivera explored the southwest and his route took him through present day Durango, Dolores and out into Utah. On his return he passed through present day Delta, where the Gunnison and Uncompahgre Rivers join; and there, he carved his name on a tree which stood into the 1960s. He reported favorably to Governor Cachupin that minerals existed in sufficient quantity to be mined. The next large expedition began August 1, 1776 under **Fathers Dominguez and Escalante** to find a route to California. They followed the general route of Rivera, attained the Colorado River and Grand Mesa, but turned west into Utah. They journeyed as far as the Grand Canyon but with winter approaching, and food and water becoming difficult to obtain, the expedition returned to Santa Fe. But the expedition had a significant impact on the region. Detailed maps made by **Captain Miera** would help guide future explorers and settlers into the region.

The Louisiana Territory reverted back to France in 1800 and then was sold to the United States in 1803. Subsequent American explorations by **Zebulon Pike** in 1806-07 and by **Major Stephen H. Long** in 1820 probed the boundaries

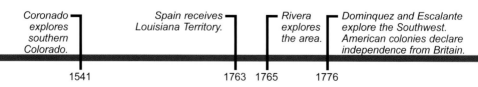

Coronado explores southern Colorado.	Spain receives Louisiana Territory.	Rivera explores the area.	Dominquez and Escalante explore the Southwest. American colonies declare independence from Britain.
1541	1763	1765	1776

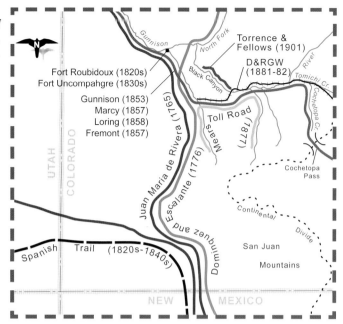

Routes of explorers around Black Canyon of the Gunnison, 1765-1901.

Fort Roubidoux (1820s)
Fort Uncompahgre (1830s)

Gunnison (1853)
Marcy (1857)
Loring (1858)
Fremont (1857)

Torrence & Fellows (1901)
D&RGW (1881-82)

Cochetopa Pass

San Juan Mountains

of the United States' new possession, but failed to penetrate into the Western Slope. However, Long's assessment of the plains as the **Great American Desert**, unfit for farming, delayed settlement for decades, and resulted in the leapfrogging of the Colorado area in general by tens of thousands of settlers bound for the Oregon Territory.

After the Dominguez-Escalante Expedition, Europeans increasingly came into the region. While the Spanish had searched for gold and silver, French trappers came to harvest beaver, otter, and fox; to satisfy the European market for fine hats and fashion. Two French trappers may have seen the Black Canyon in 1809. Mexico gained independence from Spain in 1821 and allowed other Europeans to enter the area for trade purposes. The **Santa Fe Trail**, from St. Louis to Santa Fe, and the **Spanish Trail** from Santa Fe to Los Angeles, thrived during the Mexican period. The latter trail followed a circuitous route north through western Colorado, and then south through Utah, skirting north of the Grand Canyon, continuing southwesterly through western Arizona to Los Angeles. A single caravan might consist of 4,000 horses and mules carrying wool products, clothing, luxury goods and some staple products. Such large caravans stocked the southwest with animals that later aided the United States Army and settlers moving into the region. The Spanish Trail closed at the outset of the war with Mexico in 1846.

In the 1820s, **Antoine Robidoux** crossed near today's Great Sand Dunes National Park and over Cochetopa Pass with a wagon filled with supplies. Near present-day Delta, he built **Fort Robidoux**, a trading post beside the Uncompahgre River. Trappers came from the east, and north from New Mexico, including Kit Carson. Utes burned the fort (1828) but Robidoux built **Fort Uncompahgre** at a nearby location in the 1830s. Around 1837, he and several others may have gazed into the depths of the Black Canyon.

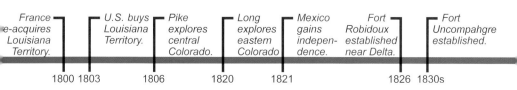

France acquires Louisiana Territory.	U.S. buys Louisiana Territory.	Pike explores central Colorado.	Long explores eastern Colorado	Mexico gains independence.	Fort Robidoux established near Delta.	Fort Uncompahgre established.
1800	1803	1806	1820	1821	1826	1830s

American Territory

The **Treaty of Guadalupe Hidalgo,** after the war with Mexico in 1848, and the boundary treaty with Britain along the 49th Parallel, vastly expanded the territory of the United States, including adding what would later become the state of Colorado. At about the same time, gold was discovered at Sutter's Mill in California. Congress called for expeditions to be sent across the west to survey a railroad to the gold fields, to tie the country together for all time.

Congress planned five expeditions to study routes at different latitudes. Missouri **Senator Thomas Hart Benton** rallied, along with promoters Asa Whitney and Robert J. Walker, for a route from St. Louis to San Francisco along the 38th and 39th Parallel, pressing for a wagon route to be built within a year and a railroad in seven. Benton provided financial backing for **John Charles Fremont**, already known for his trail blazing to California and heroism in the war with Mexico,on several subsequent expeditions. Fremont's ill-fated fourth expedition, which set out from Missouri on October 21, 1848, was to test the viability of a railroad route along the 38th Parallel by crossing the San Juan Mountains in winter near Cochetopa Pass, hoping to find a route through the Gunnison Basin and out to the Colorado River to the west. The expedition met failure and disaster in the snowy mountains, and the subsequent investigation (which included rumors of cannibalism) tarnished Fremont's image.

THE GUNNISON EXPEDITION

Despite that, Benton and others decided to finance another expedition lead by Fremont. But Congress decided to fund an alternative expedition, giving the job to **Captain John W. Gunnison**, an officer in the Corp of Topographic Engineers with considerable experience in exploring and surveying, including Captain Stansbury's Utah Territory Expedition in 1849. The exploration of the mid-latitude route for a railroad was to follow as near as possible along the 38th and 39th Parallel crossing the Huerfano region, and Cochetopa Pass to the Grand (Colorado River), Green River, and Salt Lake, then across the Great Basin, and the Sierras to the coast. The 1853 expedition started in St. Louis with eighteen wagons pulled by mules. After crossing the Sangre de Cristo Mountains, the expedition climbed toward 10,032-foot **Cochetopa Pass**. But with only an old Indian trail and no road, the men had to cut a path over the pass, felling trees and moving large rocks out of the way. On the west side, wagons were lowered with ropes wound around trees until the valley of the Cochetopa was reached. Following the creek, Gunnison reached the river that the Utes called **Tomichi**, or the river *"of high cliffs and plenty water."* Gunnison believed it to be the Grand River (Colorado) and followed it past what would become the town of Gunnison, and west to the Lake Fork. With a difficult crossing of the Lake Fork, Gunnison became reluctant to follow the canyon. He and several of his men scouted as far as the entrance of the canyon, near today's Blue Mesa Dam; and seeing the sheer

U.S. acquires the Southwest, including Colorado, after the Mexican War. Gold is discovered in California.	Fremont's 4th Expedition ends in disaster in San Juan Mountains.	Gunnison Expedition surveys possible railroad route through Black Canyon area.
1848	1849	1853

walls framing the raging river, concluded that a railroad along this route would not be feasible. The party crossed over **Blue Mesa** to the Cimarron, completely avoiding the Black Canyon. The expedition then saw the **Uncompahgre Valley** from a ridge above Cebolla Creek. For two days, they cut a trail through sagebrush, Gambel oak and cactus, descending 1,400 feet before reaching the wide Uncompahgre Valley, with its dark, shale, and clay-like soil. Here they found cottonwoods along the creeks and encountered Utes in their wickiups, where **Chief Siritschiwup** of the Utes and his son came out to meet peacefully with the whites. Despite warnings from the chief about hostile tribes farther west, Gunnison's party continued out into Utah, where a month later Gunnison and several companions were murdered by Paiutes. But his second-in-command, **E. G. Beckwith**, continued west in the following year, completing the survey out to California.

Painting of Captain John W. Gunnison.

While the Gunnison Expedition met tragedy, there were positive results. Information about the country was later used for settlement, and just twenty-nine years later, the Denver and Rio Grande Railroad used the information collected by the survey to build a railroad through the Gunnison country, and even into the upper portion of the Black Canyon. Gunnison's name became attached to the river that he partially explored and surveyed, and subsequently to the surrounding country. And the captain and his lieutenant are commemorated today by two mountain peaks, **Mount Gunnison** and **Beckwith Mountain**, in the West Elk Mountains, a dozen miles north of the Black Canyon.

Shortly after the Gunnison party passed through the Black Canyon area, two other military expeditions received orders that lead them through the area — both in response to events of the so-called Mormon War of 1857-58. The **Marcy party**, including the legendary **Jim Baker** as guide, camped near present day Delta, where they were harassed by the Utes; before embarking on another winter crossing of Cochetopa Pass, reminiscent of Fremont's attempt, but ultimately more successful. A year later, the **Loring detachment** returned from Utah through the Gunnison area, with Colonel W. W. Loring carefully recording his progress as he and his column of 50 wagons and 300 men, guided by **Antoine Leroux**, traveled up the Gunnison Valley along Tomichi Creek, and then over Cochetopa Pass to the San Luis Valley.

Lt. Beckwith completes
Gunnison's survey
after the Captain's death.

Marcy party
camps near Delta.

Loring detachment
passes through
Gunnison Country.

1854

1857 1858

FREMONT'S FIFTH EXPEDITION

Despite Fremont's disastrous fourth expedition, Senator Benton and others again backed the so-called "Pathfinder of the West" to lead yet another expedition near the 38th and 39th Parallels, closely following the same course as the earlier exploration. The party comprised 22 men, including **Solomon Carvalho** — the first photographer on a western expedition and **W. H. Palmer**, who later became Colorado's most respected railroad builder. Once again, Fremont decided to attempt a winter crossing of the Rockies to prove if a railroad could be operated during that season through the mountains.

The expedition would attempt to cross into the Gunnison area by way of Cochetopa Pass. The previous Gunnison Expedition had created a rough wagon road, obliterated at times by the snow. But at the top of the pass, Gunnison's cleared trail allowed an easy crossing and the wagons and men descended into the broad Cochetopa valley. Fremont and Carvalho decided to climb a steep, granite peak in the vicinity to take barometric readings and photos of the lofty peaks that lay all around in the distance. Standing on the summit, the two men first saw the **Gunnison River** in its canyon course. The party followed Cochetopa Creek, joining Tomichi Creek and following that west to the Gunnison River. Several days after descending from Cochetopa Pass, the trail became too difficult along the valley, and a mountain had to be crossed. As the train of mules and wagons climbed steadily up the slope, one of the mules suddenly lost its balance. The unfortunate creature pulled fifty of the mules in the train with it down the slope. Buffalo robes, blankets, daguerreotype materials and other provisions lay strewn down the slope, half buried in the deep snow. One mule and a horse died in the event, but the supplies were recovered. The accident ruined the tent — an unfortunate loss with daytime temperatures reaching minus 30 degrees below zero. After another day's march, the expedition arrived at a Ute village where they traded blankets, knives, and other goods for horses and venison. The expedition followed the Gunnison River, skirting south of the Black Canyon. Twenty-nine years later, Palmer would build his Rio Grande Railroad through the upper portion of the great chasm that refused the expedition passage. They reached the Uncompahgre River, then followed it to the junction of the Gunnison River near today's Delta and then to the junction with the Colorado River at present-day Grand Junction. Fremont ultimately reached California, in what would be one of his most successful expeditions. But once again the route between the 38th and 39th Parallel seemed to be too difficult for the construction of an all-season, continental railroad.

CONFLICT WITH THE UTES

With the discovery of **gold** in Colorado in 1859 and the subsequent rush to the gulches of the Front Range, a perception developed that a **great mineral belt** existed extending northeast to southwest in a crescent shaped arc to the San Juan Mountains. Soon prospectors and miners fanned out across the mineral belt into Ute country, with inevitable confrontations the result between gold seekers and

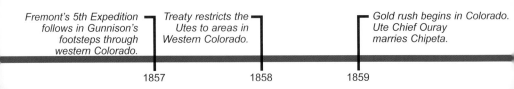

Fremont's 5th Expedition follows in Gunnison's footsteps through western Colorado.

Treaty restricts the Utes to areas in Western Colorado.

Gold rush begins in Colorado. Ute Chief Ouray marries Chipeta.

1857   1858   1859

the aboriginal inhabitants. At the outset of the **Gold Rush**, Utes ranged over the entire Colorado Rockies, including the Front Range. A treaty negotiated in 1858 restricted the Utes from entering areas where mineral had been discovered — in effect, most of the areas of the Southern Rockies and the Western Slope became the territory of the several bands of Utes. But this soon changed as miners continued to push into areas reserved for the Utes, and trouble between Mexican settlers and the Utes in the San Luis Valley required a new treaty arrangement.

The so-called **Kit Carson Treaty** of 1868, negotiated between a delegation of Utes, including **Chief Ouray**, led to Washington by Kit Carson and D. C. Oakes, resulted in a treaty that called for removal of the Utes to a line west of the

A band of Utes gathered near Montrose.

THE UTES

There were five bands of **Utes** who roamed Colorado when the first Europeans arrived. The Utes came into the **Gunnison Country** during summer from lower Western Slope valleys, finding abundant game. During winter, the Utes returned to the milder climates of the lower valleys along the Uncompahgre and Colorado Rivers.

By the time that miners and settlers began to push into Ute Territory in the mid 1800s, confrontations were often bloody. But one Ute chief sought to find a peaceful means of resolving the conflict. **Chief Ouray** was born near Taos of Apache and Ute parentage. He grew up in Mexican society, and trained in, but never converted to Catholicism. At age 17, upon his father's death, Ouray went to claim his inheritance of twenty ponies with Ute Chief Nevava's band and decided to stay with the Utes, marrying "*White Singing Bird*" — **Chipeta** — in 1859. Ouray spoke four languages, and quickly rising in stature, challenging Nevava's leadership. Invited to Washington in 1862, Ouray saw the need to take power from Nevava, believing he could better deal with the coming influx of whites. From that point on, the whites recognized him as spokesman for all the Utes; although not all of the Ute bands accepted his leadership authority.

Ouray never saw the heartbreaking removal of his band of Utes from Colorado, which he had so long tried to avoid. On a trip to confer with Ignacio, he died of *Bright's disease*. Chipeta, Ouray's wife, did move with her tribe to the Utah reservation. (There is a legend, almost certainly apocryphal, that in disgust for all the lies and broken treaties of the whites, she visited the Black Canyon and threw the money paid to Chief Ouray by the federal government into the dark chasm.)

The **Ute Indian Museum**, 3.0 miles south of Montrose on US-550 (hours: 9-4:30 M-Sa year-round, plus 11-4:30 Sunday in summer) celebrates this vibrant culture that once occupied the Uncompahgre Valley. The grounds lie on the original 8.65 acre homestead of Ouray and Chipeta (she is buried on the site) and feature a museum, a gallery, a gift shop, classrooms, a native plants garden and the **Chief Ouray Memorial Park**. For more information about the museum, see the **Local Attractions** section on page 212.

107th parallel — roughly those areas west of the Continental Divide. The **White River Agency** in the north, and the **Los Pinos Agency**, west of Cochetopa Pass, were established. Ouray attempted to set an example for the rest of his people by establishing a cattle ranch in the Uncompahgre Valley; but trespassing continued, as prospectors entered Ute territory in search of precious metals. By 1872, the San Juan Mountains supported hundreds of miners, which led the Utes to protest this illegal entry on their lands. The government decided that a new treaty would be needed to reduce tensions between the Utes and whites. This new agreement, the **Brunot Treaty** of 1873, once again was facilitated by Ouray, assisted by his white friend, **Otto Mears**. Mears spoke the Ute language and the Indians felt he could be trusted more than other whites in the treaty process. This treaty furthered stripped lands from the Ute's control, passing most of the San Juan Mountains into white hands. The Uncompahgre Agency was moved from Los Pinos to the Uncompahgre Valley near Montrose. The Northern Utes, under chiefs Douglas, Colorow, and Captain Jack, moved into the White River Agency near Meeker. The southern Utes, under Ignacio, moved to the Southern Ute Reservation, straddling the Colorado-New Mexico border.

For five years, the whites and Utes managed to co-exist under the Brunot Treaty. But as the San Juan filled with miners, they began to covet the areas north of the mining region, and discoveries near Aspen in 1878 brought prospectors in droves across the Divide into the territory of the White River Agency. Pressures boiled over into the **Meeker Massacre** at the White River Agency, where a misguided agent, Nathan C. Meeker, almost singlehandedly incited a rebellion that left him and four other whites dead. The result was the cry that went up all over Colorado that the "Utes must go."

A new treaty ratified in 1880 pushed the White River Utes, and subsequently the Uncompahgre band, to a new reservation in Utah. Two years later, the old agency at Los Pinos went on the auction block, and the long occupation of the Gunnison region by the Utes had ended.

Permanent Settlers

While still occupied by the Utes, the topography of the Black Canyon area remained something of a mystery. Beginning in the spring of 1873, the **United States Geological Survey** under **Dr. F. V. Hayden**, who the Indians called *"the white man who picks up rocks while running,"* conducted a detailed study of Colorado. Hayden's survey extensively explored the Elk and West Elk Mountains north and east of the canyon during the field summers of 1873-75, skirting the north rim of the Black Canyon for most of its length. At one point, a man was lowered 1,000 feet by rope into the canyon, and when hauled up, the frightened man said that the old Ute legend that no man could go into the canyon and live was true. Hayden's reports were distributed to schools and libraries, and assisted prospectors and settlers for many years.

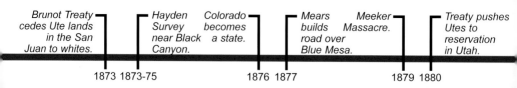

Brunot Treaty cedes Ute lands in the San Juan to whites.	Hayden Survey near Black Canyon.	Colorado becomes a state.	Mears builds road over Blue Mesa.	Meeker Massacre.	Treaty pushes Utes to reservation in Utah.
1873	1873-75	1876	1877	1879	1880

OTTO MEARS

Chief Ouray and Otto Mears.

The story of **Otto Mears** is the story of the development of Western Colorado. Throughout the last quarter of the 19th and into the 20th centuries, Mears had a hand in nearly every major event in the colorful history of the Western Slope. His story includes pioneering, road building, a railroad empire, treaties between the Utes and whites, plus he was a state legislator, and proposed the gilding of the dome on the State Capitol.

Born in 1850 in Russia and orphaned at age four, Mears came to America at age 11 and ended up in the care of an uncle in California, where he learned tin smithing. At the outset of the Civil War, he joined the First California Volunteers, serving mostly in New Mexico. While in the service, he saw the San Luis Valley; and believing it to be a good place to farm, homesteaded on Saguache Creek after the war, built a flour mill and hauled flour to Leadville. On one of his trips over Poncha Pass, a wagon filled with flour overturned, dumping the goods on the rough trace of trail. Former territorial governor **William Gilpin** happened to be passing by and stopped to help. He suggested that Mears apply for a charter and build a **toll road**. The route from Saguache to Nathrop — some fifty miles — became the first toll road in southwest Colorado, and launched the *"Pathfinder of the San Juan"* on his long road and railroad-building career. Gilpin continued to advise Mears in his road building enterprises, suggesting that roads be well-made, with gentle grades for conversion to railroads. Following that advice, his roads became famous for their well-constructed grades.

Mears enterprises included running a general store in Saguache and establishing the *Saguache Chronicle* newspaper. In partnership with **Enos Hotchkiss**, the men formed the San Juan Wagon Toll Road Company and planned a route to the San Juan before the ink on the Brunot Treaty of 1873 had dried. Hotchkiss set out to survey the route from Saguache over Cochetopa Pass, to the Lake fork of the Gunnison, and on to Lake City. While surveying around Lake San Cristobal, Hotchkiss discovered the Golden Fleece mine, touching off a rush. The men built the road from Saguache all the way to Howardsville in the San Juan, near Silverton. Mears continued constructing toll roads in the San Juan and opened a hardware store in Ouray. The men built a twenty-five mile road from Barnum on the Lake Fork to Cimarron, and a six-mile road from Barnum to Sapinero. By 1877, Mears had completed a 100-mile route from Lake City, over Blue Mesa to Cimarron, then to the Uncompahgre River, and south to Ouray. He then connected the Lake Fork with the town of Gunnison. Every twenty-five miles, cabins were built to accommodate mail carriers in winter on Norwegian skis or running dog sleds. He helped to incorporate the city of Montrose and went on to build the **Million Dollar Highway** near Ouray. Mears also built the Rio Grande Southern and Silverton Northern Railroads.

1947 D&RGW excursion train crosses Crystal Ck. Bridge.

THE RAILROADS

In the aftermath of the expulsion of the Utes from western Colorado, **Gunnison Country** was opened up to a rush of white settlement. Towns sprang up, fueled by mining for gold, silver and coal, and the development of cattle and sheep ranching. An 1880 Denver newspaper reported on the boom to the Gunnison Country, *"'To the Gunnison' is the all absorbing subject of thought and talk in Denver as well as the remotest borders of the country . . . there will be such as rush that the country cannot hold them . . ."* Such talk could not but attract the interest of the railroads, who not only wanted to tap into the market of this thriving area but also to extend their sway into the rich mining country of the San Juan Mountains, and perhaps ultimately reach California. Two narrow-gauge railroads vied to penetrate the mountain barriers of the central Rockies. John Evans' **Denver South Park and Pacific** started in Denver, and followed a route along the South Platte to South Park, then over the Sawatch Range to Gunnison through the **Alpine Tunnel** between St. Elmo and Pitkin, and finally terminating at the coal fields at Baldwin. General William J. Palmer's **Denver and Rio Grande Western** laid track through Royal Gorge, bought Otto Mears' toll road over Marshall Pass, and began grading. The Rio Grande steamed into Gunnison on August 8, 1881, greeted by an exuberant crowd and a full year ahead of the South Park, winning the race to control the Central and Southern Rockies.

With victory achieved for the Rio Grande into Gunnison, and well on its way to locking up the San Juan, Palmer's construction crews continued west for 20 miles through the wide mesa and tablelands of the upper Gunnison Valley to the head of the Black Canyon at the Lake Fork at Sapinero. Railroad construction crews of Italian and Irish workers had a relatively simple task of grading in the soft ground of the valley. Terminal towns sprang up; including Kezar, Cebolla, and Soap Creek (later called **Sapinero**.) Here at Sapinero, the railroad plunged into the spectacular depths of the Black Canyon. Railroads try to follow watercourses wherever possible, so a survey was conducted to locate a route through the entire length of the canyon in 1880. The route appeared feasible through the first 15 miles, from Sapinero to **Cimarron Creek**. After that, the sheer walls and narrow canyon seemed impossible to conquer (although a diversion tunnel to the Uncompahgre Valley was thought possible.) Throughout the seasons of 1881 and 1882, crews lowered over the cliffs, blasting a roadbed

Town of Gunnison platted.

Denver and Rio Grande Western railroad reaches Gunnison.

Denver and Rio Grande Western reaches Montrose. The Denver and South Park railroad reaches Gunnison.

Bryant party survey attempt in Black Canyon.

1879   1881 1882   1882-83

out of the hard granite walls with dangerous and volatile nitroglycerine. Many injuries occurred as a result of this unstable explosive. As the grade proceeded to the Cimarron Creek, railcars provided sleeping, eating and entertainment quarters for the immigrant workers. Following close behind, graders and tracklayers set in ties, and spiked down rails. The grade emerged from the canyon at **Cimarron** and the railroad established a town to serve the railroad, and the ranchers who had already settled in the area. The railroad built a roundhouse for the engines, a restaurant for passengers, a hotel, and accommodations for railroad crews. At its peak, Cimarron had a population of 300-500 people. The cost of construction through the canyon, astronomical for the time, came to $165,000 per mile. The first train passed the length of the canyon from Sapinero to Cimarron in August of 1882.

Construction continued from Cimarron to Montrose with the road crossing **Cerro Summit**, which required extra engines to pull the heavy trains up the steep grades, arriving in **Montrose** in 1882. At least a portion of the canyon that John W. Gunnison noted as impassable had indeed been passed. Palmer ordered a new survey be conducted, as he determined that a railroad through the entire length of the canyon would reduce grades and operating costs; so he hired **Byron H. Bryant** to survey the route. Expecting the survey to take 20 days, all but five men quit before that time and the task wasn't completed until two months later. Starting the survey in December of 1882, below zero temperatures nearly froze hands and feet. Each day the men would hike into the canyon, then climb back out the nearly 2,000 feet in the evening. When in the canyon, the men found it nearly impossible to cross the swift river when not frozen. At one point, rock fall had filled the floor so deeply that the river disappeared below it and some areas could not be reached at all. By March, when the survey finished, all agreed that building a railroad would be nearly impossible, ending any designs the DG&R had on building an all-river-route along the Gunnison.

SCENIC LINE OF THE WORLD

The section of the D&RGW through **Black Canyon** became one of the most advertised sections of the line for the tourist dollar, with the spectacular **Curecanti Needle** appearing on logos and advertisements for the *"Scenic Line of the World."* The railroad publicized the magnificence of the scenery in the great chasm, its stark straight, sheer walls, impressive rock formations, and the numerous waterfalls gushing from canyon walls — one named in honor of Chief Ouray's wife, **Chipeta**. For sixty-seven years, trains, their crews and passengers braved the depths of the Black Canyon along the D&RGW's narrow-gauge mainline. The steepness of the canyon walls, made rock falls a common occurrence; and in winter, avalanches might sweep a train into the icy river. By the late 1940s, the route had been eclipsed by other means of moving freight and passengers; and in 1949, the line closed and the rails were pulled up.

Today, at the mouth of Cimarron Creek stands a reminder of those bygone days — a **trestle** from the Black Canyon of the Gunnison portion of the route with restored **locomotive #278**, a **coal tender**, a **boxcar**, and a **caboose**. The trestle is on the National Register of Historic Places.

THE TOWNS

Today, the cities of **Gunnison** and **Montrose**, plus the small town of **Crawford**, form the three major gateways to Black Canyon of the Gunnison National Park. And while they all were settled in a few short years at around the time of the expulsion of the Utes, different interests came to create and shape each community; namely mining, farming and ranching.

Sylvester Richardson's rough cabin (shown in 1876) was the first "home" in Gunnison.

Gunnison had its beginnings with the signing of the Brunot Treaty in 1873; although the first cabin built on the site may have been about 1870 by a Mr. Wall and Mr. White at the junction of Tomichi Creek and the Gunnison River. The government established a cow camp there for the Utes of the Los Pinos Agency. Professor Sylvester Richardson, who first visited the area in 1872 and prospected in the Elk Mountains, organized a colony that arrived in the area in April 1874. Richardson's colony failed, as most left to prospect or establish ranches. **Gunnison County** was created in 1877, when it was separated from Lake County and interest revived to establish a town, as two railroads were pushing through the central Rockies to tap the developing mines in central and southwest Colorado. John Evans, Richardson, Alonzo Hartman and others established the **Gunnison City Town Company**, and the site was platted in 1879. By the early 1880s, Gunnison boasted a population of 5,000 and had two railroads; but by 1883, a decline had set in.

The hoped for finds of rich carbonate ores, like those found at Leadville, never materialized; and the high costs of transportation, severe winters, and a general slowing of silver mining ended the boom. But Gunnison did become the major town for the Gunnison Country; supporting stock raising, farming, coal, and metals mining in the surrounding mountains.

The communities of Montrose and Delta were developed as service centers for farmers that began pouring into the Uncompahgre Valley in search of fertile land soon after the Utes were forced out. Mild winters in the valley had attracted the Utes for centuries and white traders, trappers and explorers had stayed for periods of time as well.

O.D. *"Pappy"* **Loitsenhizer**, a sometime prospector turned land speculator, founded Montrose in 1882, as the Denver and Rio Grande rail lines pushed over Cerro Summit and reached the valley. Montrose became the railroad end-of-line operation for teamsters vying for the lucrative freighting business to the booming San Juan mining districts, including the legendary Dave Wood's **Magnolia Line** with its 20-mule teams. Montrose was a typical western town complete with wooden sidewalks, hitching racks, dozens of saloons where cowboys, teamsters and railmen celebrated Saturday nights, and (depending on the weather) dusty or muddy streets.

But it was agriculture that was to shape the valley's long-term future. As soon as farmers began to arrive and take up lands, it became evident that availability of water was the key to making these parched lands bloom. An extensive network of irrigation ditches, flumes, canals and small reservoirs were locally initiated and built, tapping into the Uncompahgre River, a source that proved to be inadequate to irrigate enough of the potential acreage. A tunnel carrying the live-giving waters of the Gunnison River was proposed locally as early as the 1890, but it took the creation of the federal government's Bureau of Reclamation in 1902 to bring enough financial resources to bear to accomplish the ambitious scheme. With the completion of the tunnel in 1909, Montrose and Delta evolved from frontier towns, to financial and service centers as the surrounding desert valley bloomed with everything from sugar beets to fruit orchards.

A Montrose boy holds up some irrigation-grown sugar beets in about 1900.

Crawford was founded on the Smith Fork of the Gunnison on an economy of cattle, sheep and hay; and granted a post office in 1887. Too high for agriculture, Crawford Country attracted cattlemen in the early 1880s who wintered their herds in the adobe hills on the north slope of the Gunnison Uplift. **Enos Hotchkiss**, Otto Mear's sometimes partner in road building and town founding, was among those who settled in the area. Many walked in over Black Mesa from the railhead at Sapinero, over roughly the same route as today's CO-92, liked what they saw, settled in, then drove their herds to market back over the Black Mesa route. **Sam Hartman** became the undisputed cattle king of the area in the 1880s and '90s and was characteristic of the rugged rancher that existed in this isolated area. Hartman mangled a leg in an accident with a runaway wagon and had it amputated on the spot with a de-horning saw, deadening the pain with whiskey.

Harsh winters, the end of the "open range" and grazing wars with invading sheepherders (including violence by so-called "night riders") challenged the economy and lifestyle of the area; but today, Crawford, still somewhat off the beaten path, remains at heart a ranching community. A couple of times a year, herds are driven right through this small town on their way to round-up. The creation of Crawford Rerservoir in 1963 has helped build a tourist economy with over 100,000 visitors per year.

Water for the Uncompahgre Valley

No issue is more contentious in The West than **water**. This was true when the first settlers came to the Western Slope, and remains so to this day. While the importance of water in an arid land cannot be underestimated, the problem is that rainfall is sparse in areas where agricultural can thrive, and abundant where farming is impossible. **John Wesley Powell** recognized this paradox during his explorations of the arid southwest, concluding that unless water could be moved from its source to where it was needed, The West would remain mostly unpopulated. To build dams and provide the infrastructure necessary to accomplish this, the government established the **Bureau of Reclamation;** and on the Western Slope, one of Reclamation's earliest projects involved bringing water from deep inside the Black Canyon, from the Gunnison River, to the waiting fields of the Uncompahgre Valley.

After removal of the Utes to the Uintah Reservation in Utah in the early 1880s, the **Uncompahgre Valley** soon filled with settlers, attracted to fertile lands that could bloom if the precious water could be delivered to them. Some thought the water available from the Uncompahgre River would do the task, but only 30,000 acres could come under the plow from that source. Twenty miles away, the Gunnison River, with its large volume of water, roared untapped through the Black Canyon. If only a way could be found to bring the water to the Uncompahgre Valley, then the promise of a large agricultural community could be realized. An early settler, **F. C. Lauzon**, first proposed that a tunnel be built under Vernal Mesa. The Colorado Legislature appropriated $35,000 for the purpose of building the tunnel, but the funds quickly ran out. Then the newly established Bureau of Reclamation stepped in, and offered to help with the project. Before spending millions of dollars, a detailed survey for a starting site had to be completed.

TORRENCE AND FELLOWS

Montrose Power and Light Superintendent **William W. Torrence** and four local residents determined to survey the canyon for a tunnel site by floating the river in large wooden boats, not unlike the 1869 Grand Canyon Expedition of John Wesley Powell. The party set out from Cimarron in September of 1900. On the second day, and after only one mile, the boat containing the most important provisions and survey equipment sank. Fresh supplies and equipment were brought down from the rim and the team pushed on, hoping to complete the survey in three or four days. An arduous three weeks passed and only fourteen miles — about half the distance — had been crossed. Support teams on the rim tried to follow progress of the men, but lost sight of them and considered the men to be lost. In the canyon, the explorers struggled along, until at a point below today's **Rock Point Overlook**, a series of cataracts and waterfalls ended the expedition. The boat could neither pass through or be portaged over the

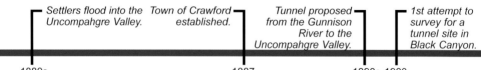

Settlers flood into the Uncompahgre Valley.

Town of Crawford established.

Tunnel proposed from the Gunnison River to the Uncompahgre Valley.

1st attempt to survey for a tunnel site in Black Canyon.

1880s   1887   1890s 1900

obstructions, and the men climbed out, upstream from the Narrows. And as they looked back at the point of their defeat, they named it the *"Falls of Sorrow."*

The next year, the United States Geological Survey assigned hydrographer **Abraham Lincoln Fellows** to the project. Experience of the earlier expedition gave any attempt to explore the Black Canyon the aura of a suicide mission. But undeterred, Fellow and Torrence (who had vowed in his journal of the previous year to return *"if I survive"*) teamed up and planned a new attempt. Torrence's experience on the first expedition provided much needed knowledge of the canyon and how to traverse it successfully. Instead of boats, air mattresses and watertight bags would be used to contain provisions. Most travel would be attempted on foot; but the men would float, if possible, and traverse back and forth when one side or the other became impassable. During June and July, Fellows and **C. A. Fitch** walked the rim along **Vernal Mesa**, scouting for places where assistant **A. W. Dillon** could bring down supplies. By bringing only some food and basic supplies, Fellows and Torrence greatly lightened the provisions they

"Our surroundings were of the wildest possible description. The roar of the water . . . was constantly in our ears, and the walls of the cañon, towering half mile in height above us, were seemingly vertical. Occasionally a rock would fall from one side or the other, with a roar and a crash, exploding like a ton of dynamite when it struck bottom, making us think our last day had come."

Abraham Lincoln Fellows, 1901

Near the foot of Long Draw.

had to carry. On August 12, 1901 they started off from Cimarron. Dillon delivered the first supplies at the present site of **Crystal Dam**. For three more days, the men floated, crossed several times, and portaged over rocks, with the river running fast and white over rocks, churning wildly and slowing their progress. Fearing the delays would cause Dillon to believe them lost, they built bonfires to alert him to their progress. At **Trail Gulch**, Dillon delivered supplies and carried out film and notes. Fellows was naturally awed by the canyon and his notes describe its rugged beauty and steep walls that "*. . . looked almost as if cut into enormous steps by some titan of old, while statues, turrets and pinnacles adorned the rugged precipices on either side.*"

At the **Falls of Sorrows**, where the previous year's expedition ended, the gorge became very narrow. The roar of the river nearly deafened the men, and mist rose so heavy that they could see only a short distance. They looked at the huge boulders and waterfalls they faced, and believing this to be the end, they bade farewell and jumped in one after the other. In just a few moments, they emerged, having sustained only bruises and cuts. But after the Falls of Sorrows, travel became even more difficult — with huge boulders requiring climbing higher and higher, to pass impassable rapids in the river. At one point, the men had to camp so high up that it took an hour to retrieve water; and at another, the Gunnison flowed under huge boulders that had crashed down from cliffs towering 2,000 feet overhead, entirely blocking the canyon floor. Climbing over on each other's shoulders and hauling supplies up with rope, took six hours to cross a quarter mile stretch. In other places, the river filled the canyon from wall to wall, forcing them into the stream for a cold swim.

Now they entered a point in the canyon so truly remote and wild that four-pound trout swam in deep pools, never experiencing the hook of a fisherman. Soon they came to a section that posed the greatest danger of any place yet traversed. Huge boulders so filled the canyon floor that the Gunnison River disappeared below. Impossible to climb over and unable to return upriver, the men had only one choice — dive into the river and hope to be carried through to the other side. Taking a deep breath, Fellows went first, while Torrence watched as his companion swirled in the swift river and disappeared beneath the boulders. Torrence followed and seconds later emerged on the other side, both men battered but still very much alive.

The provisions last brought down by Dillon had been lost, so starvation threatened to end their journey. As they climbed alongside the river, they startled two bighorn sheep standing on a ledge, causing one to jump and break its shoulder. The men had a feast and continued on, revived in body and spirit, past a series of falls that they named for Torrence. Finally, they came within sight of **Red Rock Canyon** and the last drop point for supplies. Only one stretch remained — to a ranch house, estimated to be eight miles away. Still loosing weight, ill from exertion and lack of sleep, this relatively simple section turned into an ordeal. They decided to leave the canyon, having fully succeeded in the exploration and discovery of a suitable location for the tunnel.

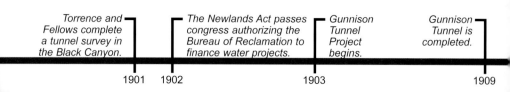

Torrence and Fellows complete a tunnel survey in the Black Canyon.

The Newlands Act passes congress authorizing the Bureau of Reclamation to finance water projects.

Gunnison Tunnel Project begins.

Gunnison Tunnel is completed.

1901   1902   1903   1909

THE GUNNISON TUNNEL

The epic exploration of the Black Canyon by Fellows and Torrence resulted in the Bureau of Reclamation selecting a suitable site for the **Gunnison River Diversion Project**, or **Uncompahgre Project** as it is also known. One of the first projects of the new Bureau of Reclamation, it would run under **Vernal Mesa** from **East Portal**, located nine miles downstream from the confluence of the Gunnison and Cimarron Rivers. First started in 1903, delays slowed construction until 1905, when work commenced in earnest. To speed completion, work progressed in both directions from Lujane (**West Portal**) on Cedar Creek (where the water moved by canal to the Uncompahgre River), and from East Portal in Black Canyon on the Gunnison River. Bringing supplies into East Portal required building a treacherous, 12-mile wagon road with grades up to 22%. Men and supplies made the dangerous journey down the road on wagons, slowed by logs chained to the rear wheels.

Unexpected problems started immediately. Some of the tunnel passed through weak *Mancos shale*, requiring special drilling, support techniques and boring through the **Red Rock Fault**, exposing the miners to unbearable high temperatures. Occasionally, superheated water broke through, scalding the men; and poisonous gas could kill at anytime. In spring, high runoff flooded the tunnel, stopping work. A workforce of hundreds labored on the 5.9-mile tunnel, but conditions were so dangerous that the average worker only stayed on the job for two weeks. After six years, the tunnel was completed at a cost, including canals to carry the water into the Uncompahgre Valley, of $10,541,560. **President William Howard Taft** presided over the opening on September 23, 1909, throwing the switch that released the first water to flow from the Gunnison River to the Uncompahgre Valley.

East Portal around 1907.

At a grade of two feet per thousand, the **Gunnison Tunnel** carries 1,300 cubic feet of water per second. At first, only half of the 146,000 acres predicted were able to be irrigated by the tunnel because of seasonal variations in the river's flow. Each year when the Gunnison ran low late in the season, crops could be lost. To alleviate the shortfall, **Taylor Park Dam** was built in 1937, a 206-foot high earthen dam with a reservoir capacity of 106,200 acre-feet. The water is owned by the users in the Uncompahgre Valley. Another unforeseen problem was that some of the land intended for irrigation proved too alkaline for cultivation. Still, today the valley is a major agricultural producer in Colorado, dependent on the life-giving waters of the Gunnison.

Creation of a New National Park

With the decline of mining as the powerhouse of the Colorado economy, beginning at the start of the twentieth century, boosters began to look at the tremendous resources the region as a magnet for attracting tourism. Tourism began early in Colorado, almost from the point when gold was first washed from eastern slope streams. The railroads, such as William J. Palmer's D&RGW, went to great lengths and expense to advertise their lines that crossed over the high mountain passes and descended the deep rugged canyons. The establishment of National Forests, National Parks, and National Monuments in the region contributed to the idea of making the Western Slope the *"playground of America."* In southwest Colorado, **Mesa Verde National Park** was created in 1906, forever protecting this rich archeological resource. Northwest Colorado benefited from the attraction of the giant dinosaur bones and skeletons found at **Dinosaur National Monument**, designated in 1915. **Colorado National Monument**, with its canyons and sandstone formations, received federal protection in 1911.

In the late 1920s, citizens of Montrose and other area towns, led by Rev. Mark T. Warner and local groups, pushed for preservation of Black Canyon. As one of the last acts of his Presidency, **Herbert Hoover** issued Presidential Proclamation 2033 on March 3, 1933 establishing the **Black Canyon of the Gunnison National Monument**. This act protected the unique resources of the Black Canyon of the Gunnison *"...for the preservation of the spectacular gorges and additional features of scenic, scientific and educational interest."* On October 20, 1976, portions of the canyon and surrounding lands received wilderness designation under the **National Wilderness Preservation Act** which defined wilderness as an area *"... affected primarily by the forces of nature, with the imprint of man's work substantially unnoticeable."* Wilderness is to remain forever a place where man is a visitor and forces of nature remain unimpaired. Designated wilderness in Black Canyon of the Gunnison are those areas encompassing the canyon's rim to the Gunnison River — the Inner-Canyon — and the western uplands of some 11,180 acres in the Park. Finally in 1999, the 106th Congress held hearings to re-designate the Monument as a National Park. The act designating National Park status expanded the size of the Park by 4,500 acres of river, inner canyon and uplands,

The Inner-Canyon of Black Canyon.

downstream of the existing Monument. The act maintained the mandate to preserve the *"... unique natural qualities and superlative scenery, as well as, recreational opportunities..."* of the original Monument.

The purpose of the new Park is the preservation of the gorges and scenic values, protection of natural, cultural, and scientific resources, and to provide educational, scientific, and interpretive opportunities. A further purpose is the preservation of the wilderness characteristics of designated lands and to provide opportunities for use and enjoyment of the resources, leaving them unimpaired for future generations. The management of Park resources is part of an integrated plan, including the Gunnison River Basin. The legislation and acts provide protection, resource management and recreational opportunities to the public, and includes an area of river with three major units; the new **Black Canyon of the Gunnison National Park**, the **Curecanti National Recreation Area** and the **Gunnison Gorge National Conservation Area.** These protected areas provide a variety of outdoor attractions to the visitor, as well as a lasting legacy of far-sighted preservation for generations to come.

Water and the Dams at Curecanti

John Wesley Powell wrote that *". . . history of the West . . . will be written in acre-feet of water."* It was true over 100 years ago when Powell wrote it, and it is so today. **Curecanti National Recreation Area**, and the dams that are at its heart, are a direct result of legal battles that raged for decades over The West's most precious resource, **water**. After the historic **1922 Colorado River Compact** which allocated water use to the various states of the upper and lower basin of the river, it became apparent that Upper Basin states such as Colorado needed to insure that water resources were developed enough to meet the commitments of that and subsequent agreements. **The Upper Colorado River Storage Act** of 1956, largely the work of Colorado Congressman Wayne Aspinall, powerful chairman of the Committee on Interior and Insular Affairs, envisioned six major dams (and several smaller, local water projects) that would be built along the Colorado for irrigation and power generation purposes. After several drawn-out battles between environmentalists and developers over the locations of those projects, three of the dams were completed between 1965 and 1976 on the Gunnison River (tributary to the Colorado River) at Curecanti, now known as the **Aspinall Unit** for the congressman who pressed so hard for their completion. While the original purpose was for irrigation and electricity, recreation opportunities became a major reason for organizing the NRA. The National Park Service manages Curecanti NRA (named for *Curecata*, a Ute Indian chief) by agreement with the Bureau of Reclamation, who built the dams and manages them and the water resource. The main goals that the Park Service has set are for Curecanti are to *"... conserve the scenery, natural, historic, archeological and wildlife resources, and to provide for public use and enjoyment . . . to ensure visitor safety and resource preservation . . ."*

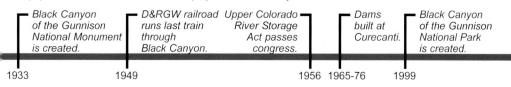

Black Canyon of the Gunnison National Monument is created.	D&RGW railroad runs last train through Black Canyon.	Upper Colorado River Storage Act passes congress.	Dams built at Curecanti.	Black Canyon of the Gunnison National Park is created.
1933	1949	1956	1965-76	1999

THE DAMS

Located 1.5 miles below Sapinero, and 30 miles west of Gunnison, **Blue Mesa Dam** was the first of the large dams to be built on the Gunnison River. Completed in 1965, its main purpose is water storage and electricity production. Blue Mesa Dam, at an altitude of 7,500 feet, is an earth and rockfill dam with a volume of 3,093,000 cubic yards of fill. It stands 390 feet high, with a crest length of 785 feet. The reservoir it backs up has a capacity of 940,800 acre-feet, and when filled, covers an area of 9,180 acres. **Blue Mesa Reservoir** is 20 miles long and has 96 miles of shoreline. Blue Mesa Power Plant consists of two 30,000-kilowatt generators powered by two 41,500 horsepower turbines, generating 43,200-kilowatts serving the upper basin and adjacent areas. A single 16 foot penstock carries water to the two turbines. The drainage basin above the dam comprises an area of 3,434 square miles — a vast and rugged region with altitudes reaching to over 14,000 feet.

Morrow Point Dam is 12 miles below Blue Mesa Dam, and was the second dam completed in the complex in 1968. With power generation its main purpose, the dam creates a narrow reservoir confined by the steep walls of Black Canyon. It is a concrete, double-curvature, thin-arch dam, 469 feet high with a crest length of 724 feet. Morrow Point contains 365,180 cubic yards of concrete with its crest

Blue Mesa Dam

EFFECTS OF THE DAMS

While over geologic time, the dams will have little impact (as the river will eventually silt up and destroy them,) the immediate effects have been enormous. Below the dams, seasonal flooding has been controlled, so that **silt** and **alluvium** (as well as camper's trash on bars and beaches), normally flushed from the canyon, now accumulates. The **canyon floor**, raised and locally dammed by talus and alluvium, has altered habitats and affected wildlife. Increased **seismic activity** has resulted from the weight of the reservoirs on formerly stable faults. The dams made a semi-desert region agriculturally productive and brought electrical power to a quarter-million users, but at the loss of 40 miles of world-class river fishing along a now-flooded stretch of the Gunnison River. **Trout Haven**'s name was perhaps evocative of the local fishing. Like *Elkhorn, Henderson Place, Tex Lodge* and other old settlements and D&RG whistle-stops nestled in bends along the river, it has sat underwater for some 40 years. Interestingly, the flooding required the U.S. Geological Survey to rename two maps. Maps "Cebolla" and "Iola", spots that also disappeared under Blue Mesa Lake, became "Carpenter Ridge" and "Big Mesa," renamed for features that remained high and dry above the waves.

elevation at 7,165 feet altitude. It is the first of its type built by the Bureau of Reclamation. The underground power plant is located in the left abutment, downstream from the axis of the dam, and contains two 83,000 horsepower turbines, producing 172,000 kilowatts. The generators are served by two penstocks, 13.5 feet in diameter. The reservoir has a maximum storage of 117,190 acre-feet. Morrow Point can be viewed by taking a one-mile side road north from the Cimarron Information Center in Curecanti NRA off US-50.

The last of the dams in the Black Canyon, **Crystal Dam**, was completed in 1976. Its purposes are power generation, irrigation storage, recreation, and to control flow through the National Park. Crystal Dam is a concrete, double-curvature, thin-arch dam similar to Morrow Point Dam. It is 323 feet high and has a crest length of 635 feet at an elevation of 6,772 feet. The reservoir stores a maximum 25,200 acre-feet. The power plant consists of one 28,000 kilowatt generator driven by a 39,000 horsepower hydraulic turbine. Crystal Dam is located 6 miles below Morrow Point Dam, near the eastern boundary of the National Park. Crystal Dam can be seen from the end of East Portal Road (closed in winter) which begins just past the South Rim Entrance Station in the National Park. The three reservoirs can store about half of the annual flow of the Gunnison River and together produce electricity to support a population of 240,000.

Additional dams built around Black Canyon and Curecanti, are **Paonia Reservoir** on the North Fork of the Gunnison, **Smith Fork Reservoir** at Crawford (see page 214), and the Bostwick Park project with its **Silver Jack Dam**, built at the head of Cimarron Creek, south of Cimarron.

The Final Piece: Gunnison Gorge

Today's **Gunnison Gorge National Conservation Area** has its roots in a 1979 **Wild and Scenic River** study that determined that the upper 26 of 29 miles of the Gunnison River, from the west boundary of then Black Canyon National Monument to near the river's confluence with the North Fork, qualified for wild and scenic river designation. Then in September of 1988, another study established that 21,038 acres of the Gorge qualified for wilderness designation. That study declared the Gunnison Gorge *" . . . to be natural, and to provide outstanding opportunity for solitude and primitive/unconfined recreation."* The NCA was designated in 1999 as part of the same Act that established the Black Canyon of the Gunnison National Park, as a way to further protect the natural and geologic features of the area, while recognizing its unsurpassed recreational opportunities. The establishment of the Gunnison Gorge National Conservation Area was the final jewel in this crown of federally protected units.

That said, recreation management in the NCA has become problematic. ATVs, motorcycles and 4WD vehicles have overrun the area, concentrated mostly in the badlands west of the gorge. Target shooters set up targets in the ravines between the adobe domes, or blast away at abandoned vehicles. OHVs indiscriminately blaze new trails — past *Closed Area* signs, across sensitive desert soils and plant communities, through creek beds, and up and down steep, soft, easily eroded slopes. The Bureau of Land Management, which manages the NCA, is aware of the situation and a **new management plan** is in the works, due out sometime in 2004.

FACILITIES

Gunnison Point Overlook.

NATIONAL PARK FACILITIES

Visitor Center at Gunnison Point on the South Rim

Welcome to the Black Canyon of the Gunnison National Park! As of 2004, the **entrance fee** per car is **$7**. Bicyclists or hikers pay $4 per person. Admission is free during periods when the entrance station is not staffed, such as holidays. If you have a Golden Age, Golden Access, National Park Pass, or Annual Permit, you and your car passengers may also enter for free. Entrance fees are good for 7 days.

OPTIONAL PASSES

One of these *optional* passes may be a good choice for you if you plan on returning to the National Park within the year or if you plan on visiting other parks in the National Park Service system. The ranger at the entrance station can accommodate you. Your options include:

Black Canyon Annual Permit (good for entrance to Black Canyon of the Gunnison NP for one year from month of purchase): *$15*

National Parks Annual Pass (good for entrance fees to NPS areas for one year from month of purchase): *$50*

Golden Age Passport (lifetime pass good for entrance fees to NPS areas if you are a US citizen 62 or older): *$10*

Golden Access Passport (lifetime pass to NPS areas if you are a US citizen with a permanent disability): *Free*

South Rim

The Visitor Center should be your first stop in the Park. You'll find Park staff and volunteers on duty to answer your questions, you'll find information about **daily programs**, **nature walks** and other events, you can obtain necessary **permits**, purchase **books** or **maps**, and you'll enjoy the **exhibits** and the **short video** in the center's theatre.

Information desk

Exhibits

Exhibits

VISITOR CENTER

If you're like most of the Park's 230,000 annual visitors, your first stop after you enter the Park will be at the **South Rim Visitor Center**, located at Gunnison Point, 1.6 miles after you pass the South Rim entrance station.

The Visitor Center on the South Rim is open daily, year-round, from 8:30 AM to 4:00 PM. (The building is closed on Thanksgiving, Christmas Day and New Years Day.) Even if you've been to the Park before, it's well worth stopping at the center for another look, especially since additional displays and improvements are being made on an ongoing basis.

Even if you arrive after Visitor Center hours or on a a holiday, the Park is never closed! However, if you plan to spend the night within the Park boundaries, you must camp at South Rim Campground (pay at the self-serve station at the campground entrance, see pg. 104.) Or you can camp at nearby East Portal in Curecanti NRA (see **Campgrounds/Campsites**, pg. 111.)

Along the South Rim Drive, you'll find **restrooms** or **outhouses** at the South Rim Campground, at Tomichi Overlook, at the Visitor Center, near Rim House at Pulpit Rock Overlook, and at the Sunset View and High Point Picnic Areas at the west end of the road.

Don't venture into the canyon or on any other hike without carrying plenty of water with you. **Drinking water**, available at the Visitor Center, the South Rim Campground and at Pulpit Rock Overlook, is hauled in by tanker truck; so it is limited. It's best to bring water with you to the Park.

The **Rim House** (open daily from about mid-May to late-September) has a coffee shop, snacks and souvenirs. It's located at the Pulpit Rock Overlook.

Pay phones are located on the east side of the Visitor Center.

Map of National Park Facilities

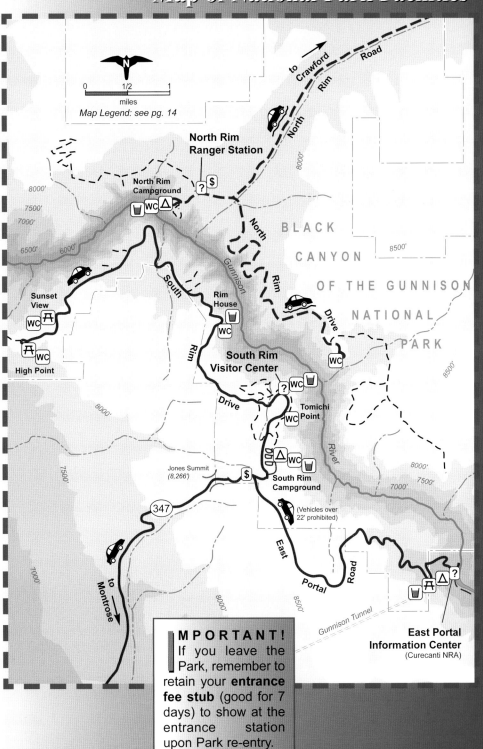

SOUTH RIM CAMPGROUND

The **South Rim Campground** offers a lovely setting in the oak/brush forest close to the rim, with a connection to the scenic Rim Rock Trail (see Hike #1, page 172), starting near Loop C. It's located off the South Rim Drive, less than 0.5 mile north of the entrance station and the turnoff for the East Portal Road. This is the only developed campground in the Park on the South Rim, with **88 campsites** — those at **Loops A and B may be reserved**, Loop C is first-come, first-served. The Park personnel report that it is rarely full, but come early anyway and choose a site close to the canyon rim. Two sites are set up for handicap access. Loop A is open year-round; Loops B & C are open from spring to fall only.

You'll find a picnic table, fire pit, and space for your tent in each site. Be sure to pitch your tent within the area marked out for your site. Loop B has 30-amp **electrical hook-ups**, although recreational vehicles greater than 35 feet are not recommended. Quiet hours are from 10 PM to 6 AM.

Firewood is not provided, not is collecting of wood permitted in the Park, so you'll have to bring your own wood or charcoal. It is also a good idea to bring your own water, as it must be trucked in and should be used sparingly. Please don't feed or tempt local wildlife with your food. Also keep all pets leashed. Maximum stay is 14 days.

> **FEES** (as of 2004)
> ▌ *Loop A & C:* **$10** per night (**$5** with Golden Age/Access pass)
> ▌ *Loop B:* **$15** per night (**$10** with Golden Age/Access pass)

Reservations at certain campgrounds at Black Canyon of the Gunnison NP and Curecanti NRA are now accepted at:

☎ www.ReserveUSA.com
   1 (877) 444-6777

There is a **$9** reservation fee, in addition to the normal campground fee. Reserve your spot at least 5 days in advance. This is a round-the-clock, nationwide reservation system for camping in virtually all federal land agencies.

PICNIC AREAS

There are two small picnic areas along the South Rim Drive. **Sunset View**, as the name implies, is our choice for a picnic in the evening because of its fine end-of-day views into the canyon. The site is wheelchair accessible, but there's no water. For a mid-day lunch stop, try shady **High Point Picnic Area**, nestled among the pinyons at the western road end, about a mile past Sunset View. High Point has tables and restrooms. Fires are not permitted at either site.

Picnic at High Point.

North Rim

NORTH RIM RANGER STATION

The **North Rim Ranger Station** serves as the "visitor center" for those Park visitors who prefer to explore the less-crowded, more-remote north rim of the Park. To reach it, turn west on North Rim Drive at the North Rim Road junction. The Ranger Station is on the right in about 0.5 mile. Inside are some exhibits about rocks and wildlife found in the Park. There's staff on duty to answer questions and to dispense backcountry permits (although there is a self-serve station for sign-ins and permits on the front porch for after-hours.)

The Ranger Station, North Rim Campground and North Rim Road are generally open from early May to November, depending on snow and road conditions. That doesn't mean you can't visit this side of the Park in winter — the Park is always open — it just means you'll have a long snowshoe or ski in during off-season (see **Winter Activities**, page 168.)

Vault **toilets** are located at the Ranger Station and at the North Rim Campground, and there's an outhouse at the turn-around at the east end of North Rim Drive. **Drinking water** can be found in the campground. You can't purchase **food** at the north rim of the Park. The small town of Crawford, 15 miles away, has a small general store with limited groceries and a handful of restaurants.

There's no direct access to the less-visited **North Rim** from the popular **South Rim**, though they are within shouting distance of each other! You'll have to either drive west on US-50, through Montrose to Delta, then east on CO-92 to Crawford, or go east on US-50 to CO-92, then north to Crawford, almost two hours drive either way. (See the map on page 33.)

North Rim Ranger Station.

NORTH RIM CAMPGROUND

The small (13 sites) **North Rim Campground** is a short stroll up the road from the Ranger Station, at the west end of North Rim Drive. The peaceful sites (first-come, first-served) are nestled in with the junipers and pinyons, and include tables and

FEES (as of 2004)
$10 per campsite per night / **$5** with Golden Age or Golden Access pass (maximum of 8 people per site.)

fire pits. You'll need to bring your own wood or charcoal. There are no hook-ups or dump stations. The very pleasant and scenic Chasm View Nature Trail (see Hike #6, page 176) starts on the south side of the campground.

North Rim Campground.

Backcountry Camping in the Park

If you're packing into the backcountry, you'll need a recommended gallon of water, per person, per day. (Two gallons for two days weighs 16 pounds. *Ouch!*) Side canyons are usually dry, so the river is your only reliable water source. Either boil, filter or treat river water as **giardia** is present.

It is also possible to camp in the National Park's designated Wilderness Area which includes all of the Inner-Canyon and its river corridor, and the western third of the Park, a vast, seldom-visited area of dry, rugged side canyons and upland mesas straddling the river. You'll need a free **wilderness-use permit** to hike, kayak, climb or camp, available at the South Rim Visitor Center or the North Rim Ranger Station (or by mail.) There are no designated campsites; but there are several suitable tent and bivy sites along the river, mostly clustered at the bottoms of ravines that enter the Inner-Canyon. The rangers can advise you and give you directions when you obtain your permit. (See **Inner-Canyon Routes** in the *Hiking* section on page 194 for further information on suitable overnight trips into the canyon.) The staff will also let you know where to leave your vehicle. You'll need to carry your copy of your permit with you and then turn it in at the end of your trip. (Failure to do so may trigger a rescue attempt, so don't forget!) There's a slot for after-hours drop-off at both issuing facilities. You might also want to jot something down about conditions in the comment book maintained at each facility that might aid other parties.

This is primitive camping; you'll need to be properly equipped (see the **Suggested Equipment List** on page 225) and practice *Leave No Trace* principles. No open fires are allowed in the backcountry — bring a stove and fuel. Pack out your trash, including *you-know-what* paper. For human waste, dig a *cat-hole*, 6" deep and as far as possible from the river, or other water source.

EMERGENCIES

For medical, fire, or law enforcement emergencies, ☎ 911.
For non-emergencies, ☎ *(970) 874-2000* (Delta County Sheriff)
☎ *(970) 240-6606* (Montrose County Sheriff)
☎ *(970) 641-1113* (Gunnison County Sheriff)

For Poison Control, ☎ *(800) 332-3073.*

For less dire emergencies:
At Black Canyon NP: stop at the Visitor Center, or ☎ *(970) 249-1915* ext 18.
At Curecanti NRA: stop at the Elk Creek Visitor Center or ☎ *(970) 641-2337*

To visit an area hospital:

Montrose Memorial Hospital
■ 800 S. 3rd. Street
Montrose, CO 81101
☎ *(970) 249-2211*

Gunnison Valley Hospital
■ 214 E. Denver Avenue
Gunnison, CO 81230
☎ *(970) 641-1456*

For the **Colorado State Patrol** (Montrose area):
☎ *(970) 249-4392*

CURECANTI NRA FACILITIES

Elk Creek NPS Administrative Center

Welcome to the Curecanti National Recreation Area! The National Recreation Area is open year-round and there is **no entrance fee**. However, an **activity fee** is charged for boaters on Blue Mesa Reservoir for all motorized and/or state registered water craft: $4 for two days, $10 for 14 days, or $30 for an annual boat permit. (Boating on Morrow Point Reservoir and Crystal Reservoir is limited to hand-carried craft only and no permit is required.) You can purchase any permit by mail after March 1 (call or write to the address on page 33) or you can buy one in person in season at the Elk Creek Visitor Center, at the marina at Lake Fork, or from the campground hosts at Stevens Creek and Ponderosa Campgrounds.

Administered by the National Park Service, your NPS **Golden Age** or **Golden Access** Passport is good for half-off boat activity fees and camping fees at Curecanti NRA. (See page 101.)

Services at Curecanti NRA

VISITOR CENTERS

Curecanti NRA is spread over such a large area and receives so many visitors (nearly 900,000 per year) that there are several visitor and information centers in the unit. All are wheelchair accessible.

The **Elk Creek Visitor Center**, 16 miles west of Gunnison on US-50, is the primary center, as well as the headquarters for the National Park Service administrators. It's open mid-May through late-September, 8:00 am to 4:30 pm, and open weekends and intermittently on weekdays during the rest of the year. It's closed on holidays. The center has exhibits and shows a video telling about the natural and cultural history of the area. You can ask a ranger about boating and fishing conditions and obtain the necessary boating permit for Blue Mesa Reservoir. There's also a large classroom used for education classes and meetings. To reach the Elk Creek Visitor Center, ☎ *(970) 641-2337 ext 205.*

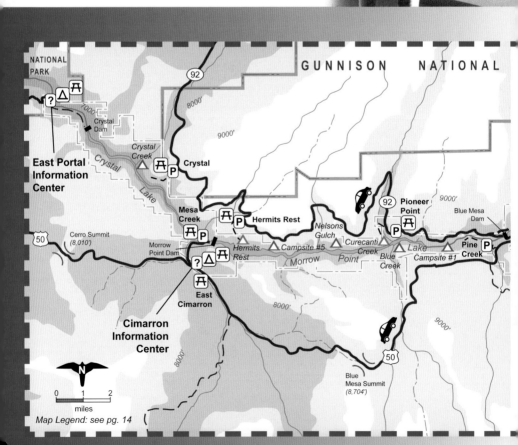

Map Legend: see pg. 14

The **Lake Fork Information Center** is located 25 miles west of Gunnison on CO-92, just north of its junction with US-50. Lake Fork is only open from mid-May to late-September, 9:00 am to 4:00 pm. You'll find a ranger on duty to answer your questions and a small retail outlet where books, maps and postcards are sold. There are also some photo exhibits relating the history and ecology of the region, including stuff about Blue Mesa Dam, just a stone's throw down the road. To contact the center, ☎ *(970) 641-3128.*

Further west along US-50, 35 miles from Gunnison, is the **Cimarron Information Center**, open summers only from 9:00 am to 4:00 pm. This is a must stop for railroad buffs who will be interested in the photo exhibit about the days when the Denver and Rio Grande Western Railroad high-balled through the canyon (see page 88 in the **Cultural History** section of this guide.) There's more history just down the Morrow Point Dam Road, heading north from the center. The road leads to an overlook with plaques telling about the dam; along the way, you'll pass an historic train exhibit (see page 164 more info.) To phone the center, ☎ *(970) 249-4074.*

From CO-347, just past the entrance to Black Canyon of the Gunnison National Park, turn right onto the 6-mile access road to **East Portal**. You'll have to pay the $7 per car National Park entrance fee. The steep, winding road (closed in the winter) prohibits trailers, buses and RVs over 22 feet long. At the bottom, there's a **visitor information station** with info about both Curecanti NCA and the National Park, open from mid-April to mid-November.

Map of Curecanti NRA Facilities

PICNIC AREAS

Several delightful picnic areas dot scenic highways C0-92 and US-50, as they wind through Curecanti NRA. Most information centers, overlooks and trailheads along these two roads have a picnic table or two. Larger picnic areas, with water and toilets, are at the extreme east end of the unit, and at **East Cimarron Picnic Area** on the west end. East Cimarron is one mile east of the Cimarron Information Center, off the south side of US-50. The picnic areas of **Neversink** and **Cooper Ranch,** a mile apart along US-50 near the unit's eastern boundary, are especially pretty in late spring and early fall, nestled among groves of cottonwood and featuring short nature trails along the Gunnison River. Generally, these areas are open only from the first of May to early October.

MARINAS AND LAUNCH RAMPS

There are two **full-service marinas,** located at Elk Creek and Lake Fork, open during the summer. Besides slips and showers, you can also hire a fishing guide or rent a boat at the Elk Creek Marina. There are boat launches into Blue Mesa Reservoir at **Stevens Creek**, **Elk Creek**, and **Lake Fork** located along US-50 at mile 12, mile 16 and mile 25 respectively from Gunnison. Access ramps are also at **Willow Creek** and **Dillon Pinnacles** on the north shore. There's a launch ramp on the southeast shore of the reservoir at **Iola**, off CO-149 about 3.5 miles south of the Lake City Bridge; and another ramp into the lake's largest arm, Soap Creek Arm, at **Ponderosa**, 7 miles north of the dam on gravelled Soap Creek Road.

A guided fishing trip just might be the ticket to finding those lunkers hiding in the depths of Blue Mesa Lake. **Elk Creek Marina** offers licensed guided trips in the NRA and rents gear, pontoon boats and larger fishing craft. Reservations are recommended.

P.O. Box 1804
Gunnison, CO 81230
(970) 641-0707
www.whresorts.com/elk_creek_marina/

GROCERIES AND DRINKING WATER

There is a limited selection of **groceries** at both the Elk Creek and Lake Fork Marinas; and there's a **restaurant** at Elk Creek as well (*Pappy's,* open summer only). For anything more than that, you'll have to drive to Gunnison (16 miles east of Elk Creek) where you'll find a couple of supermarkets and restaurants of every flavor (see the **Gunnison** section on page 120 later in this chapter.)

Drinking water can be found at all the visitor/information centers, as well as at all of the 10 road-accessed campgrounds and larger picnic areas, generally from May through September. **Elk Creek Picnic Area** has water year-round. Potable water is not provided at the several boat-accessed campsites dotting the shores of the three reservoirs. Water taken from the reservoirs and creeks at these sites should be treated chemically with pills designed for water purification, by filtering the water with an approved filter, or by boiling untreated water for several minutes.

Showers are available at Elk Creek and Lake Fork (summers only.)

Elk Creek Marina.

CAMPGROUNDS/CAMPSITES

Camping is very popular at Curecanti NRA with two distinct choices: **road-accessed campgrounds** or **boat/foot-accessed sites**. Most of the road-accessed campgrounds fill up on major weekends in the summer, so try to arrive by 10 a.m. **Elk Creek** is the only one that is open year-round; all others generally are open from April or May to late fall. Only Elk Creek has hook-ups (in Loop D). Some sites are limited to 14 days. Smaller areas at **Dry Gulch**, **Gateview**, **Ponderosa**, **Red Creek** and **East Portal** offer more seclusion from the masses and welcomed shade. Driftwood may be collected and burned.

> **Reservations** are accepted at these campsites; all others are first-come, first served.
> ☎✓ *www.ReserveUSA.com*
> ☎ 1 (877) 444-6777
> ▪ Elk Creek: Loops A & D
> ▪ Lake Fork: Sites 31-87
> ▪ Stevens Creek: Loop A
> ▪ East Elk Creek: Group site
> ▪ Red Creek: Group site

There are several **primitive campsites** sprinkled around the shores of all three reservoirs that offer much more of a wilderness experience, especially those on Morrow Point and Crystal Reservoirs. Most of these sites can only be accessed by boat, although a few can also be reached by foot (for more info, see the **Boating at Curecanti NRA** section, page 128.) Besides space for a tent, some sites also have picnic tables, grills or fire pits, and outhouses. All are free and first-come, first-served. Please pack out your trash and keep your fires small.

ROAD ACCESSED CAMPGROUNDS	Fee	# of sites	Water	Flush WC	Vault WC	RV Dump	Showers	Access	Listed east to west. See the map on page 108-109 for the location of these campgrounds. Fees are as of 2004. Comments:
Stevens Creek	$10	54	✓		✓			✓	Amphitheater, boat ramp, fishing access
Elk Creek	$10	160	✓	✓	✓	✓	✓	✓	16 walk-in, 20 pull-thru sites.*Loop D:$15
East Elk Creek	$50	1	✓		✓				1 group site (up to 50 people)
Lake Fork	$10	90	✓	✓		✓	✓	✓	5 walk-in,16 pull-thru sites, mostly paved
Dry Gulch	$10	9	✓		✓				Secluded among cottonwoods
Red Creek	$10	2/1	✓		✓				2 sites plus 1 group site ($25, 20 people)
Gateview		7	✓		✓				Access by CO-149 on dirt road, no fee
Ponderosa	$10	28	✓		✓				Gravel road access, 9 walk-in sites, corral
Cimarron	$10	21	✓	✓		✓		✓	Visitor Center, 5 pull-thru sites
East Portal	$10	15	✓		✓				No trailers over 22 feet on steep road

BOAT/FOOT ACCESSED CAMPSITES	# of sites	Boat Acc.	Foot Acc.	Blue Mesa	Morrow Pt.	Crystal	Listed east to west. See the map on page 108-109 for the location of these campsites. Comments:
Turtle Rock	1	✓		✓			On south shore, opposite Elk Creek Marina
Cebolla Creek	1	✓		✓			On Cebolla Arm
West Elk Creek	1	✓		✓			At end of West Elk Arm
Lake Fork Arm	1	✓		✓			On Lake Fork Arm
Campsite #1	1	✓			✓		South shore, between Pine Creek & Curecanti Needle
Blue Creek	1	✓			✓		South shore, near Curecanti Needle
Curecanti Creek	3	✓	✓		✓		Across from Curecanti Needle, off Curecanti Cr. Trail
Nelsons Gulch	1	✓			✓		North shore, 1/2 way point of lake at Kokanee Bay
Campsite #5	1	✓			✓		North shore, between Myers Gulch & Hermits Rest
Hermits Rest	9	✓	✓		✓		North shore, off Hermits Rest Trail
Crystal Creek	5	✓				✓	At mouth of Crystal Creek

GUNNISON GORGE NCA FACILITIES

Kiosk at the Ute Trailhead.

Welcome to the Gunnison Gorge National Conservation Area! There is **no entrance fee** for the National Conservation Area and visitors can use trailhead facilities, such as restrooms and picnic areas, at no charge in *non-wilderness* portions of the NCA. However, a **$3 per person day-use fee** is required of all visitors (children under 16 enter for free) to the **Gunnison Gorge Wilderness Area** within the NCA (see the map on page 115.) Instructions, envelopes and fee tubes for payment are at the various trailheads. One person from each group visiting the wilderness area must also sign the trail register at the Bobcat, Duncan, or Ute trailhead, the Chukar boater put-in (located on the river), or at the Gunnison Forks take-out.

An **annual day-use pass** is also available for $15. Put your money and filled-out envelope in the fee tube and use the fee receipt for that day. BLM will mail you a pass.

The fees and requirements can be a little confusing, so take note:

❚ Payment is by cash or check only (exact change required and no charge cards.) No other federal or state passes (such as National Park Annual Pass, Golden Age, Golden Access, or Colorado State Parks Pass) can be applied to user or camping fees in the Gorge.

❚ Hikers traveling from the Chukar trailhead upstream into Black Canyon of the Gunnison National Park still have to pay the user fee. However, boaters traveling downstream from the Park do not, although they must have a backcountry Park permit (for info on that, see page 106) and sign the Chukar put-in register.

❚ There is no charge for *private* walk-in fishing or camping below the Smith Fork. But visitors that use the services of the *Gunnison River Pleasure Park* (such as the jet boat, raft rental or guide services) in the four-mile section between the Smith Fork and the North Fork confluences must pay the fee.

❚ The user fee is in addition to any commercial company's advertised charge for guided rafting or fishing trips in the Gorge. The outfitter should collect the user fee from clients prior to the trip. By the way, outfitters must have a permit issued by the BLM to operate in the Gorge. For a list of permitted outfitters, see page 226.

❚ Passes are good for in-and-out the same calendar day but cannot be applied toward camping fees (more about that below.) Passes are non-transferable.

Earn a **free annual day-use pass** for volunteering four hours of work on a volunteer work day in the Gorge. Contact the BLM at the Montrose Field Office ☎ *(970) 240-5300* for details.

Whew — that's a lot! But it's part of a growing trend on public lands, including collecting fees for activities that have never had an associated fee before. The Bureau of Land Management reports that nearly 100% of what is collected remains here to be spent directly to benefit the NCA.

These fees and regulations are subject to change; as the BLM is in the midst of developing a sweeping **new management plan** (due out in 2004) which will effect not only use of the wilderness area, but may impose new regulations or restrictions on users in the entire NCA. Be sure to check in with the BLM about the latest rules before heading out.

Informational brochures about current rules at the NCA are available at major trailheads.

Services in the NCA

Restrooms and **picnic tables** are provided at the Chukar, Duncan and Ute trailheads, but you'll have to bring your own water. No day-use fee is required to use these facilities, since they are *outside* the wilderness area. (See the **Hiking** section, page 188, for driving and access directions) Primitive camping is allowed anywhere outside the wilderness area (except right at the trailheads), but the BLM encourages you to use sites that have already been impacted.

At the **BLM Gunnison Forks Day Use** site at the far northern end of the NCA, there is a boat ramp, picnic tables with shelters, grills, a restroom and a sanitation dump station. Camping is prohibited at the site, but a nearby private concessionaire (*Gunnison River Pleasure Park*, see page 114) provides camping and other services to visitors. Gunnison Forks is outside the wilderness area and so no day-use fee is required. Most of the NCA is on the far (south) side of the river, requiring a ford or ferrying by boat. However, once across, one can hike up river as far as the Smith Fork in the Gunnison Gorge Wilderness Area without paying a day-use fee. There is one free campsite at **Cedar Flats** along the trail, just outside of the boundary to the wilderness area. (For information, see **Hike #22**, page 192.) Gunnison Forks is located at the end of CR-2810, 13 miles east of Delta off CO-92.

CAMPING IN THE WILDERNESS AREA

> **CAMPING FEES**
> (as of 2004)
> **$10** per person for one night / **$15** per person for two nights (maximum stay).

Camping in the **Gunnison Gorge Wilderness Area** is restricted to **designated sites**, all of which are along the river corridor, mostly clustered at the bottom of the Chukar Trail, Bobcat Trail, Duncan Trail and Ute Trails. Overnight visitors must sign-in for campsites at time of registration and pay the required camping fee (note that this is in *addition* to the day-use fee.) There are two types of campsites, marked with blue or green-topped wooden posts with the number of the site in white. **Blue sites** are for boaters only (water access) and **green sites** are for hikers only (land access.) (See the map on the facing page for the location of these sites.) Boaters may stay only one night at any blue site, while hikers can stay two nights at the same green site. Maximum stay in the wilderness area is two nights.

There are backcountry toilets at the bottom of the Chukar, Duncan and Ute Trails for hikers. River runners and horseback groups must have *porta-potties* (for more rules for boaters see the **Boating in Gunnison NCA** on page 130.) The whole purpose of the system is to concentrate use in small, maintained areas, protecting the rest of this beautiful yet fragile canyon. As you can well imagine, there are other rules that you should be sure to follow:

▌ You must stick with your designated campsite. Check the visitor registration at the trailhead to ensure that another party hasn't already reserved your desired spot. Three **overflow camps**, below the confluence with the Smith Fork, marked with brown posts, are for boaters (or hikers coming up the Smith Fork Trail from Gunnison Forks) on a first-come, first-served basis.

▌ Wood fires aren't permitted in the wilderness area (and in the entire river corridor down to the confluence with the North Fork.) There simple isn't enough driftwood to handle the impact of so many visitors. Bring a backpacker's stove and fuel or a fire pan and charcoal (carry out the ashes.)

▌ Keep a clean camp and practice the principles of *Leave No Trace.* Pack out all your trash and strain your dishwater before returning it to the river. Bring along a water filter or purification tablets, or be prepared to boil drinking water.

▌ Maximum group size for all day-use and overnight activities is 12 persons. Groups with stock animals are limited to 12 animals.

▌ Finally, remember that typical use rules apply in a wilderness area. That means no motorized vehicles or bicycles are permitted on the trails into the gorge and motorized craft are prohibited on the river.

Map of Gunnison Gorge NCA Facilities

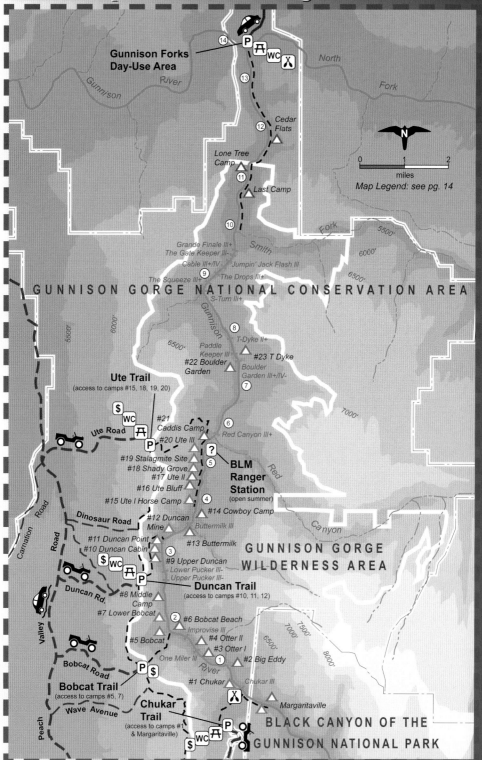

Gunnison Forks
Day-Use Area

North

Gunnison

River

Fork

14

13

Cedar
Flats

12

N

0   1   2
miles

Map Legend: see pg. 14

Lone Tree
Camp

11

Last Camp

10

5500'

Fork

6000'

Grande Finale III+
The Gate Keeper III-
Cable III+/IV   Jumpin' Jack Flash III

6500'

The Squeeze III+   The Drops III+

9

GUNNISON GORGE NATIONAL CONSERVATION AREA

S-Turn III+

Gunnison

8

T-Dyke II+

7000'

5500'

6000'

6500'

Paddle
Keeper III

#22 Boulder
Garden

#23 T Dyke

Boulder
Garden III+/IV-

7

Ute Trail
(access to camps #15, 18, 19, 20)

$

WC

#21
Caddis Camp

6

Red

Canyon

#20 Ute III

P

#19 Stalagmite Site

?

Red Canyon III+

5

#18 Shady Grove

BLM
Ranger
Station
(open summer)

#17 Ute II

#16 Ute Bluff

#15 Ute I Horse Camp

4

#14 Cowboy Camp

7000'

Carnation
Road

Dinosaur Road

Road

#12 Duncan
Mine

Buttermilk III

Canyon

#11 Duncan Point

#10 Duncan Cabin

$ WC

3

#13 Buttermilk

**GUNNISON GORGE
WILDERNESS AREA**

P

Duncan Rd.

#9 Upper Duncan
Lower Pucker III-
Upper Pucker III-

Duncan Trail
(access to camps #10, 11, 12)

#8 Middle
Camp

#7 Lower Bobcat

valley

2

#6 Bobcat Beach

7500'

7000'

Improvise III

#5 Bobcat

#4 Otter II

6500'

8000'

One Miler III

#3 Otter I

Bobcat Road

P $

River

#2 Big Eddy

Bobcat Trail
(access to camps #5, 7)

#1 Chukar

Chukar III

Wave Avenue

**Chukar
Trail**
(access to camps #
& Margaritaville)

Margaritaville

Peach

P

$ WC

**BLACK CANYON OF THE
GUNNISON NATIONAL PARK**

LOCAL FACILITIES

Montrose Regional Airport.

Welcome to Gunnison Country! Whichever of the small cities and towns you visit in the Gunnison, Uncompahgre and North Fork Valleys, you'll find these communities around the Black Canyon of the Gunnison to be some of the warmest and friendliest anywhere. Relax and enjoy their Western Slope brand of hospitality, one that embraces a slower-paced, less-stressful way of life.

All together, over one million visitors per year come to explore the Black Canyon region, with a profound effect on the economies of these communities. The largest of the communities close to the canyon is historic **Montrose**, only about a 30-minute drive form the south entrance to the National Park. This commercial center for the Uncompahgre Valley has a complete range of facilities, including first-class lodging and fine dining. For those visiting the North Rim of the Park, the small towns of **Crawford** and Hotchkiss have, at first glance, limited facilities and services. Yet, the number of fine restaurants in Crawford will surprise you; and a home stay on one of the area's working ranches is an experience in an unique lifestyle, not to be forgotten. The city of **Delta** provides many close-by services to visitors to Gunnison Gorge NCA. And any outdoor adventurer at Curecanti NRA will feel right at home in nearby **Gunnison**, whose residents and businesses celebrate the outdoors.

Nearby Services

There are a number of **close-by concessioners** that operate at the entrances or on private in-holdings within the boundaries of Black Canyon of the Gunnison National Park, Curecanti National Recreation Area and Gunnison Gorge National Conservation Area that offer services or facilities convenient to the visitor; such as gas, groceries or alternatives to camping. We list some, but not all, of the possiblities here. You'll find much more extensive services at the nearby towns of Crawford, Gunnison, Montrose and Delta, detailed starting on page 119.

CLOSE TO THE NATIONAL PARK

The city of Montrose is so close to the south (main) entrance of the National Park as to be your primary source for services and facilities. But if you just can't wait for an ice cream cone, turn in at the **Black Canyon Corner Store**. You can't miss it, nestled under the only shade trees in sight, at the turn-off for the Park entrance (the intersection of US-50 and CO-347.) They have snacks, ice, and the usual assortment of postcards and gifts that are either treasure or trash, depending on your viewpoint. They also have something called *"The Pressed Rat and Wart Hog's Rock Emporium."* For

Black Canyon Corner Store.

anything more important, like gas or groceries, you'll have to continue on down the road another 9 miles to Montrose. The store is open from about early May to mid-November.

CLOSE TO CURECANTI NRA

Despite the fact that Curecanti NRA is so spread out, with some distance between sites, there are several places along US-50 to get propane, a few groceries, or some fishing bait; perhaps saving one from running out of gas or from a much longer trip into Gunnison or Montrose for needed supplies.

At the summer-cottage village of **Sapinero**, just east of where the highway crosses the Lake Fork Arm at the southwest end of Blue Mesa Reservoir, there is a general store with food, propane and gas open year-round. One mile further west, after crossing the Lake Fork Bridge, you'll spot a sign on the bluff for **Blue Mesa Village** which has RVcamping and cabins for rent. Continue west along US-50 for a couple of miles, 1.0 mile past the turnoff for the Pine Creek Trail, to **Blue Mesa Point** which has gas, a small campground, a motel, a general store, and a bait and tackle shop. The village of **Cimarron**, 35 miles west of Gunnison on US-50 and next to the the NRA's Cimarron Information Center, serves as the year-round commercial center for the ranches of the Cimarron Valley with a post office, general store, two gas stations and a cafe. Towing and car repair is available here (including a junk yard, if your vehicle puts out its last gasp on the haul over Blue Mesa Summit.)

A pair of resorts cater more to long-term vactioners, especially RVers, offering nearly instant access to the NRA and Gunnison National Forest. **Gunnison Lakeside Resort**, 12 miles west of Gunnison on US-50, offers an alternative to camping at Curecanti NRA; including all the amenities, such as full hooks-ups for RVers (including TV), laundry and showers, Internet access and a convenience store. For reservations, call *(970) 641-0477*. A mile further west is the *Ponderosa*-like spread of the **Blue Mesa Recreational Ranch**. It is a *member-only* camping resort with luxurious features that are too many to mention here (including bingo night!) You can inquire at *(970) 641-0492*. Both are open from about May 1 through the end of October.

Ferro's Blue Mesa Trading Post, about 4 miles north of CO-92 and Blue Mesa Dam on gravelled Soap Creek Road, is another of those roadside attractions off the beaten path run by colorful characters that seem to dot The West. The friendly owner, John Ferro, can set you up in your choice of log cabin or RV, take you on a guided horseback ride on the post's 40 acres or up into the 35,000-acre West Elk Wilderness, or sell you everything from assorted gee-gaws, to fishing gear, to a hot shower. The store is open from May to the end of November.

> *3200 Soap Creek Road*
> *Gunnison, CO 81230*
> *970-641-4671*
> *www.coloradodirectory.com/ferros*

CLOSE TO GUNNISON GORGE NCA

Gunnison Gorge Pleasure Park.

970-872-2525
www.troutfisherman.net/

FEES (as of 2004)
▮ Camping, **$10** per night, per person.
▮ RV sites (self-contained), **$15** per night.
▮ RV sites with electricity, **$25** per night.
▮ Shuttle to Chukar Trail (with your vehicle), **$75**.
▮ Shuttle to Drysdale Flats, **$40**.

While the facilities at the BLM's Gunnison Gorge NCA are indeed a bit primitive, the **Gunnison River Pleasure Park**, located at the end of CR-28.10 (13 miles east of Delta off CO-92), makes up the difference with virtually anything the civilized recreationalist might need to float or fish the gorge. Located on the river, next to the **BLM Gunnison Forks day-use site**, this private concessionaire offers camping and cabins with showers, food, beer and pop, plus rentals of fishing tackle, pontoon boats and rafts. You can hire a fishing guide, whose 25 years of experience on the river might help you find the big ones, or they can haul you upriver by jet boat and drop you off. If you are interested in hiking the trail to the Smith Fork (see **Hike # 22**, page 192), they can ferry you across the Gunnison, thus avoiding a difficult and potentially dangerous ford of the river.

Perhaps the most popular service offered to floaters is a **shuttle service** between Gunnison Forks and an upriver put-in at the Chukar Trail, or a downriver take out at Drysdale Flats. Advance reservations are required. Note that activities within the NCA's Wilderness Area require fees (see pages 112-114) that may or may not be included in the prices.

Crawford Services

Located at the foot of the nearby West Elk Mountains, the authentic western town of **Crawford** serves as a base for the much less-visited North Rim of Black Canyon of the Gunnison National Park. Services are limited in this small community of about 250 persons. The main drag (CO-92) through town has a couple of cafes and the **Crawford Country Store**, which has a little bit of everything — some groceries, sporting goods, showers, a laundromat and a few motel rooms for hunters and travelers. In the late 1990s, a lot of excitement came to town with the opening of the lavish **Mad Dog Ranch Fountain Cafe**, with no expense spared by owner, rock star Joe Cocker. Unfortunately, enough business failed to materialize in this quiet corner of Colorado and the restaurant sits, at least temporarily, closed. There's also a gas station/general store about 1 mile south of town, off of CO-92 near Crawford State Park. For most other things, such as a full-service grocery store, continue north on CO-92 for 10 miles to **Hotchkiss**.

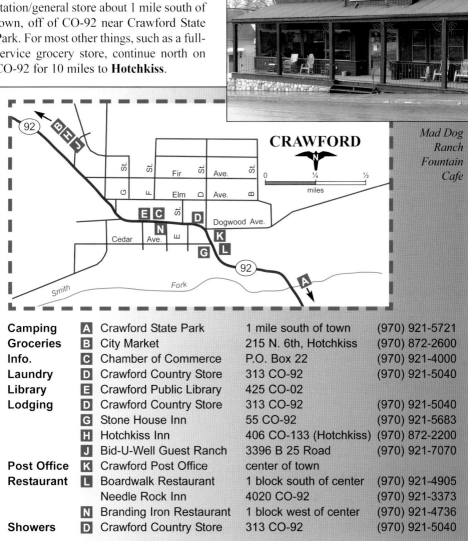

Camping	A	Crawford State Park	1 mile south of town	(970) 921-5721
Groceries	B	City Market	215 N. 6th, Hotchkiss	(970) 872-2600
Info.	C	Chamber of Commerce	P.O. Box 22	(970) 921-4000
Laundry	D	Crawford Country Store	313 CO-92	(970) 921-5040
Library	E	Crawford Public Library	425 CO-02	
Lodging	D	Crawford Country Store	313 CO-92	(970) 921-5040
	G	Stone House Inn	55 CO-92	(970) 921-5683
	H	Hotchkiss Inn	406 CO-133 (Hotchkiss)	(970) 872-2200
	J	Bid-U-Well Guest Ranch	3396 B 25 Road	(970) 921-7070
Post Office	K	Crawford Post Office	center of town	
Restaurant	L	Boardwalk Restaurant	1 block south of center	(970) 921-4905
		Needle Rock Inn	4020 CO-92	(970) 921-3373
	N	Branding Iron Restaurant	1 block west of center	(970) 921-4736
Showers	D	Crawford Country Store	313 CO-92	(970) 921-5040

Gunnison Services

Visitor Center in Gunnison.

Gunnisonians like to say, *"If you don't like to play outdoors, then this ain't your kind of town."* With the vast recreational playgrounds of Curecanti National Recreation Area and the Gunnison National Forest virtually on its doorstep, the city of **Gunnison** is well-equipped to serve visitors and tourists in any season. Even in winter, when the valley has a reputation as one of the chilliest spots in Colorado, Gunnison embraces (even revels in) the sub-zero temperatures and whiteouts with most motels, restaurants and other services in this city of about 6,500 staying open to cater to skiers at nearby Crested Butte Resort or ice fisherman at the NRA. In summer, mountain bikers and hikers, boaters and fisherman find this town an ideal base for their outdoor activities in the canyon or the surrounding high mountains.

Most of the motels are clustered at the far ends of town along US-50; while most restaurants are near the town center at Tomichi and Main.

> For more info about visitor services around town, contact or visit the **Gunnison Country Chamber of Commerce**, open year-round and located in a park on your right as you enter town from the east on US-50.
>
> *500 E. Tomichi Avenue*
> *Gunnison, CO 81230*
> *(970) 641-1501*
> *www.gunnisonchamber.com*

TRANSPORTATION

The Gunnison Airport is the only one in the U.S. above 7,500 feet able to accommodate 757 aircraft. **United Express** provides daily service to Gunnison from Denver International Airport. **American Airlines** has non-stop service in winter from Dallas/Ft. Worth. **Avis** (800) 331-1212, **Budget** (970) 641-4403 and **Hertz** offer car and 4WD rentals at the airport. **Dollar Rent-A-Car** (970) 642-0199 is off of US-50, close to the airport. Long-distance bus service is through **TNM&O** (Greyhound) with their depot on the west side of downtown.

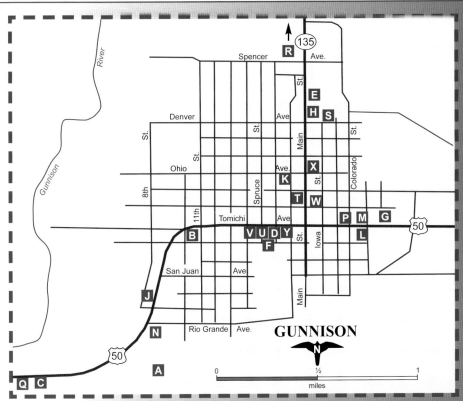

Airport	**A**	Gunnison County Airport	S. Boulevard Avenue	(970) 641-2304
Bus	**B**	TNM&O (Greyhound)	821 W. Tomichi	(970) 641-0060
Camping	**C**	Gunnison KOA	west of town on US-50	(970) 641-1358
Gear	**D**	Gene Taylor Sport. Goods	201 W. Tomichi	(970) 641-1845
Groceries	**E**	City Market	880 N. Main	(970) 641-3816
	F	Safeway	112 S. Spruce	(970) 641-0787
Info.	**G**	Chamber of Commerce	500 E. Tomichi	(800) 274-7580
Laundry	**H**	High Country Laundry	700 N. Main	(970) 641-3894
	J	High Country Laundry	221 US-50 W	(970) 641-3894
Library	**K**	Ann Zugelder Library	307 N. Wisconsin	(970) 641-3485
Lodging	**L**	Western Motel	403 E. Tomichi	(970) 641-1722
	M	Hylander Inn	412 E. Tomichi	(970) 641-0700
	N	Days Inn	701 W. US-50	(970) 641-0608
	P	Holiday Inn Express	400 E. Tomichi	(970) 641-1288
	Q	Waterwheel Inn	37478 US-50	(970) 641-1650
	R	Lost Canyon Resort	8264 CO-135	(970) 641-0181
Medical	**S**	Gunnison Valley Hospital	214 E. Denver Ave.	(970) 641-1456
Post Office	**T**	Gunnison Post Office	200 N. Wisconsin	(970) 641-1884
Restaurant	**U**	Mario's Pizzeria	213 W. Tomichi	(970) 641-1374
	V	Cattleman Inn	301 W. Tomichi	(970) 641-1061
	W	W Cafe	114 N. Main St.	(970) 641-1744
	X	Farrel's Restaurant	310 N. Main St.	(970) 641-2655
	Y	Sidewalk Cafe	113 W. Tomichi	(970) 641-4130
Showers	**C**	Gunnison KOA	west of town on US-50	(970) 641-1358

Montrose Services

The Daily Bread and Bakery in Montrose.

Montrose is strategically located to be a four-season playground for recreationalists. The South Rim of the Black Canyon of the Gunnison is only 30 minutes away and the administration for the BLM's Gunnison Gorge NCA is located here. The spectacular spires of the San Juan Mountains fill up the southern horizon and Grand Mesa, the largest flat-top mountain in the world, looms to the north. To the west is the Uncompahgre Plateau, a favorite with fall hunters, and beyond is the canyon country of the Colorado Plateau. The city of 13,000 has most everything you'll want: restaurants with a wide variety of eats, outdoor and sporting goods retailers with the gear you need, a splash of culture with galleries, cinemas and bookstores, and shopping opportunities ranging from fine antiques to *Walmart.*

Motels are mostly clustered at the east end of town along US-50, near the Visitor Bureau, and south of town along US-550.

For more info about visitor services around town, contact or visit the **Montrose Visitor and Convention Bureau**, open year-round and located on your right as you enter town from the east on US-50.

■ *1519 E. Main Street*
Montrose, CO 81402
☎ *(970) 240-1414*
🖥 *www.visitmontrose.net*

TRANSPORTATION

Montrose Regional Airport is a large, modern facility servicing the whole of west-central Colorado. Major carriers such as **United Express** ☎ *(970) 249-8455* and **America West** ☎ *(970) 249-7660* provide non-stop service to major cities, like Denver. During winter ski season, additional carriers bring visitors from places like Dallas and Chicago. Air charters also operate at the facility. Several car rental businesses are located at the airport: **Budget** ☎ *(970) 249-6083*, **Enterprise** ☎ *(970) 249-3835*, **Dollar** ☎ *(970) 249-3770* and **Thrifty** ☎ *(970) 249-8741*. Long-distance bus provider **TNM&O** has their depot near the town center.

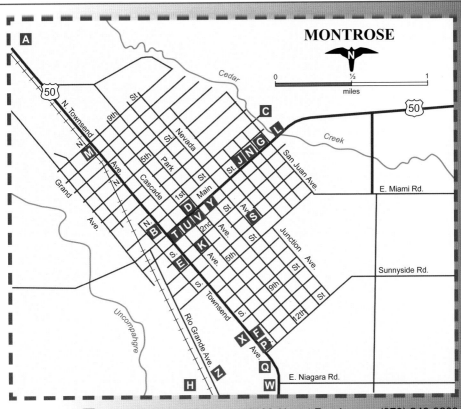

Airport	**A**	Montrose Regional Airport	2100 Airport Road	(970) 249-3203
Bus	**B**	TNM&O (Greyhound)	132 N. 1st Street	(970) 249-6673
Camping	**C**	Montrose RV Resort	200 N. Cedar Ave.	(970) 249-9177
Gear	**D**	Cimarron Creek	317 E. Main	(970) 249-0408
Groceries	**E**	City Market	128 S. Townsend	(970) 249-3405
	F	Safeway	1329 S. Townsend	(970) 249-8822
Info.	**G**	Chamber of Commerce	1519 E. Main	(970) 249-5000
Laundry	**H**	Summit Laundry	124 Apollo Rd.	(970) 252-1560
	J	Highlands Laundry	1347 E. Main	(970) 249-1741
Library	**K**	Montrose Library District	320 S. 2nd Street	(970) 249-9656
Lodging	**L**	Black Canyon Motel	1605 E. Main	(970) 249-3495
	M	Blue Fox Motel	1150 N. Townsend	(970) 249-4595
	N	Colorado Inn	1417 E. Main	(970) 249-4507
	P	Holiday Inn Express	1391 S. Townsend	(970) 240-1800
	Q	San Juan Inn	1480 US-550	(970) 249-6644
		Annies Orchard B & B	14963 63.00 Road	(970) 249-0298
Medical	**S**	Montrose Mem. Hospital	800 S. 3rd Street	(970) 249-2211
Post Office	**T**	Montrose Post Office	321 S. 1st Street	(970) 249-6654
Restaurant	**U**	Camp Robber Cafe	228 E. Main	(970) 240-1590
	V	Daily Bread & Bakery	346 Main	(970) 249-8444
	W	Glenn Eyrie Restaurant	2351 S. Townsend	(970) 249-7861
	X	Starvin Arvin's	1320 S. Townsend	(970) 249-7787
	Y	Kokopelli's SW Grill	647 E. Main	(970) 252-8100
Showers	**Z**	Montrose Rec. Center	2101 S. Rio Grande Ave.	(970) 249-7831

Delta Services

One of the first things you'll notice upon driving into **Delta** are the many large murals that decorate the sides of downtown businesses in the city. Eleven colorful murals have been created by local artists celebrating the history of the area and the bounties of local agriculture. Indeed, the city of 6,500 has a small town feel to it, reflecting the farming and ranching base of Delta County. It's too far from the mountains and the heart of the canyon to attract a lot of hikers or backpackers; so you'll find more outfitters and outdoor retailers that cater to the Black Canyon area in Montrose and Gunnison. But for mountain bikers exploring the adobe hills in the western portion of Gunnison Gorge NCA or for white-water enthusiasts and anglers at the gorge, the city of Delta is only about 10 miles west of the popular **Gunnison Forks Day Use Area** and is a convenient place to re-stock supplies or rest.

For more info about visitor services around town, contact or visit the **Delta Chamber of Commerce**, open year-round and located on Main Street (US-50), just south of the intersection with CO-92.

301 Main Street
Delta, CO 81402
(970) 874-8616
www.deltacolorado.org

The usual range of local and national chain restaurants and motels are situated mostly along the main drag (US-50) through town. For something quite different, one might try one of the bed and breakfast establishments that are more out in the *boonies*. For instance, the **Escalante Ranch B & B** is on an 100,000-acre, working cattle ranch along the Gunnison River. Besides conventional rooms for the night, the ranch also offers rustic cabins requiring a 4WD vehicle (or skis/snowshoes in winter) to reach.

TRANSPORTATION

Delta has a small airport, but most air travelers will arrive on commercial flights at the airports in Montrose or Grand Junction.

Several colorful murals in Delta extol local agriculture.

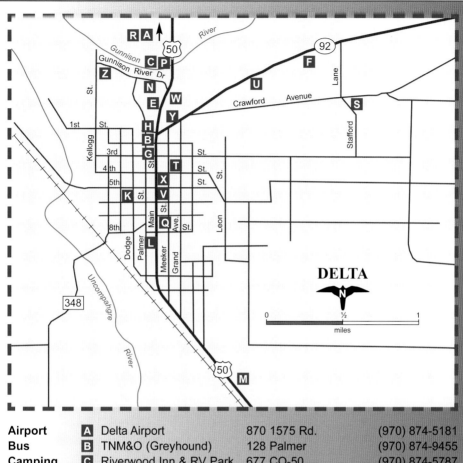

Airport	**A** Delta Airport	870 1575 Rd.	(970) 874-5181
Bus	**B** TNM&O (Greyhound)	128 Palmer	(970) 874-9455
Camping	**C** Riverwood Inn & RV Park	677 CO-50	(970) 874-5787
Groceries	**E** City Market	122 Gunnison River Dr.	(970) 874-9718
	F Safeway	1550 CO-92	(970) 874-7103
Info.	**G** Chamber of Commerce	301 Main	(970) 874-8616
Laundry	**H** Sudsy Duds	230 N. Palmer	(970) 874-7732
Library	**K** Delta City Public Library	211 W. 6th	(970) 874-9630
Lodging	**L** Best Western Sundance	903 Main St.	(970) 874-9781
	M Southgate Inn	2124 South Main	(970) 874-9726
	N Comfort Inn	180 Gunnison River Dr.	(970) 874-1000
	P Four Seasons River Inn	676 CO-50	(970) 874-9659
	Q El-D-Rado Motel	702 Main St.	(970) 874-4493
	R Escalante Ranch B & B	701 650 Rd.	(970) 874-0711
Medical	**S** Delta Cty. Mem. Hospital	100 Stafford Lane	(970) 874-7681
Post Office	**T** Delta Post Office	360 Meeker	(970) 874-4721
Restaurant	**U** Delta Fireside Inn	820 CO-92	(970) 874-4413
	V Daveto's Italian Res.	520 Main St.	(970) 874-8277
	W Starvin Arvin's	204 Ute St.	(970) 874-7288
	X Leon's Mexican Res.	420 Main St.	(970) 874-0309
	Y Ocean Pearl Oriental Res.	155 CO-92	(970) 874-1888
Showers	**Z** Bill Heddies Recreation Ctr.	530 Gunnison River Dr.	(970) 874-0923

ACTIVITIES

Biking in the adobe hills of Gunnison Gorge NCA.

THINGS TO DO

*Fly fishing in
the Gunnison River.*

The Black Canyon and Gunnison Country is a great place to camp in the wilderness, to discover the lives of critters through birding or watching for other wildlife, to cast a fly in a Gold Medal stream, to mountain bike a rugged track, or take photos, ride a horse, waterski, snowshoe or, if you dare — white-water kayak on the Gunnison or rock climb the highest cliff face in Colorado. You can use this chapter to help plan most of your activities (hiking and rock climbing are covered in the next two chapters.)

Each of the three units that make up the Black Canyon has something different to offer. **Black Canyon of the Gunnison National Park** has family-oriented activities, such as scenic drives and nature hikes; as well as extreme adventures in the backcountry for experienced individuals. **Curecanti National Recreation Area** is known for water sports and recreation, including boating and fishing on your choice of three lakes. Opportunities cater to sportsmen of many different interests; from marina-based activities, to wilderness kayaking. **Gunnison Gorge National Conservation Area** has exceptional self-propelled activities; such as rafting, hiking, mountain biking and horseback riding.

While most activities can be self-planned, the **Park Service** also schedules a lot of fun and interesting activities for visitors. You'll want to stop at the South Rim Visitor Center in the National Park or at Elk Creek Visitor Center in Curecanti NRA to check out the ranger-led nature walks and evening campfire programs in the campgrounds during the summer months. In winter, there are ranger-led outings at the South Rim of the National Park. Concessioners and outfitters also operate in these units, offering boat tours, rafting and whitewater adventures, and guided fishing trips.

Boating

Each of the three protected units shares the Gunnison River, yet each provides entirely different recreational opportunities for boaters; including rafting, kayaking, canoeing, sailing, windsurfing, and powerboating.

BOATING AT CURECANTI NRA

For water recreationalists, 20-mile long Blue Mesa Reservoir with its 96 miles of shoreline holds special appeal. The lake's three wide basins, Sapinero, Cebolla and Iola, have wide expanses of blue water to attract power boaters, sailors and water skiers. Windsurfers prefer the warmer bays, like the popular Bay of Chickens. And the lake's several major arms, Soap Creek, West Elk, Lake Fork and Cebolla, reach deep into secluded side canyons — ideal for exploration by boaters or kayakers. There are two **full-service marinas** on Blue Mesa Reservoir, located at Elk Creek and Lake Fork, open during the summer. Besides slips and showers, you can also hire a fishing guide or rent a boat at the Elk Creek Marina, ☎ *(970) 641-0402.* There are boat launches at **Stevens Creek**, **Elk Creek** and **Lake Fork** located along US-50 at mile 12, mile 16 and mile 25 respectively from Gunnison. Others are at **Willow Creek** and **Dillon Pinnacles** on the north shore. There's a launch ramp on the southeast shore of the reservoir at **Iola**, off CO-149 about 3.5 miles south of the Lake City Bridge; and another ramp into the lake's largest arm, Soap Creek Arm, at **Ponderosa**.

There are ten developed campgrounds on or near the lake and four water-accessed, undeveloped campsites tucked away on remote shores of the reservoir (for locations, see the **Facilities Map** on pages 108-109 and the chart on page 111.) Motorized and/or state registered water craft on Blue Mesa Lake will need to pay the **activity fee** (see page 107). Your safety equipment must include a personal flotation device for each person, bailing bucket, paddle or oar, fire extinguisher, tool kit, and anchor with line. Federal boating regulations apply, posted at launch points. Keep protective coves in sight in case of high winds and waves and return to shore if lightening threatens. Craft must travel wakeless in the West Elk, Lake Fork and Cebolla Arms, and east of the Lake City Bridge.

Catch sight of a startled mule deer drinking at water's edge, glide peacefully beneath impressive Curecanti Needle and supremely graceful Chipeta Falls, and camp at a remote shoreline site where stars peek through a slit framed by towering walls. Floating through the stone-wrapped corridors of Morrow Point or Crystal Reservoirs offers the chance for solitude and silence, away from the crowds and with exceptional opportunities to view park wildlife. No fees or permits are required for boating on these remote lakes, but access is by hand-carried craft only. For Morrow Point, you'll have to carry down the 232 steps of the **Pine Creek Trail** (see Hike #13, page 184) and choose a likely put-in point between the foot of the trail and the dock for the tour boat downstream. If the dam is releasing, portage down the trail to avoid any white water. At Crystal Reservoir, carry your craft down to the bridge on the **Mesa Creek Trail** (see Hike #16, page 186). While you can launch here, most people will want to avoid the rapids as much as possible be carrying downstream on the trail to any of several put-in spots. Note that motorized craft are allowed on the lakes — if you can

Boat tours are offered on Morrow Point Reservoir on a regular schedule in the summer with a park ranger on board to relate the canyon's story. To learn more, see page 150.

get it down there. Craft with small horsepower motors are a possibility and a decided advantage in going upstream during the frequent releases from the dams. **Elk Creek Marina** rents pontoon boats on Morrow Point Reservoir (they lower them over the dam at the start of the season.)

The water level in both lakes fluctuates greatly depending on water releases from Blue Mesa and Morrow Point Dams. In fact, these releases can be a hazard to boaters, complicating launches in strong, swirling currents and inhibiting (and even preventing) paddlers from returning upstream against the surge. Check with the rangers at any of the NRA visitor centers for information about scheduled releases before launching. High, violent winds can also occur on the lakes. The Park Service suggest that it is best to travel west in the morning, returning east in the afternoon. However, late afternoon and evening are also the times when releases from the dams are most likely to occur. Be aware that both of these lakes are very narrow, almost fiord-like, and bounded by steep cliffs in many places. In the event of an emergency or a capsizing in the frigid water, it can be very difficult to find a a protective cove or a suitable place to make a landing. You'll need a personal flotation device (white-water Type III/IV, as well as other prudent items; an adequate first aid kit, repair kit and a spare set of dry, insulated clothing.

You may paddle for several miles along these rugged, rock-bound shores. However, there are no other put-ins or take-outs and the areas around both dams are restricted. Camping at Morrow Point Reservoir is excellent with several free, water-accessible sites marked with posts situated around the lake (for locations, see the **Facilities Map** on pages 108-109 and the chart on page 111.) Many of these have picnic tables and a fire pit or grill. On Crystal Reservoir, there are five comfortable campsites at the mouth of Crystal Creek.

BOATING IN THE NATIONAL PARK

Kayaking through the Black Canyon within the National Park is extremely difficult and dangerous. The challenges facing the expert paddler are myriad. The river is categorized as Class V, including a very long and difficult portage between 18-foot Torrence Falls and camps below S.O.B. Draw where the river is rated Class VI to unrunnable. The river's gradient is extreme (averaging 96 feet per mile). With huge boulders and talus fallen from the cliffs, the resultant untamed rapids, currents and eddies are dangerous and unpredictable. Water temperatures year-round are very cold, usually 50° F or less. The portages can be unbearably hot down in the canyon, with progress impeded by a maze of jumbled boulders and a jungle of poison ivy. Self-rescue is absolutely necessary, as rescue by others from outside may be impossible. Fatalities of even the most experienced and respected kayakers have occurred. You'll need to obtain a **backcountry permit** (see page 106) free at the South Rim Visitor Center. The rangers can advise you on current flow conditions. Levels of 750-950 cfs are considered acceptable. Above 1200 cfs, the river is pushy with major hydraulics. Above 1500 cfs, hydraulics are extreme. Put-in is at **East Portal**, passing out of the Park at the Chukar put-in at mile 14.5 in Gunnison Gorge NCA, for take-out at the **Gunnison Forks Day Use** site at mile 27.7.

BOATING AT GUNNISON GORGE NCA

At the Chukar put-in.

Read the **day-use** and **camping regulations** on pages 113-114. Some additional rules apply to boaters in Gunnison Gorge NCA:

∎ No motorized craft are permitted upstream of the confluence with the Smith Fork.

∎ Boaters must have a portable, reusable camp toilet (no plastic bags) and pack out all trash. There's a dump station at the Gunnison Forks take-out.

∎ All boaters must wear an approved white-water (Type III/IV) personal flotation device. Each raft must carry an extra oar or paddle, adequate first aid kit, repair kit and an extra PFD.

∎ Rafts, kayaks and white water canoes are required. The use of flat-water canoes, single-chambered rafts and inner tubes is not advised.

The Gunnison River through the Gunnison Gorge Wilderness Area offers a technical and remote experience for rafters, kayakers and whitewater canoeists. The boating changes with every flow and is very dependent on winter snowpack. Expect high spring releases of 2,000 to 10,000 cfs (cubic feet per second) in late May and early June. Summer flows vary from 300 cfs in a very low water years, to 2,000 + cfs during big water years. At flows below 800 cfs, the gorge is very technical and not recommended for rafts over 12 feet in length. Flows over 5,000 cfs make the Gorge very dangerous for boating. Currents become very swift and swirly, eddies disappear, and swims are very long. Remember that once you push off into the river, rescue is very difficult in the gorge. There are no roads that reach the bottom of the gorge between the put-in at Chukar and take-out at Gunnison Forks. If in doubt, SCOUT! See the **map** on page 115 for locations, classes of rapids and designated campsites for river-runners (blue sites).

Put-in is at the foot of the **Chukar Trail** (see Hike #18, page 189). You'll need to carry your boat down the 1.0 mile trail or hire a horse packer to do so (contact BLM-permitted outfitter, Larry Franks, ☎ *(970) 323-0115.)* Pay the required day-use and camping fees, and sign into the register (see pages 112-114 for details.) The following mile-by-mile description is supplied by the BLM. For current flow information through the gorge, call their **river hotline** at ☎ *(970) 240-5312.* Flow info on all rivers in southwest Colorado is also available at ☎ *(800) 276-4828* or by visiting the USGS website at ⊕ *http://nwis-colo.cr.usgs.gov.*

Located just downstream of the put-in is **Chukar Rapid**. Chukar is a single-drop, Class III. Most choose to run center at higher water and the right slot at lower flows. Watch out for the pyramid rock, center right, thirty yards downstream. Next, you encounter **One Miler Rapid**, running left of the large center hole or rock, depending on flows. **Improvise Rapid** (Class III) is located at mile 1.5 and is recognized by a small vertical cliff on river right and a prominent rock slide on river left. Scout on river left.

At mile 2.5 and 3.0, you encounter **Upper** and **Lower Pucker**. Both consist of narrow slots at lower flows. At flows over 6,500 cfs, Upper Pucker has very large standing waves and a giant hole on river left. At mile 4.0, **Buttermilk Rapid**

(Class III) offers a wild wave ride. Run straight down the tongue and watch out for the cliff on the left.

Just below Buttermilk Rapid, you swing the corner and enter **Ute Park**. Ute Park widens out as the Gunnison River hits the Indian Fault Zone. On river right, notice the red Entrada Sandstone; and the left consists of black Precambrian granite. The river gradient drops and the canyon broadens. As you leave Ute Park, you dive back into the Black Canyon and the steepest section of the Gunnison Gorge. Gradient picks up to 35 feet per mile. Crystal Creek enters from the right at mile 6.0, forming **Red Canyon Rapid** (Class III). Red Canyon rapid is very rocky, requiring technical boating skills to navigate the run. Scout on river right.

Beyond mile 7 is the **Boulder Garden** (Class III/IV). Look for Baby T-Rex Rock on the right, upstream of Boulder Garden. Scout Boulder Garden on river left. Two routes are most commonly run. At flows above 1,000 cfs, most will navigate the narrow slot on river right. At flows below 1,000 cfs, a more technical route is required running left and ferrying back to river right at the bottom slot. Beware of Fang Rock at the bottom on river left. Many boats have high-sided here.

Just below Boulder Garden is **Paddle Keeper** (Class III). Paddle Keeper is very technical. The rapid is most successfully run on river left, ferrying back river right. Scout river right. A cliff is on river left. **T-Dyke Rapid** (Class III) is located at mile 7.5 and is the last camp until Smith Fork. At mile 9, you encounter the steepest, most difficult section of the Gorge. **S- Turn Rapid** (Class III) throws you into the cliff on river left. Immediately below is the **Squeeze Rapid** (Class III+). The Squeeze is a deceptive, rocky rapid and has wrapped rafts and pinned kayaks. The most common run is through the narrow slots river right. Scout on river right.

The 14-mile float through the gorge, with more than two dozen rapids ranging from Class II to Class IV, depending on season and flow rates, can be a heart-pounding, challenging trip even for more-experienced boaters. Consider a guided trip with one of the **BLM-permitted outfitters** listed on pages 226-227.

Next are the three **Drops**, which contain many large holes and narrow slots. Scout all from river right. **Cable Rapid** (Class III/IV) is located at mile 9.5. It is very technical. Scout river right. Many large holes enter into two narrow slots. Most run the right slot avoiding the cliff wall on river left. Below Cable is **Jumpin' Jack Splash Rapid** (Class III). Jumpin' Jack Splash is run left of the large boulder, finishing river right, avoiding the large hole on river left. Watch out for the lateral wave.

The **Gate Keeper** (Class II/III) follows, which requires navigating a narrow slot, either center at higher flows, or left against the cliff at flows below 600 cfs. **Grande Finale Rapid** (Class III) finishes the run. Scout river right. A common run is to start river right and avoid the rocks on river left. Four miles of Class II water remains until the take-out at the confluence of the North Fork at the BLM's **Gunnison Forks Day Use** site (free facilities) or at the private **Gunnison River Pleasure Park** (fee charged). The Pleasure Park also provides shuttle services to the Chukar put-in and various amenities (see page 118, for more information.)

Horseback Riding and Pack Animals

Capture the spirit of early visitors to Gunnison Country by enjoying a ride atop a horse — you can bring your own, or hire horses through an outfitter and enjoy a guided outing. Horses, mules, burros, donkeys, and llamas may be also used as pack animals in some situations (especially in Gunnison Gorge NCA or on extended trips into the Gunnison National Forest that may originate from within the Curecanti NRA.)

THE NATIONAL PARK

Most of **Black Canyon of the Gunnison National Park** is not open for horse and pack animal use. The rules aim at keeping horses out of the highest-use pedestrian and traffic areas. That's why horses are not permitted in the campgrounds, at the Visitor Center, on popular trails, or anywhere at the South Rim. (There's no need to explain why horses aren't permitted in the rugged Inner-Canyon environment.)

Bostwick Park, 4 miles south of the entrance station to the South Rim of the National Park, has spectacular scenery to ride in. **Elk Ridge Trail Rides** offers guided trips in the area.

📞 *(970) 240-6007*

However, the North Rim of the Park sees far fewer visitors, making it an attractive place for a pleasant ride. Horseback riding is ONLY permitted on the, unfortunately named, **Deadhorse Trail** (see Hike #9, page 180.) Don't let the name spook you — this double-track (an old jeep road) is a enjoyable ride of about 2.5 miles one-way, concluding at some awesome backcountry overlooks. Park your trailer at the Kneeling Camel Overlook and ride the 100 yards or so east to the turnoff for the Deadhorse Trail. Horses are only permitted on the rest of North Rim Drive (or in the North Rim Campground) while in a trailer.

CURECANTI NRA

Curecanti National Recreation Area has few trails that are suitable for horseback riding. The best one is the **Dillon Pinnacles Trail** (see Hike #12, page 183), which provides an easy ride through sagebrush meadows with sweeping vistas of Blue Mesa Reservoir and of the weirdly-shaped formations that dominate the bluff above the lake. At the intersection with the jeep road in Dillon Gulch, you can ride north into the West Elk Wilderness Area. The parking lot is

HIKERS AND HORSES ON THE TRAIL

Remember that horses have **right-of-way** over hikers, bicyclists and ATV vehicles. They are big, heavy, strong and don't always understand that a bike or off-road vehicle isn't a danger to them.

Even hikers can sometimes frighten a horse because it doesn't recognize you as human with that enormous backpack. If you do encounter horses on the trail while hiking, use these safety guidelines:

▮ Step off the trail to let the horseback riders pass.

▮ Speak in a normal tone of voice, and avoid sudden movements.

▮ If possible, allow the horse to be on the uphill side of you and the trail.

▮ Follow suggestions from the equestrian, who may know their horse's "personality" and know what might startle it.

adequate for unloading, although there is high-speed traffic only yards away

The NRA butts up on the north against the Gunnison National Forest, which offers unlimited opportunities for everything from short rides, to extended pack trips into the high country, to hunting on horseback. Several outfitters offer guided rides into the National Forest — contact the Gunnison Country Chamber of Commerce, ☎ *(970) 641-1501.* Horse parties can use **corrals** provided at the campgrounds at **Dry Gulch**, **Red Creek** and **Ponderosa** to stage trips into the public lands north of the NRA. For some ideas, check out the three trips suggested for mountain bikers, starting on page 140, that enter the National Forest and/or the Sapinero Wildlife Area.

GUNNISON GORGE NCA

Unlike the limited riding available at the National Park and in Curecanti NRA, there are unlimited possibilities for you and *Trigger* to kick up some dust at **Gunnison Gorge National Conservation Area**. Horses are permitted on all of the roads and trails in the NCA, even within the inner-sanctum of the gorge. At this time (prior to a new management plan to be released in 2004), you can pull-over on the side of **Peach Valley Road** anywhere in the adobe hills region of the western NCA and ride cross-country or on one of the many jeep roads, trails, and ATV tracks that criss-cross the area.

There are too many possibilities to mention them all here; but short rides up the **Bobcat** and **Duncan Roads** see relatively little traffic and lead to picnic facilities with fine views from the ridge. Although, further travel on horseback beyond these two trailheads on the steep and rough Bobcat and Duncan Trails (see Hikes #19 & 20 on page 190) is strongly not advised.

The gentle, gradual slope of the 4.5-mile **Ute Trail** (see Hike #21, page 191) makes it an enjoyable choice for horse travel into the inner gorge. It's also the location for the only designated campsite for overnight horseback groups within the Gunnison Gorge Wilderness Area (**site #15 Ute I** in Ute Park.) Horseback groups in the designated wilderness also must have a portable toilet (one that's a washable, reusable system — not plastic bags.) Horseman entering the wilderness area for the day or overnight have to register and pay the day-use fee at the trailhead, plus overnight camping fees (for more information, see page 112.) Group size is limited to 12 persons and 12 horses. It makes sense to leave your trailer a little ways in on the Ute Road and ride up the 2 miles or so to the trailhead, rather than try to pull a trailer up this rugged 4WD road.

The 1.1-mile **Chukar Trail** (see Hike #18, page 189) is often used by horsepackers hauling in boats and gear for river runners headed to the put-in site at the foot of the trail. It sees a lot of traffic at times and is less desirable for pleasure riding. To get to the trailhead, you'll either have to pull up rough Chukar Road or park further down the 7-mile road and ride up. You can probably drive in 2.5 miles to a stock pond, where there's a single track that exits to the left, climbing up to re-join the Chukar Road, cutting off about a mile. Known as **Horse Trail**, it starts out easy enough through adobe hills, then climbs a very steep, loose and rocky ravine to intersect the road near the Black Ridge Trail. The **Black Ridge Trail** (see Hike #23, page 193) is open to horses and would be a spectacular ride; but it's also very challenging with riding on steep, loose slopes and atop plunging cliffs. It's outside the wilderness area, so no day-use fee is required.

To arrange a pack-in of your stuff on the Chukar or Ute Trails, or to join a guided horseback trip, you must use a **BLM-permitted outfitter**. Call the BLM for a list of approved outfitters: ☎ *(970) 240-5300*

Hunting and Fishing

HUNTING

Hunting or firearm use is *not permitted* anywhere within the confines of Black Canyon of the Gunnison National Park. Hunting *is allowed* in Gunnison Gorge National Conservation Area and in the extensive acreage of BLM lands that surround the NCA and the National Park. Curecanti National Recreation Area also allows hunting in prescribed areas. In Curecanti NRA, hunting areas on the north half of the unit overlap into ones in the Sapinero Wildlife Area and Gunnison National Forest. All hunting on federal and state lands is managed by the **Colorado Division of Wildlife** (CDOW).

6060 Broadway
Denver, Colorado, 80216
(303)297-1192
www.wildlife.state.co.us/regulations

Firearms which are within your vehicle or boat must remain unloaded at all times. You must be in possession of a valid Colorado **hunting license** to carry a loaded firearm outside of your vehicle. You can obtain licenses and hunting brochures from sporting goods stores and other licensing agents in Colorado, or by contacting CDOW. Among game available in the units and the surrounding public lands are big-game species such as mule deer, elk, pronghorn, bighorn sheep and bear; as well as small game, turkey and waterfowl. In particular, elk are especially abundant in the National Forest — Colorado has the largest elk herd in the world. Length of seasons and regulations change each year, so be sure to check with CDOW well ahead of time.

FISHING AT CURECANTI NRA

The lakes and streams at Curecanti NRA attracts anglers for a variety of fun fishing experiences; from lake fishing, to stream and river angling. The construction of the three dams at the unit in the 1960s dramatically altered the aquatic environment and its fishery. Once the Gunnison River snaked through this steep-walled, arid valley; its introduced **rainbow** and **brown trout** thriving in what was reputed to be one of the finest trout streams in the country, perhaps the world. The new lake environment created a vastly different habitat, where concentrations of microscopic plants and animals, called *plankton,* could support other introduced species; such as **kokanee salmon** — today, the most commonly caught fish in Blue Mesa Reservoir. The 100-foot-plus deep waters also were ideal for cold-water loving **Mackinaw** (lake trout) that can grow to more than 30 pounds in the submerged canyons of the lake. While the lake environment is excellent for *growing* lunker fish, it is not well suited for *reproducing* them. State and federal hatchery programs stock Blue Mesa and the other reservoirs annually with trout, suckers, Mackinaw, and kokanee salmon in the millions. The trout in Blue Mesa vary in size — rainbows from 12 to 18 inches, browns at a little larger average of 14 to more than 16 inches. You can learn more about these fish species in the **Natural History** section on page 75.

At the eastern end of Curecanti NRA, river access is at Neversink and Cooper Ranch Picnic Areas. Wading in the river is slippery business, so cleats and felt-sole waders are recommended. In early season, before the reservoir fills up, there is another five miles or so of river fishing beginning at Beaver Creek Picnic Area. Several types of dry flies work well along the river and streams at Curecanti NRA. Try *Adams, Elk Hair, Goddard Caddis, Irresistible, Humpy, Rio*

Grande, King, and *Orange Asher.* Wet flies to use can be *Hare's Ear Nymph, Renegade, Western Coachman, Rio Grande King, Woolly Worms, Caddis Larvae,* and *Stone Nymphs.* Flies work best in the evenings.

In late spring and early summer, when water levels are low at the reservoir, the best fishing is with streamer flies from shore or from a boat near shore. For streamers, try *Muddler Minnows, Marabou Muddlers, Woolly Buggers,* and *Zonkers.* Inlets are good spots because of the clear, slow moving water entering the reservoir. Best times for fishing are very early in the day or around sunset, when fish are feeding. Fish may also feed at mid-day for a brief period.

As lake level rises in summer and the waters warm, fish move to deeper, colder water in the middle of the reservoir. Mackinaw enter shallow water (and can be more easily located) in spring after the ice breaks up, and then again in fall during spawning — to catch them at other times, deep trolling is required; typically at 60 feet or more. Mackinaw will hit salmon eggs, casting from shore or from a boat. Boats can be rented at the Elk Creek Marina (see page 128.)

Blue Mesa Reservoir is the largest kokanee fishery in the country. Kokanee salmon will often hit the same kinds of lures that fisherman use to land trout. Though they feed primarily on plankton, kokanee will still strike lures; including *Mepps, Panther Martins* and *Rapalas.* Traveling in schools, kokanee may surface to feed during the day, then move to deep water at night. Troll at a slow speed, less than 5 mph, for kokanee. At the start of spawning season, generally in early November, many anglers come to the area when kokanee can be snagged with weighted treble hooks. For the exact start date, when snagging is permitted, call park headquarters.

Fishing at Morrow Point and Crystal Reservoirs is much more of a remote experience; especially if you plan on fishing from a boat, as they must be hand-carried down short, but steep foot trails. The easiest fishing access for Morrow Point Reservoir is the Pine Creek Trail (see Hike #13, page 184), and for Crystal Reservoir, it's the Mesa Creek Trail (see Hike #16, page 186). Read about **Boating In Curecanti** on page 128 for more information. You can also fish from shore for short stretches from either trail. The bridge crossing on the Mesa

For **year-round information** at Curecanti NRA about current fishing conditions or temporary closures, contact park headquarters at ☎ *(970) 641-2337.* A Colorado **fishing license** is required of anyone 16 or older (available at the marinas and local sporting goods stores.) Use the fish cleaning stations provided or dispose of properly in a trash can. Note that daily bag and possession limits are often the same.

	Fish Species	Daily Bag Limit	Possession Limit
Gunnison River and Blue Mesa Res.	Total fish of the following species:	4	8
	| Rainbow trout		
	| Brown trout		
	| Cutthroat trout		
	Brook trout (8" or less)	10	10
	Kokanee salmon:		
	(angling)	10	10
	(snagging)	10	10
	Yellow perch	20	20
	Crawfish	no limit	no limit
	Mackinaw trout:	8	8
	(on Blue Mesa Res. only)		
Morrow Point or Crystal Res. (inclusive of daily bag limit caught in other reservoirs.)	Total fish of the following species:	4	8
	| Rainbow trout		
	| Brown trout		
	| Cutthroat trout		
	| Mackinaw trout		
	Brook trout	10	10
	Kokanee salmon:		
	(angling)	10	10
	(snagging)	10	10
	Yellow perch	20	20

Creek Trail provides access to both sides of the river. As the access roads are kept plowed all winter to both of these trailheads, you can continue fishing on open stretches of moving water below Blue Mesa and Morrow Point Dams.

Some of the tributary streams that flow from north and south of the unit and into the reservoirs, such as Blue, Cebolla, Cimarron and Curecanti Creeks and the Lake Fork of the Gunnison, can have fair to good fishing for brook trout, and occasionally, native cutthroat trout. Access ranges from "drive-up" convenience, to long approaches on foot or by watercraft. Make sure that you check the property boundaries and ask for permission to fish on private land.

Fishing doesn't end with the onset of winter weather at Blue Mesa Reservoir. Hardy anglers brave sub-zero temperatures, auger in hand, to plumb the depths of the lake for trout and the occasional kokanee. Winter at Curecanti NRA can be pretty brutal, with strong winds pushing windchill factors to dangerous levels. For well-prepared anglers, ice fishing begins at Curecanti NRA as soon as the ice is at least four inches thick (enough to bear the weight of an adult) — usually around the end of December. If you use your snowmobile to haul your gear out, you'll need at least seven inches of the clear, hard stuff for safe passage. Ice-out on the reservoir typically occurs in late April; although melting will make the ice unsafe for several weeks before that point. Spates of warm weather or mild winters are not unusual — be sure to call the park headquarters and check with the rangers before venturing out on the ice. The ice angler can have success using sucker meat, attached to *airplane jigs,* and dropped to appropriate depths.

Colorado streams and rivers are designated as **Gold Medal Waters** because they provide outstanding angling for large trout. Of the more than 9,000 miles of trout streams in the state, only 168 miles are designated as Gold Metal. Special regulations apply to maintain that quality experience.

■ Use artificial flies or lures; **no bait**.

■ All rainbow trout are **catch and release**.

■ Brown trout 12-16 inches must be returned to the water immediately.

■ Bag and possession limit for brown trout is (4) fish, 12 inches or less **OR** (3) fish, less than 12 inches and (1) fish, 16 inches or longer.

■ A Colorado **fishing license** is required for anyone 16 years or older..

FISHING AT THE NATIONAL PARK

Imagine casting your fly into deep, green pools fed from roaring rapids, surrounded by towering, dark cliffs thousands of feet tall, without another soul in sight. A flashing rainbow takes the fly, as you battle to land yet another lunker. From below Crystal Dam in Curecanti NRA, all through Black Canyon and Gunnison Gorge, to the confluence with the North Fork, the Gunnison River is designated as **Gold Medal Waters**. The upstream dams capture much of the river's sediment load, keeping the water clearer and at a near ideal, constant temperature for trout growth. As a result, browns and (to a lessor extent) rainbow trout are plentiful throughout the waterway; averaging 12 to 16 inches in size with many pushing over 20 inches.

The two Inner-Canyon routes in the Park used most by fisherman are S.O.B. Draw on the North Rim, and the Warner Route from the south rim. There are several other draws that can be descended from either the south or north rims that give access to different stretches of the river — ranging from a few hundred yards, to a mile or more. For information on these routes and primitive campsites — and about obtaining the required backcountry permit — read about the **Inner-Canyon Routes**, starting on page 194. All of these routes are very difficult, steep and filled with loose rock; but your reward is solitude in a magnificent setting. Warner Point is the longest of the routes into the canyon, and usually is an overnight trip.

For those who prefer to drive and are willing to put up with more people, the **East Portal Road** descends to the river from just beyond the entrance station at the South Rim of the Park. Closed in winter, the East Portal area is on the boundary between the National Park and Curecanti NRA; and includes both a campground and primitive camping downriver. You have access to a 2 mile section of the tailwaters from the Gunnison Tunnel's diversion dam by a rugged path west into the National Park's designated wilderness (you'll have to self-register for a backcountry permit at the trailhead.) To get very far downriver, you'll need to do some scrambling past an obstacle ridge — read about this Inner-Canyon route on page 199.

It takes some skill to cast into the swift moving waters of the canyon. Dry flies can be good at times, especially in early summer. The **stonefly hatch** usually begins moving upriver fromGunnison Gorge NCA in mid-June — great, if you can time it right! Deep-water *nymphs* are perhaps the best strategy for getting the big guys. The month of May brings high, roiled waters from spring run-off; while fishing at low water in fall avoids the crowds and heat of summer.

Here's the **hatch schedule** for the upper river in the National Park and Curecanti NCA. Lower on the river, in Gunnison Gorge NCA, things start a few weeks earlier.

∎ May: mayflies
∎ June: green drakes
∎ July-August: stoneflies
∎ August: wooley buggers and leaches

FISHING AT GUNNISON GORGE NCA

Gunnison Gorge NCA offers the same outstanding **Gold Metal Waters** designation of the Gunnison River as that of the National Park, with identical *catch and release regulations* for rainbows and *bag and possession limits* for browns (see above). However, unlike in the dangerous, roiling waters of the National Park, angling at the NCA is best done by floating. "River trails" (see **Hikes in Gunnison Gorge NCA**, starting on page 188) do access short stretches of the stream. The Ute Trail has almost four miles of river to fish; while the river is unsuitable for wading at the Duncan Trail because of deep pools. At the foot of the Chukar Trail, there's bank fishing for 0.25 mile downstream, as well as two miles upstream into the National Park. The North Fork to Smith Fork Trail also has about four miles of good access to the river, with clear water and several depp pools — the folks at the **Gunnison River Pleasure Park** (see page 118) can ferry you across the North Fork and also can *jet boat* you further up the river for those with *belly boats* or *kick boats*. Float fishing is best done with a professional, BLM-permitted outfitter, as the gorge has several sections of white water and seasonal obstacles (see **Boating In Gunnison Gorge NCA**, page 130.) Most floats are two-day, one-night trips through the canyon.

From the confluence of the two forks, the fish are mostly rainbows; with brown trout becoming dominant about six miles upstream. The average length of fish in the gorge is a little more than a foot. Wet flies in the deep pools and cutbanks land the largest fish. Wet flies include *Hare's Ear* from size 10 to 14, *Girdle Bug,*, *Woolly Bugger*, *Woolly Worms*, and *Muddler Minnows* in sizes 18 to 20. The *Panther Martin* lure is the first choice.

Mountain Biking

Mountain biking on Duncan Road in the Gunnison Gorge NCA.

Natural and man-made obstacles, wildlife, cars, other cyclists, and inattention can all cause accidents and injury. But there are many joys that mountain biking brings, as well: solitude, the thrill of viewing wildlife and spectacular scenery, a sense of accomplishment at successfully navigating a difficult section of trail, the pleasant exhaustion of having worked out your body. With a little knowledge and common sense, you can reduce the risk and enhance the joy.

Many of the rides recommended in this chapter take place on roads; therefore, obey all traffic laws. Ride with traffic. Use hand signals drivers will understand (if you're going to turn left, point left; if you're going to turn right, point right). Be aware of vehicles and pedestrians at all times. And ride at an appropriate speed for the conditions.

Other rides recommended here traverse a more natural environment, one that is susceptible to damage caused by irresponsible riding. To minimize the damage, tread lightly. Stay on well-defined roads and trails. Never ride through mud or soft soil. Pack out all garbage and waste. When approaching wildlife and hikers, slow down and yield the trail.

Mountain biking opportunities in the Black Canyon area range from rides on established vehicle roads, both paved and unpaved, to challenging single-tracks that penetrate to some very remote parts of Gunnison Country. We've come up with some recommended rides that explore both of these extremes, offering trips suitable for novices, to the most experienced riders.

Because of its warm temperatures and dry climate, the best times to ride in the lower Gunnison Basin are spring and fall. If you go during the summer, make sure you ride in the morning or evening, and bring plenty of **water** and **sunscreen**. Also important are a spare inner tube, tools, a patch kit, and a first aid kit. There is little shade on any of the rides we've recommended; a ten mile walk back to the car with a broken bike could be a long, hot endeavor. A good map and a cyclometer are recommended but are not necessary for most of these rides, with the exception of the rides in Gunnison Gorge National Conservation Area, where both are essential. And don't overexert yourself. Remember you are biking at up to 8,000 feet in altitude.

Mountain biking in **Black Canyon of the Gunnison National Park** is limited to the two roads open to vehicular traffic, the **North** and **South Rim Drives**. All other trails in the park are open to hiking only and are so marked; mountain biking is prohibited on those trails. Keep in mind that drivers on these two roads will most likely be dividing their attention between the road (and any cyclists using it) and the many wonderful views of the canyon. Ride defensively. Cyclists are charged a **$4 entrance fee** if they ride their bikes into the Park via either the north or south access road (or $7 per car.)

BLACK CANYON NP: SOUTH RIM DRIVE

Despite the presence of tourist traffic, an early morning or late afternoon ride along the **South Rim Drive** offers a great chance to spot Park wildlife and has spectacular views into the

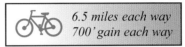
6.5 miles each way
700' gain each way

canyon from the many overlooks and pullovers. See the *Take A Scenic Drive* section on page 154 for a mile-by-mile description of the South Rim Drive. This easy ride along a paved roadbed, equally suitable for *road* or *mountain* bikes, takes 1 to 2 hours each way, depending on how many stops you make at the several scenic overlooks. Begin at the **South Rim Campground**, 1.5 miles south of the South Rim Visitor Center. The first mile or so to **Tomichi Point** is a good downhill run. From there, the road gently rolls up and (mostly) down alongside the canyon rim, reaching its lowest point at **Chasm View**, before climbing steadily to end of road at **High Point**. Bikes aren't allowed on the short

To find your way on this ride, see the *South Rim Drive Map* on page 154.

side trails that lead to overlooks. Regrettably, there has been at least one report of a stolen bike, left roadside while that rider jogged off to snap pictures, so lock your bike to a post or tree. The ride back is not too taxing, with only a steepish hill at the end. Be wary of drivers on the nearly blind curves — who, after having seen all the sights on their drive in, seem to speed up on the return.. The only water available along the route is at the campground, the Visitor Center and Rim House.

BLACK CANYON NP: NORTH RIM DRIVE

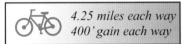
4.25 miles each way
400' gain each way

A ride along the Park's **North Rim Drive** gives just as many outstanding views into the canyon as along the South Rim Drive, but with a lot less traffic to deal

with. And the unpaved nature of the road somehow seems more in spirit with what mountain biking is all about. Nevertheless, this is an easy ride, suitable even for novice riders. Start at the **North Rim Ranger Station** (tank up at the nearby campground, as that is the only water available along the route) and turn left (east) onto North Rim Drive. Descend slightly to the intersection with the access road for the North Rim in 0.5 mile. Continue straight and begin the gradual, looping climb through rolling hills of sagebrush, oak and pinyon. The various overlooks and scenic spots are described in the *Take A Scenic Drive* section on page 160. After 4.25 miles, arrive at the turn-around at the end of the North Rim Drive. This ride takes about 1 to 2 hours each way, depending on how much time you spend taking in the spectacular views. Spring can be muddy; but autumn, before the access road closes for the winter, is an ideal time to enjoy this ride, as the oaks are in their fall colors and the tourist traffic is light to non-existent.

To find your way on this ride, see the *North Rim Drive Map* on page 160.

Curecanti National Recreation Area is best known for its water-based recreation opportunities — mountain biking in Curecanti National Recreation Area is limited to roads open to vehicular traffic. While CO-92 and US-50 are among the most scenic highways in the state, we don't recommend biking on these winding roadways because of the presence of high-speed traffic, inadequate shoulders, and steep grades. All trails within the boundaries of the NRA are open only to hiking, and are so marked; mountain biking is prohibited on most trails. However, there are several fun rides that originate within the NRA and follow tracks and trails into the surrounding public lands. These moderate to challenging rides will appeal to the experienced rider. For a portion of these rides, you may have to share the right-of-way with hikers, equestrians, motorcycles, cars, 4WD vehicles or ATVs.

CURECANTI NRA: RAINBOW LAKE ROAD (FS #724)

11.0 miles loop
1,900 elevation gain

Technically, this is an easy to moderate loop trip, taking 2 to 4 hours, with much of the ride following improved and user-created roads. The most difficult sections are a very steep 0.5 mile ascent and two moderately steep and rocky, but short, descents. To get there from Gunnison, drive west on US-50 for 14.0 miles to the **Rainbow Lake Road** turn-off, which is signed. The unsigned, unimproved parking area is 1/10th of a mile up on the right.

Turn right from the parking area onto Rainbow Lake Road and ascend gradually through pinyon, juniper and sagebrush-studded hills, passing a powerline and its steep, rocky service road at **mile 0.6** and several cattle guards along the way. Aspens crowd the bottom of **Dry Creek**, while lupines bloom on the edges of the road. At three-quarters of a mile, you'll see a large pinnacle-like butte ahead on the left, and just beyond it, at **mile 1.0**, you'll pass beneath a sheer cliff face rising on the right, with another large butte straight ahead.

The road soon turns sharply to the left and passes through more rolling hills, spotted with pinyon-juniper forest and sagebrush. Straight ahead looms a square, cake-like butte. The cliffs above you on the right rise approximately 250 feet above the sloping hillside. Watch for prairie dogs and sage-grouse. From here, the road begins a half-mile climb. Aspens shade the hillside to the right, while to the left, the hills sport pinyon-juniper and gambel oak. At the top of the hill, look for a rocky bluff to the right. A half-mile farther, the road climbs again.

Black volcanic rock decorates the slope to the right; on the left, gambel oak climbs the slope, giving way to tall aspens posed against the face of a fifty foot cliff.

You soon reach the top of the hill, and the pinyon-juniper forest yields to sagebrush. Aspens shade the banks of Dry Creek and provide shelter for an array of animals, including coyotes, foxes, bears, and deer. At **mile 3.75**, the

Riding the sagebrush-covered hills.

road passes a gate, beyond which it follows a shallow ravine. There is a big aspen grove ahead on the left; some of the trees are 18 inches in diameter and larger. It is a perfect place to stop for a snack and to listen to the wind rustle the leaves.

The road continues to climb past sagebrush-covered hills, with groves of aspen reaching down like fingers. As you ascend, the hills become noticeably higher. At **mile 4.6**, you'll come to a very steep user-created route on the right. Pass it, then, 1/10th of a mile beyond, turn left onto its counterpart. The trail ascends steeply through sagebrush, then enters an aspen grove. After about a quarter of a mile, reach the top of the climb, and be rewarded with open views to the south all the way to the horizon, with rolling sagebrush hills spotted with aspen in the foreground and remote mountains marching in the distance.

A short distance ahead, you'll climb another short hill into aspens, then follow the trail around a right hand curve. Across a small valley, see the trail cross an open hillside. Two user-created routes intersect the trail in quick succession, coming in from the right; stay left. The trail then becomes rocky and descends a short, steep hill before climbing again into forest. There is another fork; again, stay left. Ride through sagebrush for a short distance, then climb steeply into a grove of pine and fir trees. From here, you can see pleated, multi-hued hills to the north, blanketed by aspens and pines; to the west, the draws host aspen groves, while the open hillsides bristle with sagebrush; to the south, **Blue Mesa Reservoir** glistens below a pair of flat-topped buttes.

Once you've taken in the views, descend a steep, rocky slope, ignoring the user-created routes that enter on the left, and pass into an aspen grove. Beyond, ride across a smooth, sagebrush-covered hillside, where, if you're alert, you might spot coyote scat and deer prints. Soon come alongside a fenceline and pass another user-created route on the right. The trail makes several bends as it descends toward Elk Creek, then climbs again to avoid the steep walls of the ravine.

At **mile 7.5**, the trail becomes difficult to follow as it passes over rocky terrain. Look for it to veer west, to the right, and descend a short, steep hill. From here, the trail soon crosses an open, gravelly, flat-topped hill. The buttes you saw from above looming over Blue Mesa Reservoir are now immediately adjacent. Another user-created route enters from the left; stay right and descend a short, steep, rocky hill into Gambel oak-filled ravine. The descent soon mellows and smooths, as the ravine becomes deeper and wider.

At **mile 9.25**, pass yet another user-created route on the right. And a quarter of a mile beyond that, come to a sign that marks this as **Haystack Gulch**. Looking downhill, you can see the powerline and US-50, 0.5 mile away. Descend to the barbed wire fence bordering the highway, carefully climb over it, then turn left on US-50 and ride 0.9 mile back to Rainbow Lake Road and the parking lot.

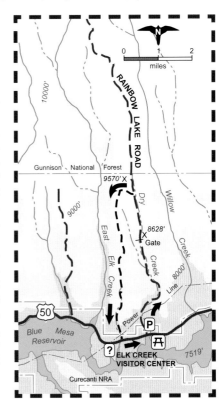

CURECANTI NRA: RED CREEK ROAD

21.0 miles total
2,900 elevation gain

Easy to moderate, with much of the ride following improved and unimproved roads, this 3 to 6-hour ride's most difficult sections are a steep, 0.25-mile climb and a short, steep, rocky descent. But it is challenging due to length and consistent climbing for the first 10.0 miles. From Gunnison, drive west on US-50 for 19.0 miles to the **Red Creek Road** turn-off, which is signed. The unsigned pull-off where you'll park is 0.1 mile up on the left, immediately past Red Creek Campground.

From the parking area, ride up Red Creek Road and through the gate, sagebrush-covered hills rising on the right, wooded Red Creek threading along the bottom of the ravine on the left. At **mile 0.6**, enter the **Sapinero Wildlife Area**, marked by a sign. The road follows the bottom of a ravine and winds through large cottonwood trees. Ahead, a tall, carved pinnacle rises from the side of a cliff. At **mile 1.5**, the road crosses Red Creek, then ascends gradually above beaver ponds and the deadfall-choked creek bed, before traversing the bottom of a pinyon-juniper, Gambel oak, and sagebrush-studded slope.

Farther along, the walls of the ravine lay back, and large ponderosa pines loom above the road on the right. On the left, sheer cliffs rise high above a steep Gambel oak and sagebrush hillside. At **mile 3.3**, pass a road on the right, continuing on Red Creek Road past a garden of small pinnacles on the other side of the creek. Soon, aspens descend to the road and more beaver ponds appear.

At **mile 4.75**, the road passes a gate, with a cattle guard and fence, and a sign stating you've entered **Forest Service** land. Just past the gate, pass another sign, this one for Lion Gulch and West Elk Creek, four miles to the left, and a road.

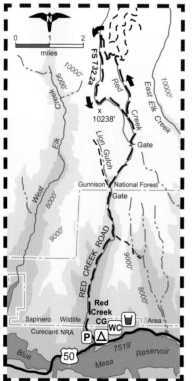

Continue on up Red Creek Road, where soon the ravine narrows and the creek thins to a trickle. At **mile 6.75**, pass another gate, and a mile past that, **FS 723.2a** comes in on your left. Continue straight on Red Creek Road, which soon runs alongside a long, grassy meadow punctuated by large spruce and fir trees.

At **mile 9.75**, the forest opens into a large meadow, and Red Creek Road enters a long switchback to the right. At the apex of the curve, an **unnamed road** intersects Red Creek Road. Take this road, climbing steeply for about a half a mile. At the top of the winding hill, the road flattens out and meanders through mixed spruce, fir, and aspen forest. At **mile 10.5**, a 4WD trail joins the road uphill from the left. This is the far end of FS 723.2a. Turn left and descend a steep, rocky slope for 0.2 mile.

FS 723.2a descends gradually for the next 2.5 miles, through thick stands of spruce and fir and past long, grassy meadows that border the creek. For a short distance, you'll be riding right next to the creek, with the walls of the ravine close on either side and a canopy of thick pine boughs overhead. The trail soon climbs a short rise, then descends briefly to the intersection with Red Creek Road. Turn right and descend the final 7.75 miles to the car.

CURECANTI NRA: FOREST SERVICE TRAIL #452

This rewarding ride to some unusual mudstone pinnacles is rated challenging due to steep, rocky climbs; and takes 2 to 4 hours. From Gunnison, drive west on US-50 for 26.0 miles to the signed **Lake Fork Visitor Center** turn-off at CO-92. Descend the hill, cross the **Blue Mesa Dam**, and turn left. A half mile past the dam, turn right on Soap Creek Road; follow it 7.0 miles to the **Ponderosa Campground** and Boat Ramp, signed on the right. In the campground, follow signs to the boat ramp. When you see restrooms on the right just uphill of the reservoir, turn right and park.

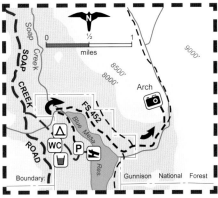

From the parking lot, turn right on the boat ramp road and descend a short distance to where you'll see a sign that says "No Vehicles, No Parking" on the left. Turn left onto the single track, following

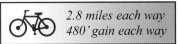

2.8 miles each way
480' gain each way

the drainage ditch around the hillside for 0.5 mile to where it intersects with the campground road. Turn right on the road and descend to where the road curves left and begins to climb again. On the right, directly across the road from campsite #18, **FS-452** departs on the other side of a gate. Ride through the hiker maze to the left of the gate and quickly enter a thick forest of Gambel oak, Douglas fir, and ponderosa pine. Traverse a steep hill that looks down on a portion of the campground and descend to a bridge that crosses **Soap Creek** at the far northern end of the Soap Creek Arm of Blue Mesa Reservoir.

Climb a short, steep, rocky hill, then descend again before passing two iron posts. At this point, you're on the other side of the Soap Creek Arm, riding through rolling hills dotted with pinyon-juniper and sagebrush, with towering palisades looming in the middle distance. The trail continues to climb and descend; and soon, look across the Soap Creek Arm and see the boat ramp, the campground, and where you parked. Sheer, mudstone cliffs rise directly in front of you, while to the left, intricately carved pinnacles decorate the hillside. Just before two miles, you'll come to a fork in the trail. The right hand fork descends through a stand of large blue spruce, crosses a creek, then quickly dead ends at a fence and a "No Trespassing" sign. The left hand fork leads to another fork, where you want to turn right and climb a steep, rocky slope. The trail soon levels out and passes through more sagebrush, with cliffs and pinnacles on all sides; like riding through a garden of statuary.

Traversing a hillside at **mile 2.5**, you'll see a stand of large cottonwoods downhill to the right. Immediately ahead, a **single track trail** leaves on the left. Take it, and climb out of the cottonwoods into Gambel oak, ponderosa pine, and sagebrush. Continue up the rocky ascent almost as if you were going to ride right into the soaring palisades directly ahead, until you enter a canopy of Gambel oak. From here, cross a steep hillside on the side of a ravine among the mud pinnacles. The trail is loose and steeply canted to the right. Just ahead, encounter a pile of dead fall logs; the trail continues beyond the dead fall, but quickly becomes unrideable. Park your bike at the dead fall, then walk the short distance up the faint trail to an **arch**, which perforates the base of the pinnacles uphill to the left. Have lunch in the shadow of the pinnacles, then remount and return to the car.

Of the dozen or so mapped trails in the **Gunnison Gorge National Conservation Area**, five are within the **Wilderness Area** and are closed to bikes. The **Peach Valley** and **Chukar Roads** are the main roads into the NCA and traverse fairly flat terrain through the adobe badlands in the western third of the NCA. The Ute, Duncan, and Bobcat Roads all climb steeply to their respective trailheads at the top of the gorge's west rim, while the Dinosaur Road, Wave Avenue, and Eagle Boulevard access the Black Ridge Trail at various points. The Ute Road also accesses the Black Ridge trailhead, although neither it, nor the Black Ridge Trail between the Ute and Duncan trailheads are recommended for mountain bikes; Ute Road is exceptionally steep and technical for three miles, and the Black Ridge Trail is even steeper, with long sections that are unrideable. The remaining trails — Black Ridge from Duncan to the Chukar Road, Horse, and Eagle Valley—are physically and technically demanding, but eminently rewarding, with spectacular views north to the Grand Mesa, east into the shadowy Gunnison Gorge, southeast to the towering cliffs of the Black Canyon, south to the rampart-like San Juan Mountains, and west to the rising terraces of the Uncompahgre Plateau.

If you choose to ride in the **NCA**, be aware of your surroundings at all times. Also, check with the BLM regarding which trails are open to mountain biking, especially after the **new management plan** takes effect (presumably in 2004.) Trails that are open today may not be open next year. Be aware that you'll be sharing trails with hikers, equestrians, motorcycles, 4WD vehicles, and ATVs. Bring plenty of **water**, as creek beds are usually dry here for most of the year. Finally, a good map, a cyclometer, and a partner are essential here.

GUNNISON GORGE NCA: LOOP #1

10.0 miles loop
1,500 elevation gain

For experienced riders only, this 3-5 hour loop ride — **Eagle Boulevard, Wave Avenue, Black Ridge Trail, Chukar Road, Horse Trail, Chukar Road, Peach Valley Road** — is technically and physically demanding, especially the Wave Avenue climb, the descent at the far end of the Black Ridge Trail, and the Horse Trail descent.

From the junction of US-50, US-550, and CO-90 in Montrose, drive west on US-50 for 9.3 miles to **Falcon Road**, which will be signed on your right. Follow Falcon Road east 3.5 miles to where the pavement ends at the intersection with 6400 Road, which comes in on the right. Continue straight onto the dirt road; this is **Peach Valley Road**. Four and a half miles from US-50, come to a sign for Gunnison Gorge National Conservation Area. One-tenth of a mile past the sign, the road forks; turn left. At 5.1 miles, you'll pass Chukar Road on the right; it is signed. Continue on Peach Valley Road up the hill. At the top of the hill, 5.3 miles from US-50, you'll come to flat area at the base of several large gray and yellow adobe domes; this is the start of **Eagle Boulevard**. Park on the right of Peach Valley Road, and to the left of Eagle Boulevard.

Follow the trail straight ahead (east) into the domes; you'll soon see it traverse a hillside directly in front of you. Climb moderately through the barren domes, then across the hillside, with views south of the San Juan Mountains rising above Montrose. At the top of the hill, pass the user-created routes on the left and take the road that heads north-northwest, left, through the flat, open plain. **Grand Mesa** is directly in front of you on the horizon, drawing a firm line across the sky. At **mile 1.25**, you'll intersect **Wave Avenue**, turn right and climb the pinyon-juniper-studded hillside. The climb starts out gradual, then becomes exceptionally steep after a quarter of a

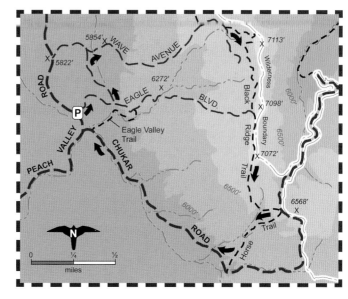

mile. The road surface alternates between dirt, gravel, and slabs of sandstone, with the gravel sections being the steepest and most technically difficult. At **mile 2.5**, after a mile of sustained climbing, the hill flattens out, and once again, you're winding through sparse pinyon-juniper forest. The forested flanks of the west rim rise, steep and wrinkled with ravines, to the east; to the south, the craggy San Juan Mountains thrust into the sky. At any point in the climb, stop and turn around to view the yellow and gray domes of the adobe badlands, the green, irrigated fields of Delta and Olathe, and the rising steps of the Uncompahgre Plateau.

At **mile 3.0**, you'll come to the top of a gradual hill and meet the **Black Ridge Trail** coming in from the left. Stay right, and follow the Black Ridge Trail as it climbs and dips and winds through the pinyon-juniper forest. The sun is warm, the breeze cool, and the air redolent with the smell of juniper. The trail becomes steep and technical again after a half a mile. At **mile 3.75**, take a right at the split; the trail soon comes close to the edge of a cliff, offering breathtaking views southeast to the towering black pinnacles of the Black Canyon of the Gunnison. The parking lot perched on the hillside below is the Chukar trailhead. Water-eroded gray, white, and yellow piles of *Morrison sandstone* slant across the hill and are bordered by yellow, orange, red, and pink domes of *Wingate sandstone*.

A maze of roads and trails intersects the Black Ridge Trail for the next mile; stay left, along the edge of the cliff. At **mile 4.75**, the upper end of Eagle Boulevard comes in on the right. Continue straight on the Black Ridge Trail. Soon, it starts to descend through the pinyon-juniper forest, and views open to the south of the adobe badlands and the impressive San Juan Mountains rising beyond. The descent becomes steeper and more technical, until you reach a 4-foot ledge you have to climb down. From here, the riding is exceptionally steep and technical, and you may choose to carry your bike the half mile or so along the narrow, exposed ridge to where the trail flattens out.

At approximately **mile 6.0**, you'll come to a dry creek bed and the bottom of the technical descent. Climb a short, steep hill, then spin through sparse pinyon-juniper, with the mountains on your right. Pass a BLM trail sign on the right and continue up the hill a short distance to the intersection with the **Chukar Road**, at **mile 6.5**. Turn right and look for a single track leaving the Chukar Road about thirty feet beyond the intersection. This is **Horse Trail**, a rolling ride through a narrow ravine that soon turns into an insanely steep and technical descent into the adobe badlands, where it rejoins the Chukar Road.

(If you choose to bypass Horse Trail, stay on the Chukar Road. Pass a road on the right at mile 6.75, another one on the left at mile 7.3, and a third on the left at mile 7.5. At mile 8.0, Horse Trail comes out of the adobe on the right.) If, however, you decide to brave it, turn right on Horse Trail and descend through the pinyon and juniper into the ravine. You'll soon come to the bottom of a dry creek bed, followed by a short, steep climb. At **mile 6.75**, the trail merges with a road that comes in from the right; beyond the road, the trail splits. Take the right hand fork, past an old wooden post in the ground. (The left hand fork cuts a switchback and rejoins the trail down lower). From here, the trail becomes very steep, loose, and rocky.

At the bottom of the descent, enter rolling badlands; the Chukar Road should be visible straight ahead, about a quarter of a mile distant. Turn right on the Chukar Road and ride through multi-colored sandstone formations; pink, yellow, and orange aprons topped by cliffs and pinyon-juniper-forested slopes. The road dips and twists through the alien landscape. Soon, the domes part to reveal the Grand Mesa standing silent and aloof on the northern horizon. At **mile 10**, you'll reach the intersection of **Peach Valley Road**. Turn right and climb the short hill back to the car.

GUNNISON GORGE NCA: LOOP #2

> *12.0 miles loop*
> *2,150 elevation gain*

With several *hike-a-bike* sections, riding up and down over slabs of sandstone, and a steep, rocky descent through a narrow ravine on the Eagle Valley Trail, this loop ride — **Duncan Road, Black Ridge Trail, Eagle Boulevard, Eagle Valley Trail, Chukar Road, Peach Valley Road** — is a very demanding but rewarding trip. Expect it to take 3 1/2 to 5 hours.

From the junction of US-50, US-550, and CO-90 in Montrose, drive west on US-50 for 9.3 miles to **Falcon Road**, which will be signed on your right. Follow Falcon Road east 3.5 miles to where the pavement ends at the intersection with 6400 Road, which comes in on the right. Continue straight onto the dirt road; this is **Peach Valley Road**. Four and a half miles from US-50, you'll come to a sign for Gunnison Gorge National Conservation Area. One-tenth of a mile past the sign, the road forks; turn left. At 5.1 miles, you'll pass Chukar Road on the right; it is signed. Continue on Peach Valley Road up the hill. At the top of the hill, 5.3 miles from US-50, you'll come to flat area at the base of several large gray and yellow adobe domes; this is the start of Eagle Boulevard. Continue past the Eagle Boulevard trailhead until you reach the intersection of Peach Valley Road and Duncan Road, 8.5 miles from US-50. Turn right and park on the right of Duncan Road.

Head east on the **Duncan Road**, which soon begins a moderate ascent through open hillsides. Ignore user-created trails along the way. At just about a mile, the North Duncan Road enters from the left on a corner; stay right. At **mile 1.5**, you'll crest the ridge and see the Duncan trailhead directly in front of you.

The Black Ridge Trail crosses from left to right; turn right, and enter the pinyon-juniper forest. The hills to your right are forested and seamed with ridges of flat rock that run their length from top to bottom. To the north is Grand Mesa; to the west, the adobe badlands stand in stark contrast to the green, irrigated fields of Olathe and Delta. Below, you can see the Duncan Road hugging the hillside as it climbs from Peach Valley Road.

The ride follows the western rim of the gorge (background) before descending steeply into the adobe hills (foreground).

You'll soon come to a short, steep, rocky descent, beyond which the trail climbs steeply again. This is the beginning of the first hiking section. Climb a quarter of a mile to the top of the peak, where you'll be greeted with views southeast into the Black Canyon of the Gunnison. To the right of the Black Canyon, in the foreground, you'll see the next peak you have to climb. Remount your bike and ride across the open hilltop. Turn right, descend the loose, sandy slope, then enter a field of flat boulders. Just beyond this, you traverse a narrow, steep-sided ridge that connects the first two peaks and affords views east and west. Ahead is a very steep, loose ascent. This is the start of the next hiking section.

With your bike on your shoulder, look down and to the left into the Gunnison Gorge. The pinyon-juniper forest extends down the slope right to the edge of the precipitous cliffs. Two-thirds of the way up the slope above the Gorge, sherbet-colored domes of *Wingate sandstone* swell above the trees. The further you climb, the deeper you can see into the Gorge. After about a quarter of a mile, you reach the top of the climb and ride across an open hilltop, through loosely scattered pinyon and juniper trees and past mustard yellow rock formations. You'll soon come to another steep climb, with large slabs of rock to maneuver your bike over. At the top of the next open ridge, look east and get a glimpse of the Gunnison River through an open "V" in the side of the Gorge. Follow the ridge, descend a short distance, then climb through more rocks.

At the top of the next peak, you get a full 360 degree view. To the southwest, a spinelike ridge topped with cliffs extends due south; just beyond it is an open area in the pinyon-juniper forest. This is the Bobcat trailhead. Descend gradually through the pinyon and juniper and over moderately technical slabs of volcanic rock. Traverse a hillside, then descend again toward Bobcat, which is directly in front of you. The trail here is rocky and bright yellow.

At **mile 3.5**, intersect the Bobcat Road. Turn left, ride through the parking lot, and begin the last big ascent on the **Black Ridge Trail**. At **mile 3.75**, you'll reach the top of the final climb, a flat, open ridgetop spotted with pinyon and juniper. Have fun riding over the sandstone slabs and winding through the sparse forest. A number of user-created routes intersect the trail on the right; ignore

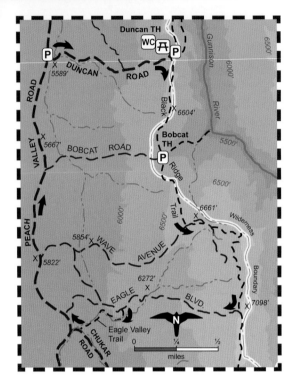

them. Just past **mile 4.0**, Wave Avenue comes in on the right. Continue along the Black Ridge Trail, left, as it twists and turns through the open forest and climbs over slabs of sandstone.

Eagle Boulevard intersects the Black Ridge Trail at **mile 5.9**. Turn right and descend the steep, winding road through the forest and over more sandstone slabs. After a short distance, the road leaves the forest and descends an open hillside, which allows uninterrupted views north, west, and south. The road becomes steeper and more technically difficult, with loose rock and bigger ledges to drop off. At **mile 7.25**, the road merges with a dry wash; follow the road until it climbs out of the wash, then take a left, continuing along the wash. This is the start of the **Eagle Valley Trail**.

(Like Horse Trail, Eagle Valley Trail provides an exceptionally steep and technical descent. If you decide to bypass it, continue along Eagle Boulevard, ignoring all intersecting roads. You'll soon pass the Wave Avenue connector and descend the slope behind the adobe domes. At approximately mile 8.5, Eagle Boulevard intersects Peach Valley Road. Turn right on Peach Valley Road and ride 3.0 miles to the car.) To continue on Eagle Valley Trail, stay in the wash. The single track soon climbs out of the wash on the left, crosses a dry, rocky gulch, then descends again back into the wash. The trail is loose and sandy here, with lots of loose rocks and big drops to negotiate. The banks of the wash eventually become closer and higher, with gray, pink, and purple slopes of *Morrison sandstone* to the left and tall undercut cliffs of pink and yellow sandstone to the right. There are several places where the trail winds through large boulders that have fallen from the banks into the wash.

At **mile 8.0**, come to a 5-foot high spillway. Climb around it to the left. Below the spillway, the trail becomes steeper and narrower, passing over large, sloping slabs of sandstone. This is where the riding becomes technical. The further you travel down the wash, now a ravine, the steeper and more steeply canted the trail surface becomes, until you're riding only on sandstone. The crux of the descent is a 6-foot wide slot through sheer shale walls where water has cut directly through the rock. Below, the trail flattens and widens, and you're riding on sand again. Adobe domes rise on both sides, then lay back as the trail passes into sagebrush flats.

At **mile 8.5**, Eagle Valley Trail intersects the **Chukar Road**. Turn right, follow the Chukar Road to the intersection with **Peach Valley Road**, where you'll turn right again, ascend the short hill, and ride the 3.0 miles back to your car.

Park Organized Activities

When visiting the Black Canyon, you have opportunities to learn a lot about the history, botany, geology, climatology and biology of this fascinating area from the experts, the **interpretive rangers** of the National Park Service. The NPS, which administers both Black Canyon of the Gunnison National Park and Curecanti National Recreation Area, offers a full list of free ranger-led activities and programs during the summer months, and even has many scheduled activities in the off-season.

You can find out about scheduled summer programs and activities at the National Park by picking up a copy of the **park newspaper** at the South Rim Visitor Center or the North Rim Ranger Station. Topics and times for slide shows and ranger talks are also posted on bulletin boards at the campgrounds. In the evenings, take a stroll from your campsite at South Rim Campground over to the amphitheater for a **slide show** or other presentation, six nights per week all summer. These presentations are given in a way that will fascinate and enlighten the adults in the audience, and also entertain the kids. You'll come away from these programs with a better understanding of the natural world around you, and you'll be able to impress your friends with your knowledge!

Ranger-led **nature walks** also occur daily in summer (late May through late September),may involve a short walk to a Park overlook or a moderate hike on one of the rim or backcountry trails. Read the posted description of the activity or ask a ranger for advice on appropriate footwear or hiking gear.

There are also ranger-conducted **snowshoeing** and **moonlight cross-country skiing** activities on the closed portion of the South Rim Drive in winter

FOR KIDS

Kids from 4 to 12 can begin the process of learning to care for and protect our natural environment while having a great time. How? By becoming a **Junior Park Ranger**, of course!

Start by picking up a Junior Ranger workbook for free at the South Rim or Elk Creek Visitor Centers. Activities that lead toward the goal of *Junior Rangerhood* (we made that up) are divided into three age groups. The book is filled with puzzles and challenges, including our favorite — *Canyon Crossword*. De-scramble the names of critters seen in the Park, then solve the crossword puzzle.

Once a child has completed the training activities in the book, they can have an adult ranger check their book and then take the **Junior Ranger Pledge**:

"As a Junior Park Ranger, I promise to do my best to protect the rocks, the flowers, and the wildlife of Black Canyon, as well as all of the other National Parks"

Now your Junior Park Ranger can proudly wear the official Junior Park Ranger badge.

After reviewing the workbook, we think all the "big kids" from 13 to 102 would benefit from this training, too.

A ranger-led visit to an overlook.

(the road is unplowed beyond Gunnison Point.) Snowshoe outings occur on weekend days, giving visitors a chance to explore Black Canyon in the winter. The moonlight ski trips are held once a month during the full moon — a 2-mile tour along the road to Pulpit Rock. Participants must provide their own equipment and dress for the weather.

At Curecanti NRA, the Park Service also offers **evening programs** at the amphitheaters in Loop A at Elk Creek Campground and at the Lake Fork Campground, usually every Friday and Saturday night during the summer. Special programs, designed for kids 5 through 12, accompanied by an adult, with hands-on activities, stories and games are offered at the Elk Creek Picnic Pavilion at 2 p.m, every Saturday and Sunday from mid-June to about Labor Day. Or join the rangers for a daily **fish feeding** at the fish pond at the Elk Creek Visitors Center during summer months.

The National Park Service is committed to fostering appreciation of the mission of the NPS to preserve the natural and cultural resources of the two parks. Their **educational outreach** programs provide for over 10,000 pre-school, K-12, college students and lifelong learners in 11 communities, 6 school districts, and colleges across the nation. Most of the curriculum involves a classroom component and a field trip to one of the parks. There is also a distance learning series that uses a satellite downlink and the Internet to allow students to take a virtual field trip in the canyon. Teachers can view the curriculum at

www.nps.gov/blca/webvc/edu/outreach.htm and reserve a program date on the web or by calling *(970) 641-2337 x203.*

RANGER-LED MORROW POINT BOAT TOUR

Operated by the Elk Creek Marina, this 42-passenger, pontoon boat tours the fjord-like **Morrow Point Lake** daily from Memorial Day to Labor Day with a NPS interpretive ranger on board to explain the geology, natural history and human history behind the magnificent canyon scenery. Highlights include viewing lovely Chipeta Falls (named for Chief Ouray's wife) and famous Curecanti Needle (carved by nature from the canyon's granite-like rock), and hearing stories of the days when the Denver and Rio Grande's *Scenic Line of the World* braved the gorge and when dams were built to harness the power of the river.

The tour lasts about 1.5 hours and runs twice-a-day, at 10 a.m. and 12:30 p.m. **Reservations** are strongly recommended, *(970) 641-0402* or stop by the Elk Creek Marina in Curecanti NRA. The tour begins at the Pine Creek boat dock, reached by the one-hour Pine Creek Trail (see Hike #13, page 184), just off US-50, one mile west of the CO-92 junction. The entire trip takes about 4 hours. Bring water, a lunch and a jacket (it can be cool on the water.) Pets and alcoholic beverages aren't permitted on the boat.

It costs (as of 2004):		
	Children (infants under 2)	*Free*
	Children (2 to 12)	*$5*
	Adults	*$10*
	with Golden Age/Access	*$5*

Photography

The savage beauty and haunting solitude of the Black Canyon of the Gunnison draws both amateur and professional photographers, intent on capturing the essence and mood of this remarkable place. With the juxtaposition of great extremes of light and dark surfaces in the deep gorge, photographing Black Canyon can be difficult. To get good results, you need to understand the effect of big differences in contrast on your camera's light meter and make intelligent choices.

❚ **Choose locations carefully:** Depending upon the prevailing direction of the canyon, different locations receive light at different times in the day. Since the canyon runs roughly east and west, most deep spots in the gorge receive light either early or late in the day. For instance, if you want to photograph the "camel" at Kneeling Camel View, you'll find it a disappointment in the morning, when the formation is in deep shadow. Return late in the day for perfect lighting.

❚ **Embrace contrast:** Instead of fighting the contrast problem of light and dark surfaces, embrace it. Images with one side of the canyon in bright light and the opposite in dark shadow can be very dramatic. But metering for that situation and getting the exposure right is tricky. Use a "bracketing" technique of consecutive frames with several different exposure settings.

❚ **Winter equalizer:** Snow, lying stark white on countless ledges and reflecting light into the darkest corners, equalizes contrast problems in the canyon.

Professional photographers know that early or late in the day are best for optimum color saturation in your photographs, avoiding intense mid-day light. If your interest is in photographing wildlife, you'll find that animals are more likely to be seen at those times of the day. For best results, use a tripod to steady your shots, especially since metering of dark walls will slow shutter speeds.

Great contrasts of light and dark surfaces can create drama in your photos of Black Canyon.

PHOTOGRAPHY TIPS

▌ At **Warner Point**, the canyon is so situated that light, late in the day, pours like water into the canyon. Using a wide-angle lens, shoot northeast up the gorge with the West Elk Mountains as your backdrop. Sunset can be an especially dramatic time at Warner Point, as the far mountains and the rim rocks become infused with alpine glow.

▌ Everyone wants to photograph colorful **Painted Wall**. Several overlooks — both South and North Chasm View, Painted Wall View, Cedar Point and Dragon Point — provide excellent perspectives. But to get an eye-popping image requires some knowledge and work. Take advantage of the fact that Serpent Point (the top of the wall) faces southeast and is one of the highest spots on the North Rim. That means it's the first thing struck by the sun each morning. Get your butt out of bed at dawn to Chasm View for some gorgeous images of alpen glow on this magnificent wall. Painted Wall is a poor choice to photograph in the late afternoon and early evening, when it is largely in shadow.

▌ For capturing shots of your buddies hanging out at the overlooks, try **Gunnison Point** and **Chasm View** for their dramatic backdrops, especially well before noon. Gunnison Point sits out on a jutting outcrop; and an interesting photo can be created by staying back on the trail and shooting down at the overlook, with your excited friends crowding the railing. At Chasm View, a short telephoto lens is useful for snapping fun shots of groups of tourists waving from the opposing overlook, barely 1,000 feet way. On the North Rim, the ultimate canyon shot is at **Exclamation Point** (see Hike #7, page 177.) If your subject isn't too fazed by great heights, you can position them inches from the brink.

▌ For an investment in effort, the summit of **Green Mountain** offers a very unusual *birds-eye* view of the "big bend" area around The Chasm from a vantage point nearly 1,000 feet above the North Rim. This moderate hike (see Hike #8, page 179) is best done in spring or fall when the scrub oak are in their best colors. An extreme wide-angle lens is needed to convey the enormity of the snaking canyon. Late in the day is the optimum time for shooting here.

▌ For those who are willing to venture into the **Inner-Canyon**, your efforts may be rewarded in discovering spectacular places, seldom photographed by Park visitors. Use a well-padded camera pack to protect your gear from the inevitable knocks from descending one of the side-canyon routes (see page 194.) Choosing "portrait" (vertical) format with a wide-angle lens will emphasize the narrowness and depth of the gorge. Use a slow-speed, fine-grained film and a small aperture for great depth of field, capturing fine details on lichen covered boulders and crystal-studded walls. A slower shutter speed will give an attractive "blur" to waterfalls and rapidly moving water. Because of the extreme contrasts of light and dark in the depths of the canyon, pay close attention to your light meter readings and "bracket" your critical exposures.

▌ Almost anywhere along CO-92, winding beside the rim between Blue Mesa Dam and Crystal Picnic Area in Curecanti NRA, is superb for **fall scenes** of colorful aspen and oak-clad slopes. Stay high on the hillside and use a wide-angle lens to get in the rugged front of the snow-clad San Juan Mountains to the south. Correct use of a polarizing filter will remove haze from the scene and increase saturation of those deep reds and golds.

■ **Pioneer Point Overlook** on CO-92 is a popular stop for photographers, but shots of dramatic **Curecanti Needle** can be disappointing from this height and angle. The Needle looms much more impressively at water level from the Morrow Point Boat Tour. All three dams at Curecanti NRA can be photographed from downstream, preferably in the afternoon to avoid placing their faces in deep shadow. **Morrow Point** is perhaps the most graceful of the three; and if you are lucky or have advance knowledge, you might capture a release of water falling hundreds of feet from its upper spillway.

■ **Winter scenes** almost seem enhanced by the intense cold at Curecanti NRA. Photograph shimmering effects of sunlight on early morning frost on the huge

Colorful scrub oak at Curecanti NRA.

cottonwoods at Neversink and Cooper Ranch Picnic Areas. Then capture scenes of "lake smoke" (water vapor from the warm lake) enveloping the air above Blue Mesa Reservoir from Middle Bridge. Keep an extra set of camera batteries warmed up in your pocket.

■ For action shots, position yourself at Cedar Point or Dragon Point and use a long, telephoto lens for photographing **rock climbers** on Painted Wall. No need to use fast film, as the "action" moves like a glacier. However, you'll need lots of high ISO film (400 or 800) to keep up with the **rafters** and **kayakers** at Gunnison Gorge. Since few of the foot trails get really close to many of the rapids (where the action is), join a raft trip. Have yourself placed ashore below a rapid and shoot upstream, as boats approach the white water.

■ For places to **photograph wildlife**, see some of the suggestions in the *Watching Wildlife* section, starting on page 166.

Take a Scenic Drive

SOUTH RIM DRIVE

A leisurely drive along the National Park's paved, 6.5-mile **South Rim Drive** is a wonderful way to experience the grandeur of Black Canyon. The 12 major rim overlooks, spaced along this beautiful drive, feature spectacular views of the river, the canyon and of the surrounding high mountain ranges. Some overlooks are wheel-chair accessible, while most feature a short walk from the parking area to the safety-railed viewing area. Many have signs that help to interpret for you the natural history, cultural history and geology of the area. We've indicated here if restrooms, picnic tables or other facilities are present.

Take your time and visit several of the overlooks; for each is different and provides a unique vista or singular perspective about this special place. For most people, including an in-depth stop at the visitor center, it will take 2-3 hours to finish at High Point at the west end of the road. Please observe the speed limit and follow the safety precautions outlined on the facing page. Note that the road is closed to vehicles beyond the Visitor Center in the winter.

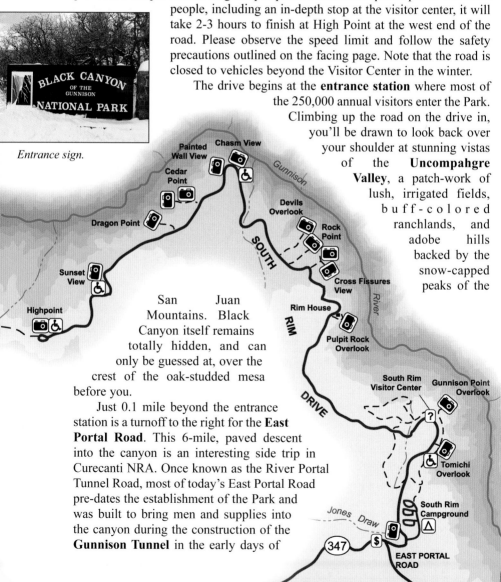

Entrance sign.

The drive begins at the **entrance station** where most of the 250,000 annual visitors enter the Park. Climbing up the road on the drive in, you'll be drawn to look back over your shoulder at stunning vistas of the **Uncompahgre Valley**, a patch-work of lush, irrigated fields, buff-colored ranchlands, and adobe hills backed by the snow-capped peaks of the San Juan Mountains. Black Canyon itself remains totally hidden, and can only be guessed at, over the crest of the oak-studded mesa before you.

Just 0.1 mile beyond the entrance station is a turnoff to the right for the **East Portal Road**. This 6-mile, paved descent into the canyon is an interesting side trip in Curecanti NRA. Once known as the River Portal Tunnel Road, most of today's East Portal Road pre-dates the establishment of the Park and was built to bring men and supplies into the canyon during the construction of the **Gunnison Tunnel** in the early days of

SAFETY ON THE RIMS

The weathered rock of the canyon edges makes the rims hazardous. Snow or ice on the rim can increase the danger. While visiting the developed overlooks along both rims of the Park, stay behind the safety rails and keep back from places on the rim where no guardrails are present. Don't allow kids to climb or play on the rails and keep your pets leashed. Yes, there have been people who have taken fatal falls at the overlooks!

Be sure to keep your speed within posted limits (20-30 mph) on the rim drives. These roads, with their sharp curves and slight shoulders, weren't designed for fast driving. Folks need to refrain from *rubber-necking* while you drive; and keep a close eye out for animals, hikers, cyclists, horseback riders and other drivers who may suddenly stop.

Lock your car doors when visiting the overlooks, even for just a few moments. And above all, DON'T THROW ROCKS into the canyon! Even a small stone can be fatal to someone below.

the 20th Century. The road was so steep and treacherous that wagons were chained to logs to control the descent. (Today, vehicles longer that 22 feet are prohibited down the sharp hair-pin curves. Trailers may be unhitched at the parking area at the entrance station.) Later, the road was extended along the south shore of the river during construction of **Crystal Dam** in the 1960s. There are pullouts along the way where you can marvel at the scene; rugged cliffs, dark towers, soaring buttresses, and the muffled sound of the river below. Along the route one sees one of the largest bodies of pegmatite in the area. (You'll see much more of this light-colored ore in the Park, shot through Black Canyon's dark walls.) Once at East Portal, you'll find a visitor information station, a shady campground and a pleasant picnic area. There's a

Diversion dam at East Portal.

small reservoir and diversion dam where river water is sent through the tunnel to farmers in the Uncompahgre Valley. Upstream is the 323-foot high face of Crystal Dam.

Jones Draw.

Once back on the South Rim Drive, continue past the entrance to the campground. Near here, the road crosses a dip at Jones Draw, a major fault line known as the **Red Rock Fault** that passes by the campground and continues through to East Portal. Descend along South Rim Drive steadily to **Tomichi Point Overlook**, your first view from the rim into Black Canyon, taking in a long look east upstream. Awesome as this first look is, it only gets better further along. The rimrocks here are *Dakota sandstone* which sometimes harbors small fossils, like ripple marks and worm trails. The **Rim Rock Trail** (see Hike #1, page 172) passes by the overlook and there's a restroom (wheelchair accessible) at the parking lot.

View east at Tomichi Overlook.

About 1.7 miles in on the drive, you'll come to the **South Rim Visitor Center**, just updated in 1999. You'll want to check out the displays, pick up some Park literature, and be sure to take in the short video about Black Canyon shown in the theater. The **Gunnison Point Overlook** is a scenic masterpiece. You can reach it by a short path from behind the center. Perched out on an airy outcrop, centered in a big, wide bend in the gorge, the overlook has unobstructed, sweeping vistas up and down the canyon.

Gunnison Point Overlook.

The drive continues west beyond the center through the scrub oak uplands of Vernal Mesa, offering tantalizing views of the gorge. At **Pulpit Rock Overlook** there are restrooms, a drinking fountain and **Rim House**, where light snacks and souvenirs are sold. A short path leads out to the overlook where your easterly gaze takes in the river. Across the canyon to your left are the Island Peaks, towers that have been separated by erosion from the canyon wall.

A jumble of rock islands at Cross Fissures View.

Leaving Pulpit Rock Overlook, the road snakes back and forth close to the rim for a mile — be careful to watch for cyclists and walkers around these blind curves! It arrives at three, closely-spaced viewpoints that look out on a jumbled portion of the gorge. The viewing stations are perched out on narrow fingers that reach out to massive islands of rock that stand back from the rim. A short walk leads out to two railed overlooks at **Cross Fissures View**. They afford close-up views of these spectacular formations, including one of the largest, Big Island.

Stress cracks that developed as the surrounding rock was uplifted have been exposed to the forces of erosion. These weak joints widen by weathering, creating open fissures hundreds of feet deep, and forming great isolated monoliths of rock. Note that the joints strongly trend to the northwest. **Rock Point** and **Devils Lookout** can also be reached by short trails that venture out on thin tongues of land. On either side, narrow troughs, like Echo Canyon, slice down some 1,800 feet to the barely glimpsed river, which is trapped between sheer cliffs at the spot appropriately termed The Narrows. Looking across the canyon to the northeast, you can see several peaks of the **West Elk Mountains** through the gap between Fruitland Mesa and Grizzly Ridge.

Looking down Echo Canyon at The Narrows from Rock Point.

South Rim Drive drops into Big Draw, the site of the original ranger station in the former Monument, before descending to the big bend at **Chasm View**, the lowest point on the drive at 7,761 feet. Situated at the apex of a dramatic bend in the gorge, and where the canyon rims are only 1,110 feet apart, the wheelchair-accessible overlook at Chasm View is one of the most dramatic spots in the Park. Beneath you, the thundering river is mostly a ribbon of foaming whitewater. The river's drop in the stretch from below Pulpit Rock to here is 240 feet/mile, an incredibly steep gradient. The sheer cliffs at Chasm View are carved from a dark gray, coarse rock called **Vernal Mesa quartz monzonite**. Hard and granite-like, it forms up the most rugged reach of the canyon, extending along the cliffs of the South Rim from Rock Point downstream to High Point.   Close by is another overlook, **Painted Wall View**. It looks west from the big bend, providing the first views of famous **Painted Wall**, beneath the North Rim's Serpent Point. Due north across the gorge is the deep cleft of **S.O.B. Draw**, one of the steep, rugged side canyons used by adventurers intent on reaching the river. Interpretive plaques at this overlook tell the story of the amazing birds that are frequently observed from this overlook — the *"hunters of Black Canyon,"* including peregrine falcons, and their sometimes prey, those *"masters of flight,"* the white-throated swift and the violet-green swallow.

Painted Wall.

Plaques at Painted Wall View.

From Chasm View, the South Rim Drive begins an easy climb to the southwest, reaching **Cedar Point** in 0.5 mile. Both this overlook and the next one west, **Dragon Point**, offer stunning, close-up views of the Painted Wall — at 2,270 feet, Colorado's highest cliff. Approach Cedar Point by its short nature trail with plaques along the way that showcase the canyon's flora and fauna. The opposite wall is largely a dark, metamorphic rock called **gneiss**. But what gives Painted Wall its great beauty are the threads of brightly-colored **pegmatite** that intrude the dark matrix in sinuous bands that suggest dragons and serpents — thus the names *Dragon Point* and *Serpent Point*. The dikes of pegmatite are white to rose in color; and were they to be examined up close, would reveal lustrous crystals of quartz and sheets of mica up to 6 feet across. Dragon Point, 0.25 mile further west of Cedar Point on the drive, sits out on an airy outcrop reached by a short path. If you've visit either of these outcrops in early to mid-morning, sheer Painted Wall will be at its best for photographing.

As the South Rim Drive continues its climb toward the summit at High Point, the canyon deepens and widens; and remarkable vistas begin to unfold, stretching westward where the river glistens and tumbles towards Gunnison Gorge. Lovely **Sunset View** is reached in 0.75 mile after Dragon Point. As the name implies, this is a wonderful spot to watch the sun slowly dip into the gorge at the end of the day. There's a wheelchair-accessible picnic area and a restroom.

Road end for the South Rim Drive comes at the parking loop at **High Point**, which indeed sits near the crest of the **Gunnison Uplift**, the elevated block through which the river cuts. There's a shady picnic area with restrooms, nestled in the pinyon/juniper forest that caps the mesa. **Warner Point Nature Trail** (see Hike #5, page 175) leaves the parking area. From the overlook, you have a view of the canyon at its deepest point of about 2,660 feet. Off to the west, the canyon widens and softens as it meets the less-resistant rock of the Gunnison Gorge. Looking northeast, some 15 miles away, are the laccolithic peaks and volcanic mesas of the **West Elk Mountains**. To the north across the valley of the North Fork is massive, flat-topped **Grand Mesa**. Through the trees to the south is the impressive mountain front of the **San Juan Mountains**, featuring three 14,000-footers. Big, bold Uncompahgre Peak is to the southeast with the thin spire of Wetterhorn Peak to its right. To the southwest, majestic Mount Sneffels commands center attention above the Uncompahgre Valley.

The Gunnison River glistens as the sun sets west over the gorge.

NORTH RIM DRIVE

North Rim Campground

North Rim Ranger Station

NORTH RIM ROAD Gulch

Chasm View Overlooks

Grizzly

NORTH

The Narrows View

The Narrows

Draw

RIM

Balanced Rock View

Long

Big Island View

DRIVE

River

Island Peaks View

Kneeling Camel View

For those seeking some solitude, the much-less-visited North Rim of the Black Canyon is well worth the extra time and effort to reach. Especially in the fall, when tourist traffic is light and these oak-draped hills offer glorious colors, a leisurely tour along the winding, 4.3-mile **North Rim Drive** offers scenic rewards without the crowds from its six, safety-railed overlooks. North Rim Drive is unpaved (but suitable for all vehicles) and is closed from about late November to early May. Be watchful for riders on horseback and mountain bikers on the road, as well as frequent stops by drivers around the overlooks. Read the do's and don'ts pertaining to safety on the rims on page 155.

The access road passes through the tranquil ranchland around Crawford, with fine views of the close-by high peaks of the **West Elk Mountains**,

The Painted Wall from the North Rim's Chasm View Overlook.

before gradually climbing the uplift that created the canyon. The broad expanse of the Gunnison Uplift hides the canyon from view, until the road pierces the rise and descends gently along Grizzly Gulch. Intersecting the North Rim Drive, turn right (west) and follow it for 0.5 mile to the **North Rim Ranger Station**, where you may pay the entrance fee, pick up literature and view the exhibits.

Continue west along the drive into the campground loop. An easy, short trail, the Chasm View Nature Trail (see Hike #6, page 176), leads south from the campground to two viewpoints on the rim. From these overlooks, you have a heart-pounding look into **The Chasm**, a point on the rim some 1,800 feet above the river and only 1,100 feet away from the opposing side — the narrowest width at the rim in the canyon. You'll be able to wave to people on the overlook on the far side. Look downstream and marvel at the highest cliff face in Colorado, the magnificent **Painted Wall**, with its wavy bands of light-colored pegmatite, seemingly alive and struggling to break free from the dark wall. Bring a pair of binoculars to keep a lookout for swifts, swallows and raptors cruising in the skies above.

The path loops back shortly to the campground, from whence the North Rim Drive commences its tour. Drive back past the ranger station, drop slightly to the junction with the access road, then continue southeast on the drive and begin a gradual climb through uplands of sagebrush, oak and pinyon. From this point on, the road loops sharply, matching the winding contour of the rim — first west towards some jutting overlook, then east around the head of a draw — for several times. The first overlook encountered is **The Narrows View**; where, as you might guess, there is a terrific view down some 1,700 feet to a pinch-point at river-level, the narrowest spot in the canyon. The actual spot called **The Narrows**, a little upstream from the overlook, is seemingly always in deep shadow, even at mid-day.

The Narrows lies in shadow even in the middle of the day.

The dark walls, made up of a rock called *gneiss*, heavily laced by dikes of lighter-colored *pegmatite*, are only about 40 feet apart at water level. The extreme steepness and grandeur of the canyon walls at any given place depend largely on the relative quantity of pegmatite, a very hard, igneous rock. The river is incredibly aggressive in this stretch, tumbling down to Chasm View at a drop of 240 feet per mile. Gazing down, you'll see the dangerous rapids and short waterfalls that turned back the early surveyors of the canyon and continue to pose grave danger to white-water enthusiasts.

Fissures and "islands."

A short distance past The Narrows View is the wheelchair-accessible viewpoint at **Balanced Rock View**. The name comes from a large rock formation that waits on time and the forces of nature to send it crashing into the gorge.

The North Rim Drive loops around the head of Long Draw, a route used by scramblers to reach the river, then snakes back south to the viewpoint at **Big Island View**. It is named for a very large, mostly flat-topped monolith that sits directly across the canyon. There are fine views up and down the river, including downstream to The Narrows.

After another big sweep to the east, the road swings south in 0.75 mile and arrives at **Island Peaks View**. This part of the canyon, on both sides, has a collection of monoliths, pinnacles, spires and fins of various sizes. Most are a result of vertical stress cracks that have been attacked by erosion over eons, forming isolated masses of rock. By the gradual enlargement of such openings, masses become separated from the main canyon wall, eventually toppling to the floor below in huge blocks of talus that contribute to the rapids that encumber the river. Some of these joints are so deep, that these monoliths are essentially free-standing, 1,600-foot high "islands."

The North Rim Drive moves away from the rim a bit, touring through Gambel oak and mountain mohagany for a mile before reaching the last overlook, **Kneeling Camel**. Look below the rim, to the ridge jutting out into the canyon. Can you see it? It doesn't take too much imagination to spot the one-humped "camel," gazing out across the abyss. Beyond the camel is a long view upstream of the river, and directly across canyon is Gunnison Point on the South Rim, perched out on its large outcrop of *pegmatite*. Several of the overlooks in the National Park (and in Curecanti NRA) stand on outcrops of this very hard, resistant rock.

From the parking lot at Kneeling Camel, you can stroll 0.1 mile east along the road to where a side road leads north in a few minutes to the site of the original ranger station on the North Rim. A couple of old structures mark the spot. A track continues from here as the Deadhorse Trail (see Hike #9, page 180), visiting viewpoints that overlook the eastern third of the Park. Back at the North Rim Drive, the road ends shortly to the east at a turn-around and a restroom.

The "camel" looks out over the gorge at sunset.

Touring History: Trains, Tunnels & Dams

For the history buff interested in man's attempts to alter the natural landscape for human purposes against great odds, Black Canyon bears the imprints of not one, but three, great construction projects that challenged our forebearers during a period from the 1880s through the 1970s, when winning control of the Black Canyon and its resources was paramount. The stories of the D&RG narrow-gauge railway, the Gunnison Tunnel, and the dams of the Upper Colorado River Storage Project are told in the **Cultural History** section (starting on page 76), but a fascinating, half-day auto tour along US-50 gives the visitor a better understanding of the engineering challenges, hardships and struggles it took to complete these three ambitious projects.

Begin your tour at the junction of US-50 and CO-92. Take the short drive north on CO-92, descending down to cross the canyon on the causeway atop **Blue Mesa Dam**. You can park on the right, at the north end, where plaques describe the history and workings of the dam, completed in 1965 as the first and largest of the three dams in the Wayne Aspinall Unit. The large vertical structure at the front of the dam is part of the intake. To get an idea of the immense size and height of the dam, you can cross the road to peer down into the narrow canyon that was plugged by this colossal structure of earth and concrete.

BUREAU OF RECLAMATION
COLORADO RIVER STORAGE PROJECT
BLUE MESA DAM

DAM EMBANKMENT	3,100,000 CU. YD.
RESERVOIR CAPACITY	941,000 AC. FT.
HEIGHT ABOVE RIVER	341 FT.
SPILLWAY TUNNEL DIAMETER	21 FT.
POWER PLANT OUTPUT	98 MW.
CREST LENGTH	800 FT.

Now return to US-50 and head west away from Blue Mesa Reservoir. In about a mile, you'll want to turn right and follow a short gravel road steeply down to the parking area for the **Pine Creek Trail** (see Hike # 13, page 184.) Take the short trail down its 232 steps of railway ties to the river, pausing at an overlook to inspect the face of Blue Mesa Dam upstream. At the bottom, the trail continues along the old railbed of the Denver and Rio Grande. This is one of the few places in the entire canyon where the original narrow-gauge railbed can still be seen. With the flooding of the valley upstream by Blue Mesa Reservoir, miles of railbed were submerged along with sites of bridges, railstops, and even whole towns that had sprung up beside the line. With the subsequent construction of the Morrow Point Dam downstream, the old railbed, which hugged within yards of the river in this narrow canyon, was largely inundated downriver as well. During periods of low water, stretches of the bed reappear between here and Cimarron Creek, visible only to kayakers who venture out into Morrow Point Reservoir.

Only a hundred yards or so upstream is a point where the railroad bridged over from the north shore, carrying the line briefly along the section of the south bank that you are walking on, before crossing back to the north side a few miles downstream near towering Curecanti Needle (which became the advertising symbol for the line.) It then stayed on that bank, before crossing a final time to exit the canyon entirely near the site of the present Morrow Point Dam. Crews of Irish and Italian workers spent more than a year braving rockfalls, avalanches, and intense cold to blast a shelf for the road through the canyon in 1881-82. If you listen closely above the roar of the river, perhaps you'll hear the faint echo of the train's whistle which resounded through the narrow chasm for nearly 70 years; a trip described by one early passenger as *". . . glorious and frightening beyond belief."*

Return to US-50 and continue west on the highway, climbing through the narrow gorge of Blue Creek, to crest over 8,704-foot **Blue Mesa Summit**. Descend into picturesque Cimarron Valley, fringed to the south with rugged, turreted ridges and the high peaks of the San Juan Mountains. Early homesteads and ranches dot the valley, some dating back more than 100 years. Soon you'll arrive at the **Cimarron Information Center** for Curecanti NRA which has interesting photo displays about the history of the old D&RG line. The close-by town of Cimarron marks the spot where the line exited from Black Canyon and began its arduous climb west to Cerro Summit, following close to the route of the present highway. The crews reached Cimarron on August 9, 1882, setting up their "hotel" trains, a veritable city on wheels, which followed their progress and provided sleeping and kitchen quarters.

Take the side road going north from the Visitor Center, descending along the old rail grade through narrow Cimarron Creek Canyon to reach a not-to-be-missed highlight of the tour. Soon come to an amazing reminder of those bygone railroading days. On the left, sitting on a trestle, is narrow-gauge, steam **locomotive #278**, with its coal tender, a boxcar and a caboose. The trestle, built in 1895 and originally 288 feet in length, replaced a former wooden trestle at this location. The masonry piers date from that earlier span. The display is set up as the line would have been in 1940, including a telegraph line extending from the ties on the south side.

Locomotive #278 was built in 1882 by the Baldwin works in Philadelphia as a freight and "helper" engine, and was used for 70 years on the Crested Butte branch and in the Gunnison railyards. The coal tender replaced the original on

Rail exhibit at Cimarron.

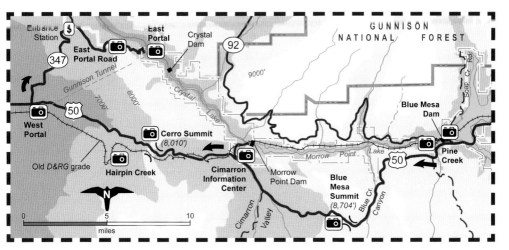

this engine around 1935. The boxcar was built in 1903 and able to carry 25 tons, mostly local agricultural products and ore. The caboose is from the mid-1880s and was used on this run of the D&RG. Due to its significance as the last remaining structure of the narrow gauge line through Black Canyon, the trestle was placed on the National Register of Historic Places in 1976.

If you continue past the rail exhibit to the end of the road, you can see the 469-foot high face of the **Morrow Point Dam**, the highest of the three dams, completed in 1968. Return to US-50 and continue your sojourn west over historic 8,010-foot Cerro Summit, just as the old rail line did until 1948. Descending the west side towards the broad Uncompahgre Valley, the old railbed leaves the modern highway to lose elevation more gradually at **Hairpin Creek**, named for where the line made a tight 180° bend. The much steeper highway bottoms out near the site of Lujane, where a side road goes left, close to the **West Portal** of the Gunnison Tunnel. You can view where the diverted waters of the Gunnison River enter a canal system to be delivered to the thirsty fields below.

Turn north onto CO-347 from US-50, following it to the entrance of the National Park. You'll have to pay the entrance fee, then turn right onto **East Portal Road**, just past the entrance station. The bottom half of this steep road, with its many, sharp switchbacks, is the original service road used to bring men and materials down to the river during construction of the **Gunnison Tunnel,** finished in 1909, and **Crystal Dam**, the last of Black Canyon's dam projects, completed in 1976. The 5.9-mile tunnel, a pilot project for the nascent Bureau of Reclamation, proved difficult and dangerous, costing the lives of six men and running into huge cost overruns. Bringing supplies into East Portal on the treacherous, 12-mile long road was equally frightening, with grades up to 22% (since smoothed out a merely nail-biting 16%.) At the bottom of the road, a diversion dam collects water from the Gunnison River and sends it through the **East Portal** of the tunnel under Vernal Mesa.

West Portal of the Gunnison Tunnel

Watching Wildlife

Mule deer

Great blue heron

Bald eagle

The **Gunnison River Valley** with its canyons, mesas, lakes and streams, is a wonderful place to observe a wide variety of fascinating animals. A visitor in a single day can observe vast differences in plants and wildlife from where the river flows into Curecanti NRA, to its exit downstream at Gunnison Gorge. Represented in the three units are very diverse ecosystems ranging from tall stands of ponderosa pine and fir, to *pygmy forests* of oak and pinyon, to sage and cactus in a near desert environment. *Microclimates* exist also in small areas of the canyon where moisture and temperature are just right. Each ecological zone has unique resources of food and cover, supporting a matrix of terrestrial wildlife — mammals, reptiles, amphibians, insects and birds. Aquatic life of fish, otters, and waterfowl are abundant in the reservoirs and river. Read the **Natural History** section, starting on page 52, for insight on many of the species of wildlife you are likely to see in and around the canyon. For a rewarding viewing experience, planning and patience are necessary.

You can improve your success in seeing wildlife up close. Binoculars, a spotting scope or a good telephoto lens on your camera will let you observe much more detail than you'll generally manage with the naked eye. Consider carrying a field guide to the birds and animals likely to be found here in southern Colorado (see a list of books on page 222.) The **Resource Guide** on page 229 also contains a check off list of many of the birds found in the National Park.

Learn about the behaviors of animals that you wish to view, by reading books and obtaining local information about the species. This will greatly aid your success in the field. Animals like **beavers** and **bats** are *crepuscular*, most active at dawn and dusk. **Mountain lions** and **ringtails** mostly come out at night, while **rock squirrels** and **whitetail prairie dog** are active during the day. Some species, such as **yellow-bellied marmots**, hibernate during the winter; while others, such as **mule deer** and **elk**, actually may range more widely and for a longer part of the day in search of food during this challenging time. All animals require water. Finding a watering location is a good place to start. The observer should find cover in a good viewing location, get comfortable, and wait quietly. Most wildlife will ignore you if there is no perceived threat. National Parks are excellent places to view wildlife, since they are protected and usually do not view humans as a threat. An early start is best for success — an the hour or two before and after daylight is an ideal time to view wildlife. If you've brought *Fido* with you (on a leash, of course), you'll have much less luck spotting wildlife. Even if your dog doesn't bark, animals will likely smell your pooch and regard it as a danger. Avoid fawning, calving, and denning areas during the birthing season, to avoid stressing the mother and young at this critical time. Never offer food; and know what to do if confronted by a threatening animal (see page 28 for more about wildlife encounters.)

TIPS SPOTTING WILDLIFE

❚ Some animals will undoubtedly come to you, especially in the National Park where many have lost their fear of humans. The developed overlooks and campgrounds are frequented by opportunistic **Colorado chipmunks, golden-mantled ground squirrels** and **mule deer**, looking for an easy snack. **Ravens** and **magpies** loudly announce their search for food as well. **Gunnison's prairie dogs** can be viewed in their towns right next to the Elk Creek Visitor Center.

❚ The Dillon Pinnacles Trail in Curecanti NRA is one of the best places to view both **elk** and **bighorn sheep** in late fall. Elk come virtually down to the edge of the reservoir; with the number wintering here depending on the severity of the weather. Look for bighorn sheep higher up-slope, never far from the haven of rugged ground. Bighorn have been reintroduced into the seldom-visited western third of Black Canyon of the Gunnison National Park. Your best chance of spotting them is to hike down the Chukar Trail (see Hike #18) into Gunnison Gorge, investigating the rugged canyons near the boundary of the two units.

❚ Any of the rim overlooks in the Park are ideal birding stations, at any time of the day. At dawn, look for **turkey vultures** hunched over on dead tree limbs along the rim. As the sun comes up, they turn east and spread wide their huge wings, warming them before launch. During the day, there are **red-tailed hawks**, **golden eagles**, ravens, and **peregrine falcons** on wing above the rims, with **violet-green swallows** below. Near dusk, the **common nighthawk** flits about the overlooks. (Species of **bats** also appear in the skies above the rims at dusk.) Listen closely at an overlook for unforgettable sounds drifting up from just below the rim — the sweet song of a **canyon wren** in the morning, or the sunset serenade of a **hermit thrush**, perched in the crown of a fir.

❚ Birding is also excellent at the east end of Curecanti NRA. The Neversink area is known for its **great blue heron** rookery, but the riparian habitat there and at nearby Cooper Ranch is also good for a variety of songbirds. During winter, **bald eagles** sometimes perch in the large cottonwoods that line the river in this stretch, feeding on fish while the lake waters remain open. The uplands of Curecanti NRA, where CO-92 climbs along the rim of Black Canyon, are good habitat for "mountain" birds. Look in the open meadows for sky-blue **mountain bluebirds**. Late June along the Crystal Creek Trail is a good time to view **broad-tailed hummingbirds**, attracted to wildflowers in bloom along the trail.

❚ Observe and learn about species of **fish** at Curecanti NRA by visiting the fishing pond at the Elk Creek Visitor Center and join a ranger for a fish feeding.

The **Gunnison sage grouse** of the Gunnison Basin, including in Curecanti NRA, account for the majority of the 4,000 or so birds that still remain after a decline in numbers of almost 60% since the 1950s. Not officially recognized as a separate species from the more common *Northern sage grouse* until 2000, this rare bird is endangered by habitat loss and habitat degradation. Through the Colorado Division of Wildlife's **Watchable Wildlife** program, you can view them from late-March to mid-May at a designated spot around Curecanti NRA where birds predictably display on a *lek*, or mating site. Please observe the protocol, designed to prevent disturbing the birds during this critical time. It's especially important that you remain quietly in your vehicle at all times. You can learn more about annual viewing times and regulations at the **Waunita Lek** viewing site by visiting the website of **Sisk-A-Dee**, a Gunnison sage grouse conservation organization, *www.siskadee.org*.

Winter Activities

Skiing on the South Rim Drive.

Black Canyon is full of things to do in the winter time. Because of the great range in temperatures and snowfall at the three units along the canyon, you can cross-country ski or ice-fish one day, and hike or mountain bike the next.

The canyon itself is transformed in the winter season — dark cliffs are softened by ledges draped in white; frosted branches on oaks shimmer like silver in the cold sunshine; and the gorge, and all its creatures, seem to pause, rest and reflect.

WINTER AT THE NATIONAL PARK

Snowfall at Black Canyon of the Gunnison National Park varies quite a bit from year to year. Usually, conditions are fair to good for snowshoeing or cross-country skiing from late December to early March. Early or late in the off-season, there are still opportunities to hike.

The **South Rim Drive** is kept plowed in winter only as far as the South Rim Visitor Center at Gunnison Point. Snowshoers and cross-country skiers are free to venture as far as they like beyond the road closure, all the way to road end at High Point (about 5 miles one way.) The wide, gentle track is suitable for even novice 'shoers or skiers; however, you'll need to leave your dog at home. Other trails near the Visitor Center, the **Rim Rock, Oak Flat Loop**, and **Uplands Trails** also make for a nice outing, especially if combined in a circle trip (see Hikes #1, 2, & 3, page 172.) You can also tour through the unplowed loops of the South Rim Campground, connecting with the Rim Rock Trail near Loop C.

The **South Rim Visitor Center** remains open daily (except for federal holidays) all winter. You can call them at ☎ *(970) 249-1914 x423* to ask about snow conditions or to sign-up for a ranger-led **snowshoe trip** or moonlight **cross-country ski tour**. Snowshoe trips (limited number of snowshoes available) are held weekdays. The ski tours are held once a month at the full moon. The latter is a 2-mile trip to Pulpit Rock Overlook beneath a fantastic dome of stars and that heavenly orb — with hot cocoa at the Visitor Center! Winter **star parties** are also held at the Visitor Center. All activities are free.

The **North Rim** is closed to vehicles at the Park boundary from roughly late November to early May. But if you crave solitude, a snowshoe trip or ski tour to the snowy rim from the winter road closure, 6 miles in from the turn-off from CO-92, will be a long-remembered winter experience. While the touring is easy along the gently rolling terrain, you might consider turning this into a winter camping trip because of the distance involved (about 5 miles each way). There's certainly plenty of space for you at North Rim Campground!

Descending on any of the snow-covered routes into the Inner-Canyon is NOT recommended. Also, there's no snowmobiling allowed in the National Park.

WINTER AT CURECANTI NRA

Depending on how much snow cover there is, snowshoeing and cross-country skiing at Curecanti NRA can be pretty good or pretty bad. Certainly, there is no lack of suitable terrain, although it's all on an informal basis — there aren't any groomed trails. You can tour on **Blue Mesa Reservoir**, when it's frozen; traveling virtually anywhere for miles if you like. The wind is the big determiner — besides making for brutal windchill factors, it can strip snow off the lake and the surrounding lakeshore meadows, and pack it into unappealing crust. Many NRA facilities, like picnic areas, are closed, with access roads gated and unplowed; but that creates fine opportunities for short tours into wind-sheltered places like Neversink, Cooper Ranch, and Dry Gulch.

Immediately after a snowfall, the **Dillon Pinnacles Trail** is an excellent tour, with a chance to spot wildlife wintering in the area. Trails at **Hermits Rest** and **Pioneer Point** (Curecanti Creek) that descend into the canyon are too steep and narrow for comfortable skiing, but make for challenging adventures for ambitious snowshoers. There are several roads and trails that originate from US-50 and CO-92 in Curecanti NRA and lead into the Gunnison National Forest, offering long extended tours; conditions permitting. Many of these Forest Service access roads are closed to vehicles in the winter, but permit recreational uses like snowshoeing, skiing and snowmobiling. Snowmobiling is permitted in Curecanti NRA on the frozen surface of Blue Mesa Reservoir (seven inches of hard, clear ice required) and on designated fishing access roads.

The **Elk Creek Visitor Center** is open weekends and intermittently on weekdays during the winter season. There's a novice-level ski trail marked off and the campground remains open all winter (there's drinking water at the picnic area.) In good ice years, a rink is maintained for skaters near the boat ramp.

WINTER AT GUNNISON GORGE NCA

There is seldom, if ever, enough snow at Gunnison Gorge NCA to engage in snowshoeing, cross-country skiing or snowmobiling. However, you can enjoy hiking and mountain biking nearly year-round.

Dark cliffs at Black Canyon, softened by ledges draped in white.

HIKING

Hiking down the Curecanti Creek Trail.

There's a lot more to see at Black Canyon then just the Visitor Center, and then, grab a quick look over the rim. Don't limit yourself by coming to the Park and spending 30 minutes, or just an hour. Spend the day, hit the trails, soak up the incredible beauty of this place and come to understand the fascinating creatures that live here. With all the hiking experiences here, and at Curecanti NRA and Gunnison Gorge NCA, you may find yourself wanting to come back again and again. Hiking options range from a stroll along a nature trail suitable for even novice hikers, to challenging, overnight backpacking adventures into the canyon. Come and explore some of the diverse treasures that await you.

Maps on the following pages shows the general locations of the hikes described in this chapter: **Hikes in the Park: South Rim & North Rim** (page 171), **Hikes in Curecanti NRA** (page 182), and **Hikes in Gunnison Gorge NCA** (page 188). Due to numerous stops you will undoubtedly be making for photographic purposes, we have used approximate hiking times in our descriptions. Hikes in the Park and Curecanti NRA are on trails maintained by the Park Service and typically are of a very high standard. You'll find that it's a bit slower going on the Gunnison Gorge NCA's more primitive trails.

A box with each hike lists the *loop* or *one-way* **hiking distance** and approximate **elevation gain** or **loss** for that hike. The latter indicate hikes which *descend* into the canyon, requiring you to make up the elevation loss on the return. While some hikes are described with optional destinations, the distance listed is to the farthest described destination. See page 24 for an explanation of the "difficulty" ratings for each hike.

Map of National Park Hikes

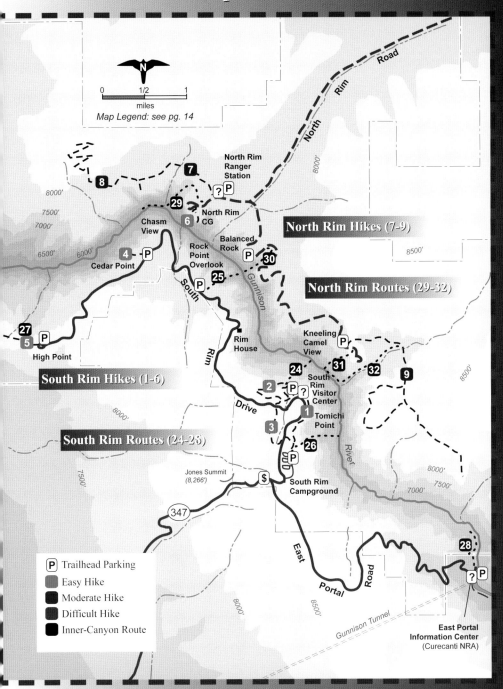

N

0   1/2   1
miles
Map Legend: see pg. 14

North Rim Ranger Station

North Rim Road

8000'

8

7

29

6

North Rim CG

8000'

7500'
7000'

Chasm View

Balanced Rock

30

8500'

6500' 6000'

4 P

Cedar Point

Rock Point Overlook

25

Gunnison

North Rim Hikes (7-9)

North Rim Routes (29-32)

27

5 P

High Point

Rim House

Kneeling Camel View

31

32

9

8500'

South Rim Hikes (1-6)

24

2 P

South Rim Visitor Center

South Rim Routes (24-28)

8000'

Drive

1 Tomichi Point

3

River

26

P

7500'

Jones Summit (8,266')

$

South Rim Campground

347

28

8000' 7500'

7000'

East Portal Road

8000'

8500'

Gunnison Tunnel

East Portal Information Center (Curecanti NRA)

P Trailhead Parking
■ Easy Hike
■ Moderate Hike
■ Difficult Hike
■ Inner-Canyon Route

Hikes in the Park: South Rim Trails

There are several — albeit short — hiking options along the **South Rim** of Black Canyon of the Gunnison National Park. What they may lack in length, they make up in diversity, as each features something different about the environment of the South Rim. For instance, the three short hikes that originate at the Visitor Center include a spectacular rim walk, a hike that explores the world below the rim, and a stroll into uplands away from the canyon. These three, the **Rim Rock**, **Oak Flat** and **Uplands Trails**, can also be combined into one, longer *loop hike* that will satisfy hikers wanting a fuller experience.

Off-trail, cross-country hiking is discouraged because of difficult travel through nearly-impenetrable thickets of Gamble oak, pinyon pine and Utah juniper.

RIM ROCK TRAIL

If you've only time for one short hike on your visit to the Park, this one would be your best choice for experiencing the Black Canyon. As the

1 | *0.5 mile each way minimal elev. gain*

name implies, this relatively flat trail takes you on a walk along the rim with many wonderful views of the river and the sheer walls of the canyon, plus occasional views of the distant West Elk Mountains to the north. Pick up a copy of the ***Rim Rock Trail Guide*** pamphlet at the South Rim Visitor Center or at the trailheads. It provides an explanation of how the canyon was formed and interesting information about canyon ecology. Numbers in the guide correspond to posts encountered along the trail.

You can start the trail from either end; from the north end of the South Rim Campground in Loop C or from the South Rim Visitor Center at Gunnison Point. (We recommend starting from the campground, reserving the most spectaclar views for the finish.) You can also pick up the trail at the Tomichi Overlook, at about the half-way point. There's water and rest rooms at each end of the trail.

The sunny trail meanders in and out of the *pygmy forest,* pausing for frequent dramatic views into the gorge. (This trail is suitable for kids; but keep a close watch on them, as there are several steep dropoffs.) Nearer to Gunnison Point, you'll notice several detached **monoliths** (or *islands*) just out from the canyon walls, created where erosion has attacked cracks and widened fissures. Keep an eye out for birds, such as hawks, ravens and swifts, that use these as safe resting spots and launching points.

A view east from Tomichi Point along the trail.

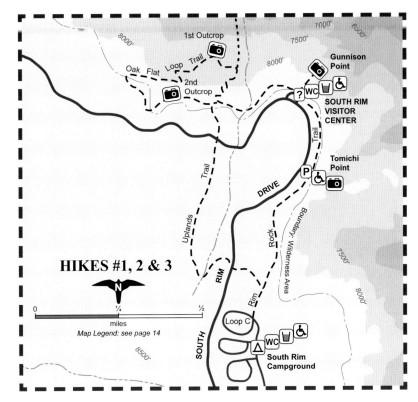

OAK FLAT LOOP TRAIL

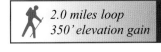

2.0 miles loop
350' elevation gain

2

This hike dips into the unique environment beneath the rim of the canyon, without the commitment and challenge required for a descent all the way to the river. Begin at the South Rim Visitor Center, hiking west, then following the signed route as it drops through quaking aspen and thickets of Gambel oak into the ravine. In a short distance, you'll encounter a sign for the *Gunnison Route*, a route to the river (see **Inner-Canyon Routes**, page 196.) Instead, go left here as the Oak Flat Trail continues through the oaks to an outcrop; a great place to rest, have some lunch and enjoy a view of the canyon.

The trail turns west, then rises through oak brush intermixed with cool stands of aspen and Douglas fir. These ravines are **microclimates** where species of plants, not normally found at this elevation, can thrive because of moist soils, shaded from evaporation by the sun. A relatively lush environment is created that supports not only trees, but other moisture loving plants, including serviceberries and wildflowers such as *Indian paintbrush* and *larkspur*. Animals, especially birdlife, and insects find this an attractive place to live. Mule deer rest in these cool thickets during the heat of the day, climbing back up to the rim to feed in the early evening.

Another overlook is reached before the trail traverses back up the ravine and turns east, paralleling the South Rim Drive, to complete the loop back to the Visitor Center. Currently, the Park Service is planning to extend the Oak Flat Trail an additional 2 miles or so west to Pulpit Rock Overlook.

UPLANDS TRAIL

Had enough of gazing down into the "big hole?" Well, the Uplands Trail has none of that — in fact, you may wonder where the canyon went on this short path

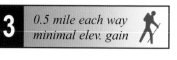

3 *0.5 mile each way minimal elev. gain*

A thick stand of Gambel oak.

Soil is poor along the rims. Low rainfall, combined with a short growing season at this elevation, means the soil here is little more than dry gravel in most places. **Gambel oak** grow into low, stunted thickets in these harsh conditions; but in places, such as along seasonal creek beds where soil has built up and moisture content is better, these oaks can grow into sturdy 30-foot tall trees. The mast crop (acorns) are winter food for **mule deer** and some birds. Hiking along the Uplands Trail in the evening provides opportunities to spot deer emerging from their daybeds in the tangled thickets. **Scrub jays**, perched atop the oak shrubs, will scold you with their raucous call as you pass.

which has absolutely no views of the gorge. However, this is a pleasant hike through a typical uplands environment with a good chance for seeing wildlife, especially early or late in the day.

The best place to park is at the South Rim Visitor Center, then walk west up the road for a hundred yards. After a dog leg in the road where it turns northwest, a small sign on the left marks where the Upland Trail goes south along the right side of a shallow drainage. Hike gently uphill, cross a small ravine in 0.25 mile, and top out in a mature, Gamble oak forest with trees up to 20 feet tall.

The trail is a little faint in the gravelly soil. Walk alongside the dry ravine, then cross it on a small log bridge and turn briefly north before the trail rises to meet the South Rim Drive. This is the end — either turn to retrace your steps, or better yet, cross the road and follow the short path east to hook up with the Rim Rock Trail (see Hike #1). Turn left and follow that trail back to the Visitor Center.

CEDAR POINT NATURE TRAIL

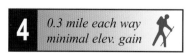

4 *0.3 mile each way minimal elev. gain*

This very short nature trail leads to a pair of overlooks, situated directly across from the famous **Painted Wall**, Colorado's highest cliff. Interpretive signs along the way describe the local flora and fauna.

WARNER POINT NATURE TRAIL

0.75 mile each way *200' elevation gain*	**5**

This hike, which honors Rev. Mark T. Warner, a Montrose citizen who fought hard and eloquently for the establishment of the original National Monument, starts at the west end of South Rim Drive at the parking lot for the High Point Picnic Area. There's a pamphlet at the trailhead, *A Walk With Mark Warner*, that describes features that are indicated by numbered posts along this nature trail.

The trail leads west along the high ridgeline, losing and gaining elevation along the way. There are shady benches thoughtfully placed at intervals so that you may study the local flora of the *pygmy forest* — pinyon pine, Utah juniper, mountain mohagany, serviceberry — or you may just study your navel! Rested and refreshed, continue on up the trail to be rewarded with wonderful views in all directions. Looking south you can see the mountain front of the beautiful San

Juan Mountains rising above the Uncompahgre Valley. To the north are the equally stunning West Elk Mountains. Good views of the river and gorge greet you at the end of the trail. Despite the name, the Warner Point Trail stops at a high ridge point just east of Warner Point.

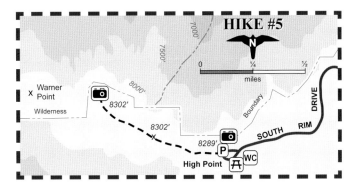

Toward the west end of South Rim Drive, the **pygmy forest** grades from scrub oak into a pinyon pine/juniper woodland, much in evidence along the Warner Point Trail. **Pinyon pines** are a familiar tree in The West, important as a food source for many animals and for people too that still collect the tasty nuts. It's hard to imagine that if present conditions continue, the state could lose most of its pinyon pines in just a few short years.

The culprit is a tiny insect, the **ips beetle**, sometimes known as the "engraver beetle." Helped by a four-year drought that has weakened the resistance of the trees, ips beetle infestation has exploded over the past few years. In some areas of Colorado, losses have been put already at 50% of pinyon pines. Perhaps 50% of the state's 1.7 million acres of pinyon pines are now infested, and some authorities have even begun using the word "extinction."

Pinyon pines.

Beetle larvae burrow into the tree's nutrient-rich cambium layer and feed; eventually girdling the tree and killing it. The bugs are highly dependent on weakened trees; only a return to normal rainfall patterns will end the plague.

You may see the distinctive **pinyon jay** close by, named for its preference for nesting in these pines.

Hikes in the Park: North Rim Trails

While there are few developed trails on the **North Rim** of the National Park, you're not likely to complain of overcrowding. North Rim trails receives far fewer visitors than do those on the South Rim — yet scenic rewards and chances to spot wildlife are exceptional on the less-visited side. In fact, most hikers would agree that **Exclamation Point** is the most thrilling and spectacular overlook in the Park. And birders find that avian life abounds in the varied habitats of the North Rim.

Hikers need to be aware that there is some cattle grazing allowed on the North Rim — be sure to keep all gates closed. Also, horses are allowed on the **Deadhorse Trail**. Hikers should give riders the right-of-way, stepping off the trail and avoiding any sudden movements. Get an early start and bring plenty of water, as it can get hot on these south facing slopes. The North Rim Road is closed from about late November to April, effectively closing down these trails for the winter (although the Park is still open to intrepid skiers or snowshoers.)

CHASM VIEW NATURE TRAIL

Located at the end of the one-way loop in the North Rim Campground, this short walk visits two overlooks on the rim.

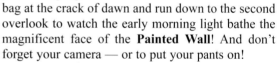

6 *0.3 mile loop*
minimal elev. loss

Get out of your sleeping bag at the crack of dawn and run down to the second overlook to watch the early morning light bathe the magnificent face of the **Painted Wall**! And don't forget your camera — or to put your pants on!

You can pick up a copy of the self-guide *Beyond The Brink of Time* at the ranger station.

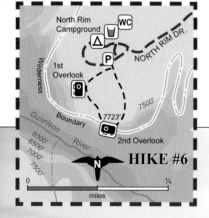

HIKE #6

Wave! Those folks opposite you on the South Rim are less than a quarter of a mile away.

NORTH VISTA TRAIL TO EXCLAMATION POINT

Don't miss this one! The views alone are breathtaking. The trailhead is at the **North Rim Ranger Station**. You can tank up with water at the campground, just up

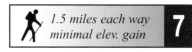

1.5 miles each way
minimal elev. gain

7

the road. The beginning of the trail is along a maintained gravel path, encountering a gate in about 50 yards. After the gate, the next 100 yards of the trail passes through an area of sagebrush and oak thickets. For the next 0.25 mile, descend into an area of concentrated Gamble oak, with some reaching a height of 10 feet. The trail switchbacks a few times, leaving the oak thickets behind, and enters sparse stands of western red cedar, Utah juniper, and stunted and dead ponderosa pines. It is obvious that the existing forest is a transitional one, as most of the pines have died and given way to the cedars and junipers.

At mile 0.5 is a marker indicating the first of three undeveloped overlooks. The site is about 100 feet off the trail, nestled in sandstone boulders that rest on the edge of the canyon. The view of steep walls on the south side of the canyon is excellent, but the river can't be seen well from this point. Continuing on, the trail meanders, matching the configuration of the canyon rim, until it arrives at a sign marking the second overlook at mile 0.75. The view is even better here; but the location requires great caution, as the edge is abrupt and there are no rails or barriers. Keep a close eye on children; don't allow them to run ahead on the trail!

But the best is saved for last! At mile 1.5, a marked path leaves the main trail and follows the rim for about 250 feet. At this point, the path forks — the right one continues along the rim, while the left one cuts through the trees and meets up with the other at a large open area with wonderful views of the canyon. Parents with young kids should use this approach, as there is less exposure to the rim from this direction.

No arguments here — this spot deserves an *exclamation point!* Falling away before you is the stupendous canyon; its nearly vertical walls cut deeply by the relentless river whose roar drifts up on the breeze. If your companions are brave enough to approach the edge of the 2,000-foot deep defile, take their picture — *just don't ask them to take one step back!* Enjoy the views and keep on eye out for birds cruising out over the gorge.

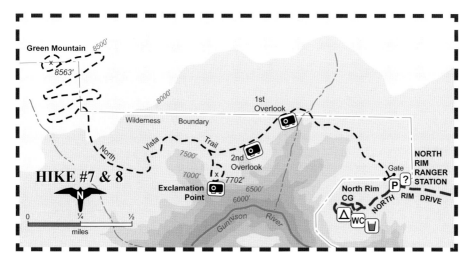

PEREGRINES

There's a vertical order to the air and sky above the canyon. Little speedsters, swallows and swifts, zip around just beyond and below the rim. Above them are the hunters — prairie falcons and peregrine falcons perched intently on high ledges or cruising the air; or American kestrels, hovering on rapid wingbeats. Gliding on thermals above them are ravens or soaring in wide circles are golden eagles and red-tailed hawks. Higher still, circling effortlessly for hours over large areas in search of carrion, are turkey vultures.

Exclamation Point is an excellent spot to observe birds on the wing, as it is

The view downstream at Exclamation Point.

situated atop the Painted Wall, where peregrines and other birds nest in isolated "scrapes" on ledges high on the cliff. Once endangered by over-use of pesticides (in particular DDT) and loss of habitat, peregrines have made a remarkable comeback, mostly because of a recovery effort, begun in Colorado, which included releasing 4,000 captive-raised birds in 28 states since 1974. In the Rockies and the Southwest, peregrines numbered 559 breeding pairs in 1994, a success that lead to delisting from the Endangered Species List in 1999.

Known for "stooping", a vertical dive at speeds up to 200 mph that knocks its feathered prey out of the air, peregrines are successful only 10-30% of the time and must hunt over a 10-mile range during breeding to feed the 3-5 nestlings. Fledglings leave the area in July.

Peregrine falcon

NORTH VISTA TRAIL TO GREEN MOUNTAIN

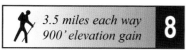

*3.5 miles each way
900' elevation gain*

8

A fantastic aerial view of the Black Canyon's "big bend" awaits you on the summit of this high point. Follow the North Vista Trail from the North Rim Ranger Station as far as the turnoff for Exclamation Point (see **Hike #7**, page 177, for directions.) From there, the high point of the trail is some two miles away. The first mile of the trail begins to move away from the canyon's edge, very gradually heading up the south slope of Green Mountain. The size and density of the trees, now primarily pine and cedars with a few junipers, increases. Buffalo grass, yucca , and shrubs fill in most of the open spaces.

After a mile from the Exclamation Point turnoff, there's a cattle fence with a ladder to allow hiker-access. The trail works its way up the slope, approaching the base of the ridge. In the process, it crosses over two ravines, rising above a meadow that borders the rim of the canyon. Panoramic views are available along this portion of the trail — from here on up, the hiker is well above the level of both the north and south rims of the canyon.

After a sharp turn north at the base of the ridge, the trail begins the first of several switchbacks that accomplish most of the hike's elevation gain. The slope steepens from one switchback to the next, with occasional rock cairns to mark the trail. At the last switchback, the trail crosses a section of scree, then climbs up through some rock steps. Once clear of these minor obstacles, the high point is just a short walk away. On top there's a loop; the right juncture penetrates a dense thicket of Gamble oak, while the left half of the loop swings around to the north and west. Coming together again on the summit, you're afforded an magnificent view of a large portion of the canyon and the surrounding countryside. Off to the southwest, on a clear day, the rugged peaks of the **San Juan Mountains** are easily spotted. To the north is massive **Grand Mesa** and 15 miles to the east are the old volcanic peaks and mesas of the **West Elk Mountains**.

Best of all, you have a grand *bird's-eye* look down into the "big bend"at The Chasm, where the river has carved a remarkably sharp turn to the southwest. You'll kick yourself if you forgot your camera for this one!

An aerial view of the canyon's "big bend."

DEADHORSE TRAIL

The Deadhorse Trail is an enjoyable walk through stands of scrub oak, serviceberry and across sagebrush meadows to several remote overlooks in the eastern part of the Park. Despite being rated as moderate because of its distance, this is really a gentle hike with little elevation gain. Be alert for horses, as this double track (an old jeep rail) is the only trail in the Park open to riding. Also, on some of the land on the North Rim, cattle grazing is allowed.

9 — *2.5 mile each way / 300' elevation gain*

Start your hike at the parking area for **Kneeling Camel View**. Walk 100 yards east on North Rim Drive, then turn onto an old road heading north. Soon you'll come to several small buildings, remnants of the original ranger station on the North Rim. Go right at a junction and descend slightly over the next 0.5 mile to cross **Poison Spring Draw**. This drainage is one of the few in the Park to maintain some flow into early summer. Hike east uphill out of the draw and pass a stock pond on your left, bearing along a fence line. Shortly you'll come to a trail marker where you may turn south to visit a pair of overlooks with fine views across the canyon at **Gunnison Point** and **Tomichi Point** on the South Rim. For a shorter hike, either overlook can be your final destination for the day.

Otherwise, the overlook side trail loops back northeast away from the rim in 0.25 mile to rejoin the main trail. Follow it southeast, then turn south along a stock fence to the third, and final, overlook above **Deadhorse Gulch**. Here you have an excellent look upriver all the way to **East Portal**.

The old ranger station.

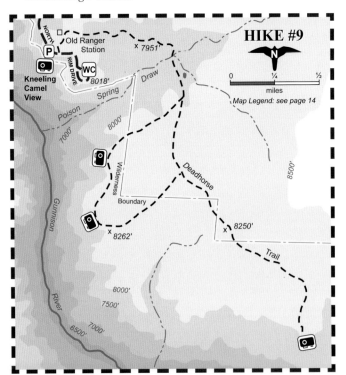

HIKE #9

N

0   ¼   ½
miles
Map Legend: see page 14

HIKING WITH YOUR DOG

*A*hh Fido — he'd ask for nothing more on a hot summer day than the chance to plunge into a cool pool in the Gunnison River. But if it's your idea to make that doggie dream come true in the three units described in this book, there's some not-so-good news; there's some pretty good news; and there's something to really wag your tail about.

First let's dispense with the not-so-good. The Park Service has never taken a liking to dogs in National Parks, related to fears of harassing wildlife or bothering other visitors; and in most National Parks, dogs are not even allowed beyond your car or your campsite. But **Black Canyon of the Gunnison National Park** allows some exceptions. You are permitted to hike with your dog, leashed of course, on some of the short trails on the South Rim — including the Rim Rock Trail and the Cedar Point Nature Trail. You *cannot* bring your canine companion along on the Oak Flat, Uplands and Warner Point Trails. On the North Rim, your dog on a leash is welcome on the Chasm View Nature Trail and the Deadhorse Trail, but *not* the North Vista Trail. And while your pooch may visit any of the overlooks in the Park, it can only gaze longingly down at the Gunnison River. Pets are *not allowed* in the Inner-Canyon or in the designated wilderness. Nor in winter are they permitted on the unplowed road beyond the South Rim Visitor Center. Area pet boarding kennels are listed on page 227.

Despite the fact that **Curecanti National Recreation Area** is also administered by the Park Service, your pooch will find a lot more to like about the NRA. Dogs are welcome on all the trails, although they *must be leashed throughout the recreation area.* Since most trails in the NRA lead to water, your dog will

Cooling off in the Gunnison River at the foot of the Hermits Rest Trail.

love it. But be cautious; with the chance of unannounced releases from the dams, the waterways along the Pine Creek and Mesa Creek Trails may not be safe for your dog.

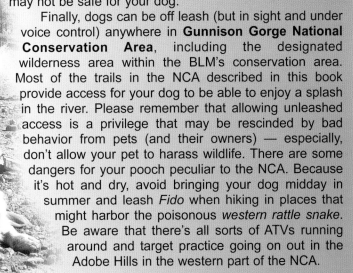

Finally, dogs can be off leash (but in sight and under voice control) anywhere in **Gunnison Gorge National Conservation Area**, including the designated wilderness area within the BLM's conservation area. Most of the trails in the NCA described in this book provide access for your dog to be able to enjoy a splash in the river. Please remember that allowing unleashed access is a privilege that may be rescinded by bad behavior from pets (and their owners) — especially, don't allow your pet to harass wildlife. There are some dangers for your pooch peculiar to the NCA. Because it's hot and dry, avoid bringing your dog midday in summer and leash *Fido* when hiking in places that might harbor the poisonous *western rattle snake*. Be aware that there's all sorts of ATVs running around and target practice going on out in the Adobe Hills in the western part of the NCA.

Hikes in Curecanti NRA

Known more for its water-based recreation, uninformed hikers don't know that **Curecanti National Recreation Area** has many excellent places to hike; offering everything from short nature walks, to backpacking trips deep into the canyon. The range of habitats explored is very diverse and there are opportunities to view some of the area's unique wildlife.

You don't need to obtain a permit or pay a day-use fee to hike at Curecanti NRA, or to use and enjoy several primitive campsites in the NRA, some of which are accessible by trail (more are accessed by boat only.) Curecanti NRA is open year-round and some of these trails are suitable for snowshoeing or cross-country skiing. Curecanti NRA shares most of its northern boundary with the **Gunnison National Forest**. Some of these hikes actually originate in the National Forest before passing into the NRA (and there are unlimited opportunities for other hikes within the NF.) We list the hikes east to west in the NRA.

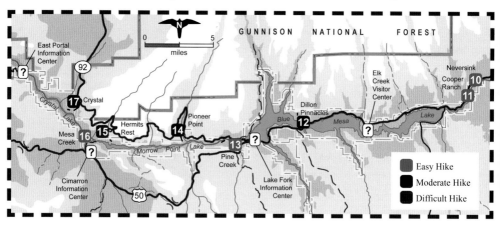

NEVERSINK TRAIL

10 *0.75 miles each way minimal elev. gain*

The pretty Neversink Trail is a favorite with birders because of its proximity to a **great blue heron** rookery. This flat, easy-to-follow trail is wheelchair accessible, winding its way along the north bank of the Gunnison River through a riparian environment of cottonwoods, willows and wildflowers. There are benches to rest at along the way, perfect for observing the rich bird life. The river is sometimes wadeable, attracting fisherman and children intent on exploring around the pools and shallows. (If the river is wadeable, the trail actually continues on the far side, meandering south to cross a second channel of the river.)

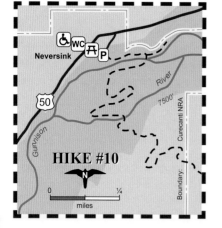

The trail leads east from the parking lot of the **Neversink Picnic Area**, 5 miles west of Gunnison off the south side of US-50. Pick up a *Neversink Trail Guide* at the parking area.

COOPER RANCH TRAIL

11 · *0.25 mile each way, minimal elev. gain*

Less than 1.0 mile west on US-50 from the Neversink Picnic Area is another pretty spot along the river. The Cooper Ranch Trail begins in the parking lot of the picnic area with the same name. Once again, the river is often wadeable here and you can follow trails along either bank. The easy trail goes west, in and out of groves of cottonwood, brush and grassy meadows. Eventually the "good" trail peters out; but a fainter, "fisherman's" trail continues along the river all the way to the north shore of Blue Mesa Reservoir. The access road to the picnic area is closed in winter, but you can park out at the gate closure and walk, ski or 'shoe in.

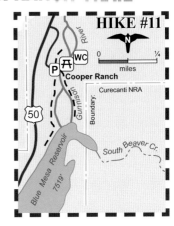

DILLON PINNACLES TRAIL

12 · *2.0 mile each way, 300' elevation gain*

The interesting Dillon Pinnacles Trail explores the contrast between the semi-arid landscape, with its weirdly-eroded volcanic pinnacles, and Blue Mesa Reservoir. Drive west on US-50 for 21 miles from Gunnison and turn off into the parking area at the north end of **Middle Bridge**, which spans the lake. Walk down toward the boat ramp and take a right turn onto the path. It follows the shore of the reservoir a short distance, then climbs through open sagebrush before dropping into Dillon Gulch. At a fork with a jeep track (which continues up the gulch), go left and, traversing below the pinnacles, reach a lookout point marked by a short loop. There are wonderful views of the lake, the distant San Juan Mountains and the pinnacles, with benches along the way and plaques

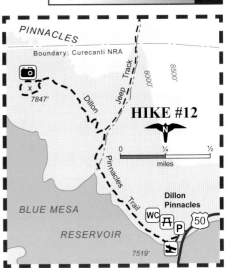

that explain the geology. The rock is a conglomerate called **breccia**, formed by volcanic activity north in the West Elk Mountains, then carved by erosion into strange shapes called *hoodoos*. For a longer, harder hike, go north up the jeep track in the gulch for about 1.0 mile, then bushwhack left (west) steeply up to the top of the mesa for fantastic views.

PINE CREEK TRAIL

This short, popular trail provides access to the Black Canyon below Blue Mesa Dam for hikers, fisherman, boaters (hand-carried craft only) and especially, for those taking the ranger\led boat tour on

| **13** | *1.0 mile each way*
200' elevation loss |

Morrow Point Reservoir (see page 150 for more details about this informative tour.) The handsome Pine Creek Trail descends 180-feet into the canyon via 232 steps, following lovely Pine Creek as it cascades merrily down to the river. There's an overlook along the way with an upstream view of the nearly 400-foot tall face of **Blue Mesa Dam**, straddling the canyon's steep walls.

The trail crosses the creek, then descends to the riverbank, where you stroll west along the old narrow gauge railroad bed beside the river to the launch point for the boat tour. The path follows the route of the so-called **Denver and Rio Grande Western's** *"Scenic Line of the World"* which plied through the eastern end of Black Canyon for nearly 70 years. Interpretive signs along the way explain the history and geology of the area. There are several picnic tables that offer shady resting spots. At times of low water, you may continue along the historic rail bed beyond the boat launch, to a point where it is submerged by the lake waters.

To get to the trailhead for the Pine Creek Trail, head west on US-50 for 1.0 mile beyond its junction with CO-92. Turn right at the sign unto a steep road (trailers need to be dropped off at the top) and follow it shortly to a small parking area.

Looking west along the Pine Creek Trail.

CURECANTI CREEK TRAIL

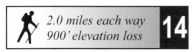

**2.0 miles each way
900' elevation loss   14**

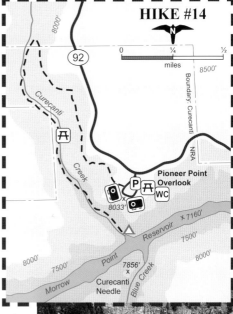

Lovely **Curecanti Creek**, rollicking, tumbling, crashing down to **Morrow Point Reservoir**, is the highlight of this potential overnight trip that descends from the north rim of upper Black Canyon to the lake's shore. While most folks choose to hike it as a day trip (about 2-3 hours round-trip), fine campsites at the bottom, with good fishing and a view of the famous Curecanti Needle, encourage a lingering stay.

The hike begins at the **Pioneer Point Overlook**, off CO-92, 5.7 miles west of its junction with US-50. Take a moment to check out the railed overlooks for one of the best views in Curecanti NRA. Your route descends the canyon to the west. Follow the sign from the parking lot, traversing northwest down through open pine and scrub forest. Once into the canyon alongside the cascading creek, the trail turns south and becomes steeper, descending through rock steps, alongside talus slides and crossing the creek on two foot bridges. About half-way down, there's a pretty picnic area set in a meadow with table and grill.

The trail ends where the creek spills out into a small inlet on the reservoir. Nearby are a couple of tent sites with picnic tables, fire grates and an outhouse. The sites are free — first-come, first-served — shared by both hikers and kayakers on the reservoir. Across the inlet and the narrow lake, towers the 700-foot spire of the **Curecanti Needle**. Once world-famous as the marketing symbol for the D&RG's rail line through the upper part of Black Canyon, it's made up of **Curecanti quartz monzonite**, a light-colored, fine-grained granite, widely exposed in the upper canyon.

Curecanti Creek descends in a foaming torrent.

HERMITS REST TRAIL

This is the most strenuous hike in Curecanti NRA; but although it's rated *difficult* due to the elevation that must be regained on the return, the trail is of high standard with plenty of switchbacks to

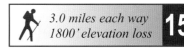

**3.0 miles each way
1800' elevation loss   15**

spread out the rise and with benches thoughtfully placed for resting. Bring lots of water — there's none along the way and this south-facing slope can get pretty warm when climbing out on a summer afternoon.

From the junction of CO-92 and US-50, drive 17 miles west on CO-92 to a sign for **Hermits Rest**. Hop on the trail at the west end of the parking lot and begin zigzagging down the long, looping switchbacks through sage and scrub oak

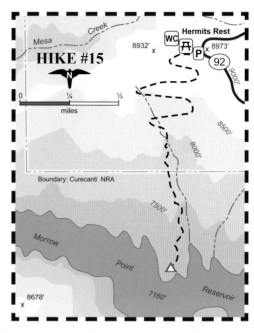

Dog tired? Rest on benches along the way.

with an occasional big pine for shade. The bottom half of the trail is steeper, arriving at a pine and fir-dotted lakeshore with numerous tentsites, picnic tables, fire grates and an outhouse.

It will take at least 4 1/2 hours round-trip, but why hurry? This is a very remote part of **Morrow Point Reservoir** with only the occasional tour boat or kayaker to interrupt your contemplation of this beautiful spot. Stay and camp — the nights are dead quiet, except for the soft lapping of the lake against the shore, the eerie call of a coyote, and maybe, the ghostly whistle of the former D&RG train, echoing faintly through the gorge.

MESA CREEK TRAIL

16 *0.75 mile each way*
100' elevation loss

From a vantage point on a bridge that spans the river below **Morrow Point Dam**, you get a true appreciation for the extreme depth and narrowness of the Black Canyon. The Mesa Creek Trail is the only dry-land crossing of the gorge open to the public between where CO-92 bridges the canyon at Blue Mesa Dam and that highway's second crossing of the river nearly 50 miles downstream. The trail continues a short distance beyond the bridge along the north shore of the river.

To get to the Mesa Creek Trail, turn north on to the Morrow

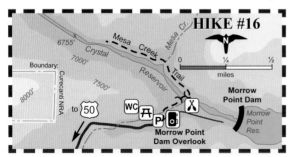

Point Dam Road, next to the **Cimarron Information Center**, 35 miles west of Gunnison and 30 miles east of Montrose on US-50. Follow the paved road for 1.0 mile to the Morrow Point Dam Overlook, passing an exhibit on the left from the old Denver and Rio Grande Western line. The site of the present dam is where the old rail line bridged over from the north shore; and giving in to the sheer walls of the Black Canyon, climbed out by way of Cimarron Creek. The small piece of trestle and the train sitting on it are remnants from that past.

From the picnic area, follow the path down to the river and cross the steel footbridge to a picnic spot on the far bank. Morrow Point Dam, the tallest of the three dams, is an impressive sight upriver. The trail continues west, gently up and down along the wooded shoreline, until it's cliffed out by the narrowing canyon walls.

CRYSTAL CREEK OVERLOOK TRAIL

Beginning in the National Forest at the **Crystal Picnic Area**, off CO-92 and 24 miles west of its junction with US-50, the Crystal Creek Overlook Trail winds along a ridge to two exceptional viewspots with

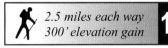

2.5 miles each way
300' elevation gain

17

abundant blooms of wildflowers along the way. The trail begins at the sign in the parking lot, traveling through scrub oak and sagebrush, then switchbacking up through Douglas fir, ponderosa pine and juniper. Benches along the way provide spots to rest and enjoy the unfolding views of the surrounding mountains.

Crossing unnoticed into Curecanti NRA, you'll reach a fork in the trail. Take the right fork and descend slightly through an area recovering from a fire in 1974. Wildflowers can be pretty here, including *Indian paintbrush* and *purple aster*. Shortly, arrive at the Crystal Lake Overlook, some 1,600 feet above the narrow reservoir. Below is Crystal Creek's deeply-etched side canyon feeding into the multi rock-spired depths of the Black Canyon.

Return to the fork and take the left-hand route to a second marvelous overlook atop the 9,000-foot high point of the ridge. Here you have a 360-degree sweep that includes the **West Elk Mountains** to the north and the long, beautiful Cimarron Valley backed by the rugged **San Juan Mountains** to the south. This is an especially wonderful place to be in the autumn, with the aspen and oak in their gorgeous fall colors and with snow on the distant mountains.

To the south are the San Juan Mountains.

Hikes in Gunnison Gorge NCA

Hiking in **Gunnison Gorge National Conservation Area** can be more of a intense wilderness experience than on the manicured trails of the Park Service. The primitive trails within the NCA are often not as clearly distinguished, requiring good navigation skills; and you'll need sturdy footwear to negotiate the steep ups and downs, sometimes on scree or bare rock.

Most hikes in the NCA are "river trails" providing access for hikers, backpackers, equestrians, fisherman and river runners to the Gunnison River, the lifeblood of the gorge. You'll need to pay the day-use fee and sign-in at the trailhead (see page 112-113 for details) before entering the **Gunnison Gorge Wilderness Area** which makes up most of the inner canyon and river corridor. If you plan to camp in the wilderness area, you'll have to register for a designated site and pay a fee for that as well. There are no fees for activities in that part of the NCA outside the wilderness area (see the map on page 115.)

While the cliffy terrain of the inner gorge discourages off-trail travel, it's easy to hike cross-country almost anywhere on the sage flats or gray and yellow adobe domes that make up the western third of the NCA; although you may have to contend with ORVs, motorcycles, mountain bikes or horseback riders. Four access roads that reach developed trailheads on the west rim, the Chukar, Bobcat, Duncan and Ute Roads are described in this guide. But there are several other former jeep trails and old mine roads that originate in Peach Valley and climb up to the pinyon/juniper-clad west rim of the gorge, providing alternatives for hikers who wish to get away from it all.

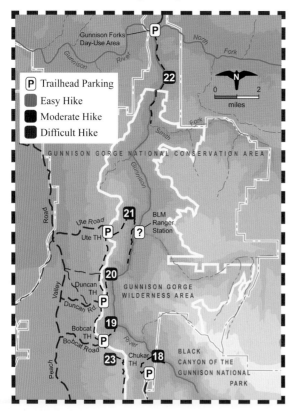

With relatively little snowfall, you can hike year-round at the NCA; but certain times of the year, especially spring, can produce wet access roads that become nearly impassable. While some of the trailheads can be reached in a regular passenger vehicle when the roads are dry, four-wheel drive is strongly recommended in any season. Summer temperatures can be quite hot, so get an early start on your hike. The seasonal streamcourses and the few, old stock ponds in the area are unreliable sources for water. So bring plenty of drinking water.

While the trails that originate on the west rim are in typical canyon country, with arid hillsides of sagebrush, juniper, Mormon tea and prickly-pear cactus, be alert along the river banks for **poison ivy** among the tall grass and heavy brush.

CHUKAR TRAIL

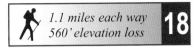

*1.1 miles each way
560' elevation loss*

18

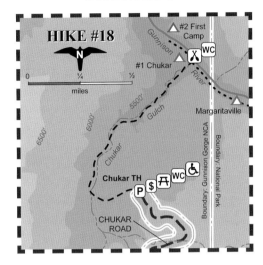

HIKE #18

#2 First Camp
#1 Chukar
Margaritaville
Gunnison River
Chukar Gulch
Chukar TH
CHUKAR ROAD
Boundary, Gunnison Gorge NCA
Boundary, National Park
0   ¼   ½
miles
6500'   6000'   5500'

The Chukar Trail, the shortest of the four "river trails" from the west rim, is the most heavily used trail in the NCA, especially in spring or early summer when higher water levels draw white-water enthusiasts. Weekend paddlers carrying their gear down to the put-in (or horsepackers doing the heavy lifting) can keep the trail busy, but off-season hikers may have the place to themselves.

To get there, head north from Montrose on US-50 for 9.0 miles and turn right on Falcon Road. travel 3.5 miles to the end of the pavement, then follow the road left as it becomes **Peach Valley Road**. Drive 5.1 miles from the highway to the BLM sign for the **Chukar Road**. Turn right to follow the Chukar Road 7.0 miles to the trailhead, where you'll find a restroom and picnic facilities.

Sign-in and pay the required fees at the self-serve station at the trailhead, then follow the path down a winding course to the river bank through a narrow ravine. The route descends through the gorge's unique "double canyon" structure, passing from 1,000-foot thick, upper rock layers of pastel and buff-colored sandstones, mudstones and shales to the inner canyon carved from a darker, harder granite-like rock called *granodiorite.*

At the river is one campsite for hikers, a backcountry toilet and a river put-in. You can hike further on along the river, following a path south through scrub and over rock for less than a mile to some additional campsites within the National Park.

A view upstream into the National Park from the foot of the Chukar Trail.

BOBCAT TRAIL

19 *1.5 mile each way*
800 elevation loss

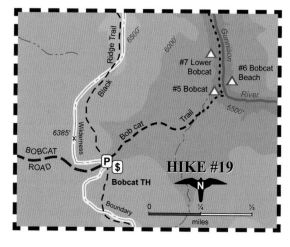

The somewhat difficult to follow Bobcat Trail is reached by taking the rough, 1.5-mile long **Bobcat Road** from its turnoff, 7.3 miles north on Peach Valley Road from US-50. At the trailhead, pay the day-use fee and register for your hike, then follow the trail east, descending steeply in the ravine. The last 0.25 mile is a steep descent down a rock face. Once at the river, there are two designated campsites for hikers. You can follow a primitive path downstream without too much trouble for about 1.5 miles, reaching the camps situated at the Duncan Trail access.

DUNCAN TRAIL

20 *1.5 mile each way*
900 elevation loss

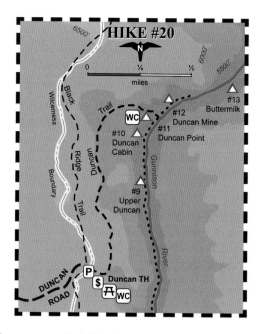

The Duncan Trail, another river access from the west rim of the gorge, is reached by continuing north on the Peach Valley Road for a total of 8.6 miles from US-50, then turn east on **Duncan Road** at the sign and drive 2.4 miles to the trailhead. There's a shady picnic area, restrooms, trail register and pay slot. The trail begins by descending slightly, then traversing north along the hillside for a 0.5 mile or so before starting a very steep descent over some loose scree to the river. To avoid the possibility of running into a problem, stay to the left in the last gully, cross below an old mine and climb slightly up a ridge, before dropping the last few hundred yards to the river. There are three hiker camps at the bottom, plus an outhouse. You can hike south along the river to reach the Bobcat Trail in about 1.5 miles. A hike north along the river soon runs into streamside rocks and cliffs near Buttermilk Rapids that limit further progress.

UTE TRAIL

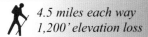

4.5 miles each way
1,200' elevation loss

21

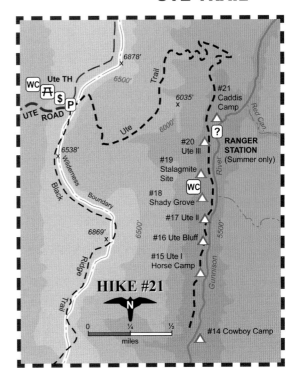

As the longest trail into the gorge from the west rim, the Ute Trail offers a pleasant grade, great views and a chance to take in and savor the wild landscape. Portions of the route were originally used by the Ute Indians in their annual migration from the Uncompahgre Valley to summer hunting grounds in the West Elk Mountains to the east. The trail access is by way of the **Ute Road**, located 11.4 miles north on Peach Valley Road from the US-50 turnoff. The rough, 2.5-mile long road climbs up to the trailhead (with picnic facilities, a restroom and fee-station) on the gorge rim.

The easy-to-follow trail soon descends to the southeast for 0.5 mile, before turning sharply northeast for a more gradual descent. The trail drops into the inner gorge through a series of steeper switchbacks, then turns and heads south to meet the river. There's a seasonal ranger station located here (open June through September); and you may continue hiking south along the west bank of the stream for quite aways, passing several pleasant campsites and a backcountry toilet, before encountering a rugged ridge running down to the river, blocking easy passage.

Exploring an
old mine along
the Ute Trail.

NORTH FORK TO SMITH FORK TRAIL

22 *4.0 mile each way*
200' elevation gain

If you'd like to experience the river up close, but don't relish a steep climb back out of the canyon on a hot day, perhaps this moderate river walk is right for you. Drive to the BLM's **Gunnison Forks Day Use** site off CO-92, 13 miles east of Delta. Turn right on paved CR-28.10 and follow the signs south for a mile. No day-use fee is required for this hike, even as you enter the northern bounds of the **Gunnison Gorge Wilderness Area**.

A view upstream from Gunnison Forks.

You'll need to get across the North Fork to access the east bank of the Gunnison River. While people do wade across during periods of low water, it is very dangerous and drownings have occurred. The safest course is to arrange at the nearby **Gunnison River Pleasure Park** for a ferry across. (Alternately, the Pleasure Park folks can take you upstream to Smith Fork by jet boat and you can hike back.)

Follow the dirt path south, never far from the shore of the stream. This stretch of river is wide and gentle, with many good fishing holes along the way. At times, the route becomes faint, scrambling up on benches 100 feet above the river, then dipping back down to shoreline.

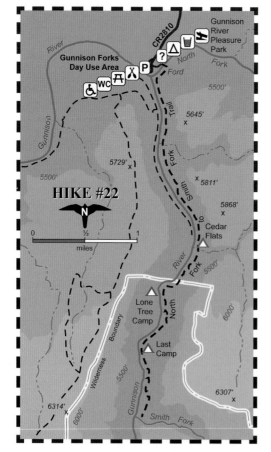

About halfway, arrive at a campsite at Cedar Flats at the mouth of a side-canyon that cuts abruptly into Scenic Mesa. The trail begins to climb again above the river as it enters the Wilderness Area, before dropping for a final time to the water's edge at Last Camp. Over the last 0.75 mile, traverse uphill in the narrowing canyon to a dramatic, trail-end overlook, 150 feet above the confluence with the **Smith Fork**.

BLACK RIDGE TRAIL

10.0 miles each way
1,950' elevation gain

23

The Black Ridge Trail follows the high ridge that defines the western rim of the gorge in the NCA, just outside the boundary of the Wilderness Area (no day-use fee is required.) All of the access roads climb up from **Peach Valley Road** to intersect the Black Ridge Trail, creating possibilities for hikes of varying lengths. To hike the entire trail would require a camp somewhere along the way. There is no water on the route, although you can drive up one of the access roads and stash a cache. Expect to share the trail with intrepid mountain bikers (see pgs. 144-148), horses and even motorcycles, especially the easier southern half of the route.

Starting at the south end, drive up the **Chukar Road** about 4.25 miles to the top of the ridge. The trail heads off to the left, passing a BLM trail sign and dropping to cross a gully, before grinding steeply up the nose of the ridge. At the top, the trail climbs and dips and winds through the pinyon-juniper forest, sometimes close to the edge of the cliffs, offering breathtaking views southeast to the towering black pinnacles of the Black Canyon of the Gunnison. A maze of roads and trails intersects the trail; stay right, along the edge of the cliff. Behind you are views of the adobe badlands and the impressive San Juan Mountains beyond.

From the 7,000-foot highpoint of the trail, descend steadily through the forest to the clearing of the **Bobcat trailhead**. Continue north, climbing again over the tops of several small peaks before dropping swiftly to the **Duncan trailhead** at mile 6.

This is a good turnaround point, as the route between Duncan and Ute trailheads is even more rugged. Another steep grind up a hill follows, before the trail begins to contour around several rugged peaks along the crest. Intersect a jeep track (Dinosaur Road) in another 1.5 miles, then begin a steady climb north along the rim to a saddle between a final summit pair. Below to the north, you'll see your destination in another mile at **Ute trailhead**.

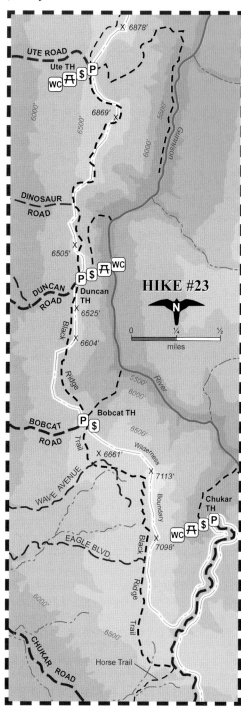

INNER-CANYON ROUTES

Looking down the Gunnison Inner-Canyon Route to the river.

Hiking the **Inner-Canyon** of Black Canyon of the Gunnison National Park can be a rewarding and fascinating adventure. The canyon's unique architecture, its great depth and complex geology, the remarkable adaptations of its plants and wildlife, and the thundering river itself are all things that add up to an experience long to be remembered. There are no maintained or marked trails into the designated **Wilderness Area** that makes up the Inner-Canyon, but several **primitive routes** have been established down to the canyon floor by hikers, fisherman, rock climbers and river runners. Only those in excellent physical condition, with strong route-finding skills should attempt any of these very strenuous routes. You are strongly urged to descend only well-established routes, for not all ravines go all the way to the river, and some may cliff out. While descending, carefully note your surroundings and memorize your route and any important landmarks, so as not to take a wrong turn on the return ascent.

We've noted the location of each route on the map on page 171. A box with each route lists the *one-way* **distance** and approximate **elevation loss** for that route. Of course, you'll have to make up that elevation loss on the return! Note that we don't assign a "difficulty" rating to any of these routes — they are all very difficult!

Canyoneering is often called "mountaineering in reverse." And whether you aspire to climb to a summit or to descend into a abyss, preparation is always essential. Read the following "do's and don'ts," observe the regulations, be cautious of the dangers, observe low impact hiking and camping techniques, and leave nothing but your footprints.

INNER-CANYON DO'S AND DON'TS

▌PERMITS: All activities in the Inner-Canyon require a free **backcountry permit**, available at the South Rim Visitor Center and the North Rim Ranger Station. Posted instructions also allow permits to be obtainable after-hours at those locations. The number of permits and free campsites are limited to protect the resources of the canyon. The rangers can monitor the safe conclusion of your adventure by letting them know your itinerary beforehand and returning your permit, or notifying the Park staff, at the end of your trip.

▌BE PREPARED: Bring high energy foods and at least one gallon (4 liters or quarts) of water per day. **Giardia** is present in the river, so be prepared to filter, purify or boil any drinking water. Wear stout footgear that protect and support ankles, not running shoes or sandals. Wear long-sleeved shirts and pants, plus light gloves to avoid cuts and abrasions while grabbing sharp rocks and brush for hand holds. Refer to the **Suggested Equipment List** on page 225 for day hikes or overnight trips. A hiker may gain a false sense at the ease of reaching the canyon floor, and then find the climb out arduous and time consuming. Plan carefully, start early, and allow plenty of time to hike out before sunset and cold sets in.

▌PROTECT THE WILDERNESS: You're a visitor to the Inner-Canyon and its wilderness environment. Practice **"Leave No Trace"** hiking and camping techniques. Don't harass or stress wildlife. Leave rocks, driftwood and all naturally occurring features in their natural state. Bring a camp stove, as fires are prohibited. Pets, firearms and hunting also are not allowed. Keep group sizes small and camp in established campsites only. Choose campsites wisely, remembering that releases from the dams upstream can cause the river level to rise in a short time. Bury human waste at least 6 inches deep and as far from the river as possible. Pack out your trash, including toilet paper.

▌BE CAREFUL: No developed trails exist into the canyon, so bushwhacking through heavy brush and scrambling on rock, scree or talus is the norm. Avoid jumping off boulders and follow the draws or sketchy human and animal paths that already exist. Loose rock abounds and a hiker can kick off rocks that endanger hikers below or set off rockslides. Always hike so that one hiker is never directly above or below another hiker.

Wading or swimming in the river is not recommended; nor should you attempt to cross the river and ascend a draw to the opposite rim. The river is deadly at flood stage and dangerous even when low. People have been swept to their deaths in the fast-moving waters of the Gunnison River.

*Y*ikes! **Poison ivy** is one of those things that people tend not to think about — unless you've had a nasty case of it in the past. But it's abundant in the ravines of the Inner-Canyon and along the riverbanks (but not on the rim); so learn to recognize, watch for and avoid this troublesome plant. It is a low-rambling, shrubby plant with three-fingered, shiny leaves, inconspicuous flowers and white-to-yellowish berries.

Every part of the plant can cause a skin rash — and at any time of the year. Wash the infected area immediately with soap and water. Anti-itch treatments or oral antihistamines may help some after the fact. But the smart strategy is **avoidance**, cover up any bare skin and, most important, wear gloves. It's almost impossible to keep from grabbing things on the way out of the canyon.

South Rim Routes

GUNNISON ROUTE

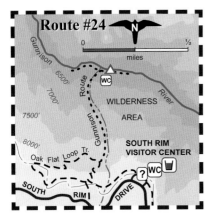

24 | *1.0 miles each way*
1,800' elev. loss

The Gunnison Route, one of the easier routes, is also the favored one for hikers into the Inner-Canyon. Plan on about 1.5 hours for the descent and 2 hours to return back up to the rim. Begin at the South Rim Visitor Center and follow the **Oak Flat Loop Trail** (see Hike #2, page 173) through aspen and oak thickets for 0.35 miles to the "river access" sign. An alternative start is to stay left (west) at the sign and follow the Oak Flat Loop Trail towards the prominent overlook, then drop over the bank just before the overlook. Circle

Descending with help from the chain.

around the promontory and down onto the slope. The trail is steep, with several trails made by previous hikers switchbacking down through the Douglas fir. Stay on the main route leading to the obvious draw, remaining in it except where terrain requires detours. The ridges are covered with loose rock and should be avoided. Avoid the right-hand draw, directly below the major overlook at Gunnison Point. It descends to the river; but it's very steep and made dangerous by loose rock.

Along the Gunnison Route in August are ripe gooseberries, currant, raspberries, chokecherries, serviceberries and fairybells; all thriving in the cool, moist soil of this shaded ravine. At about a third of the way down, there's an 80-foot length of chain to hold on to in negotiating some loose footing. Leaving the drainage near the bottom, angle diagonally to the right

One thin spire across the river is called the Dog's Paw.

through oak and serviceberry thickets to the river's bank. You then can explore about 300 yards in either direction along the river before being cut off by cliffs. Three primitive campsites and an outhouse are located upstream, beneath a tall, shady stand of ponderosa pine. Across the river are the Slide Rock and Poison Spring Routes, descending from the North Rim; and tall pinnacles and spires of gneiss and pegmatite called the **Great Pillars**.

ECHO CANYON ROUTE

Beautiful Echo Canyon was named by the major supporter for the establishment of the original National Monument, Reverend Mark Warner of Montrose. His shouts reverberating off the far canyon walls while he descended this route in the 1930s. From the parking lot for **Rock Point Overlook,** off the South Rim Drive, walk the short path toward the overlook and drop immediately right (east) into the steep, brush-choked draw. Pick a route from all of the admittedly poor choices available, through the thickets and broken, high-angle slopes, descending through oak and serviceberry brush until you reach a stand of Douglas fir on the left. The largest tree in the Park may be located here, a fine specimen — look for a large fir, stretching 85 feet high with a diameter of five feet.

0.75 mile each way
1,600' elev. loss

25

The drainage remains steep (but the brush becomes easier to pass through,) as you continue down the draw, with occasional scrambling and a *vegetable* hold here and there. The lower quarter of the descent is much more gentle, and soon, the river is easily attained. Mobility alongside the stream is limited, with overhanging cliffs blocking extended travel along the shoreline. But the area has abundant waterfalls and rapids, giant boulders and towering walls above a delightful camping area.

A short walk upstream brings you to **The Narrows**, where the sheer, dark walls are only forty feet apart — the narrowest point in the canyon. Just below the gap is the infamous rapids known as the **Falls of Sorrow**, where the unsuccessful expedition of 1900 had been forced to end their exploration of Black Canyon. Across the river from Echo Canyon is Long Draw, another Inner-Canyon route that descends from the North Rim

For climbers or scramblers used to exposure, a large, sloping rock, doming on the south side of The Narrows, takes the climber over steep slabs to a shelf and stands of Douglas fir and juniper. Ascending further around the corner, and south, takes one to a possible route up a long, unnamed draw or a return to the river by circling on around, above The Narrows. An overhanging chimney (watch for poison ivy) at the base provides a step to reach either of these routes.

TOMICHI ROUTE

Although the Tomichi Route is difficult over its entire length because of loose rock and full exposure to the sun,

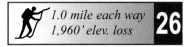

1.0 mile each way
1,960' elev. loss

26

fisherman find this entry point attractive, as it gives access to long stretches of the river during low water. Great care must be taken when descending to avoid knocking large rocks on hikers below; or even starting a general slide. Hikers can choose alternate routes to descend or ascend, since all the routes converge into one draw at about a third of the way down. You can begin the route from either the **South Rim Campground** or from the **Tomichi Point Overlook** on the South Rim Road.

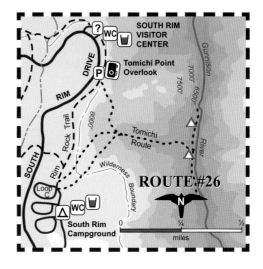

To begin from the campground, pick up the **Rim Rock Trail** (see Hike #1, page 172) near Loop C and take it to post #14, then backtrack 25 feet. The route begins here and descends steeply, meeting a junction with another draw. Follow the main drainage down the very loose, talus-covered slope to the river.

Another route begins in the campground as well. Begin either at Loop C, or the lower end of the amphitheater, and follow the sagebrush slope to the head of the draw, where there is a large stand of Douglas fir. Scramble through brush and down a boulder-covered slope to the junction with the route from Tomichi Point (see below). Trend to the right and continue down the slope to the river. A variation on this route involves heading to the left (west) side of a knife-edge ridge, paralleling the other campground route. This steep variation requires hands, but it's on a solid slab, rather than loose talus. The slabs are easier to ascend then descend. You can see and study this variation from Tomichi Point.

To start the route from Tomichi Point, drop into a brushy draw, south of the parking lot. It's pretty steep, very slippery in the upper section, and is probably best done as a descent route. Whichever route you choose, turn around often to memorize landmarks and your surroundings. While you may slip and slide down the draw in about 1.5 hours, count on your tedious ascent back up, with copious loose rock underfoot, to take about 3-4 hours.

You can stroll along the banks in both directions for quite aways. Downstream are large, deep pools for fisherman and good camping at one site. There are additional campsites near the foot of the draw.

WARNER ROUTE

The Warner Route is the longest, and perhaps, the most difficult of the South Rim descents. That's because it has a whopping 2,660 feet of elevation that must

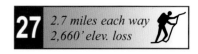

be gained on the return (although the slope is more gradual than other routes and the footing is somewhat better.) In any case, unless you're in truly great shape, you'll want to do this one as an overnight. And why not? For there is excellent camping with five spots along the river, great fishing on a Gold Medal stream (Colorado fishing license required), and a chance to spot bighorn sheep and river otters that have been reintroduced into the remote western wilderness of the Park.

Begin at the Warner Point trailhead, at **High Point**, at the west end of the South Rim Drive. Follow the **Warner Point Nature Trail** (see Hike #5, page 175) west to the third bench, shaded by a Douglas fir, where the trail then climbs a short distance and levels out. The Warner Route leaves the nature trail near a serviceberry bush (marked by descriptive plaque,) going left, away from the canyon. The route skirts around the backside of the point, passes the first drainage, and then continues west to the lowest saddle on the ridge. Turn north here, dropping through Douglas fir, and following an obvious path. But you need to

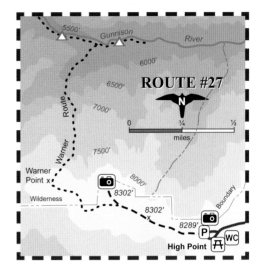

pay very close attention to the route, as several side drainages may make for confusion on the return. Near the bottom, cairns mark the way to the river. You can hike both upriver or downriver for about 0.5 mile, with good campsites along either route. There's a backcountry toilet as well. Allow about 2 to 2.5 hours for the descent, with the return trip taking up to 4 hours.

EAST PORTAL ROUTE

2.0 miles each way
300' elev. gain

28

The East Portal Route is for those that wish to get a taste of hidden depths of the Inner-Canyon, without suffering through the character-building experience of hauling themselves back out of the "big hole." From just inside the entrance station of the National Park on the South Rim Road (Park entrance fee is required), turn east and drive down the winding **East Portal Road** to the canyon bottom inside Curecanti National Recreation Area. A trail begins at the west end of the parking lot, by the **East Portal Campground**. You'll be passing into the National Park's designated wilderness, so you need to self-register for a **backcountry permit** at the trailhead station. From here, there's a route west into the canyon, a primitive trail along the south shore of the river, that involves little elevation gain or loss; but it does include a short,

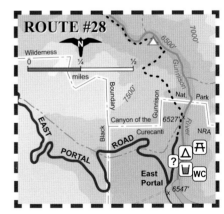

very exposed, scramble on a rock spine poised above the foaming torrent.

Begin by hiking downstream into the Park for 0.25 mile, until you encounter a long, rocky ridge (called the Devil's Backbone) blocking the route. Scramble up the ridge, following a faint trail, for about 100 yards. Cross the ridge and immediately traverse to the left, then drop into a steep gully leading back down to the river. That's the worst of it — from here on in, it's boulder hopping, with an occasional short scramble above the river, for a couple of miles downstream, before finally cliffed-out for good. There are several nice campsites and fishing pools to linger at.

North Rim Routes

S.O.B. DRAW ROUTE

29 | *1.8 miles each way*
1,800' elev. loss

Soaring buttresses and sheer cliffs loom above you on the route.

Despite any bad vibes from the name, the S.O.B. Draw Route is the most frequently traveled route to the river from the North Rim; and it's easy to see why. You can explore a long stretch of river downstream from The Chasm, with most of Black Canyon's highest and boldest cliffs looming above you. Vehicles may be parked in the pull-through near the **North Rim Campground** registration station, or at the **North Rim Ranger Station**. The route begins at the access ladder, along the fence line on the **North Rim Drive** about 100 feet east of the junction of the campground circle road, or a short distance west of the ranger station. Descend slightly through scrub oak, walk along a sage meadow, then traverse across the top of the drainage gully and descend on the far right of the ravine. Once you drop out of the heavy vegetation at the top of the route, things can get quite hot on a summer day. The descent is steep and loose the whole way, with a couple of small ledges of exposed pegmatite to scramble down through. Watch out for the lush growths of poison ivy in the gulch and along the river.

Once at the river, giant boulders make upstream travel nearly impossible. However, you can hike and boulder hop downstream for nearly two miles, encountering a half-a-dozen pleasant campsites on the way. Famous **Painted Wall** rises above the shoreline about a mile downstream from the draw. The trip down will take about 1.5 to 2 hours, with perhaps double that for the steep climb back out of S.O.B. Draw.

S.O.B. Draw from downstream.

WHAT'S PEGMATITE?

Pegmatite — in the form of countless dikes, sills, and irregular shapes and ranging from pencil thin threads, to massive outcrops — is seen from every overlook in Black Canyon. It is wonderfully abundant, a happy accident that has shaped the canyon's grand scenery. The striking, sinuous patterns of light-colored rock on famous **Painted Wall**, seen by every visitor to Chasm View, is pegmatite.

But while overlook visitors view from afar, hikers who venture into the canyon can scramble on, touch and see the stuff up-close. One of the things you might notice is how a pegmatite body often stands proud by several inches, or even feet, out from the matrix of surrounding rock. That's because this igneous rock is much harder than the metamorphic rocks, such as *schists* and *gneisses*, that make up in volume most of the structure of the canyon. (On several Inner-Canyon routes, it is often rugged outcrops of pegmatite that form any steep steps or ledges that the

Light patterns of pegmatite in a darker matrix of gneiss.

hiker must scramble or climb through.) Intruded into another, very resistant igneous rock, like *quartz monzonite*, the pegmatite erodes less boldly than the "country" (or base) rock; but it still forms striking tonal patterns against the darker base.

Pegmatite, while still molten, was forced (or "intruded") into existing cracks in the country rock, a billion years before the canyon formed. Up close, you'll see three main types of large crystals created by slow cooling of the magma: glittering **feldspars**, which are mostly pink; massive, milky-white **quartz** crystals; and sheets or books of **mica**, either black or — rare and somewhat valuable — clear sheets. Single crystals can be enormous at three, even six feet across.

As erosion has worked its way over the eons at Black Canyon stripping away weaker rock, towers, pinnacles, spires, fins, and razerbacks of pegmatite or, more often, of country rock buttressed by pegmatite have formed. Nearly free-standing, spectacular formations are often seen at river level at the foot of one of the Inner-Canyon routes; for instance, the aptly-named **Great Pillars** seen across the river from the Gunnison Route.

LONG DRAW ROUTE

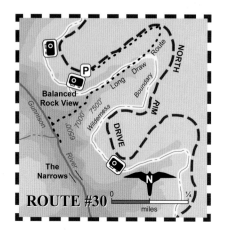

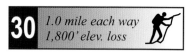

30 *1.0 mile each way*
1,800' elev. loss

The Long Draw Route begins at **Balanced Rock View** on the North Rim Drive, about 1.2 miles east of the junction with the North Rim access road. An early explorer appropriately named this narrow, shady corridor "Devil's Slide" for its loose footing, yet it is a relatively easy and direct descent of about 1.5 hours. Scrambling back up is another matter, taking about 3 hours.

Park at the overlook, then walk northeast to the bend in the road, where the descent begins past a wooden sign. Pass through a small stand of box elder at the rim and drop down the rubble-filled chute. About midway down is a narrow bottleneck that presents no real difficulty. At the foot of the draw, where you are opposite Echo Canyon, access along the shore of the river is limited to a few hundred yards; the poison ivy grows up to five feet tall; and camping is possible only at a few poor bivouac sites. Yet this is a special place of exceptional beauty, embodying the true nature of this wild gorge. A little ways upstream at **The Narrows**, the river is pinched tightly by sheer canyon walls (barely 40 feet apart) as it rushes down the steep gradient, thundering over short falls and pounding atop boulders. (You can only get so far towards The Narrows — the slabs leading to the top are deceptive, requiring climbing gear.)

A view west from the foot of Long Draw towards the bend at Chasm View.

SLIDE DRAW ROUTE

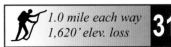

1.0 mile each way
1,620' elev. loss

31

Slide Draw is also known as Kneeling Camel Draw for the distinctive rock formation, located nearby. The route is notorious for — you guessed it — sliding rocks! A very steep and direct route to the river, some people swear by it. Most people swear at it. Begin just east of **Kneeling Camel View** on the North Rim Drive or walk west a short ways from the loop at the east end of the drive. A trail passes a sign announcing "Slide Draw" before dropping quickly into the narrow gully, steeped walled and floored with ever-shifting talus. Use great care in working your way down the loose field of rock. There's little vegetation to grab hold of and only the occasional bare spot for a trail. You'll find a good camping area downriver and some excellent fishing pools along the 0.75 mile stretch of river that is accessible. While you might slip and slide down in 1.5 hours, count on a tedious, teetering ascent, lasting up to 4 hours.

POISON SPRING ROUTE

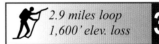

2.9 miles loop
1,600' elev. loss

32

Poison Spring Draw is one of the larger side canyons slicing down from the North Rim and requires scrambling ability and excellent route finding skills. But, it is possible to descend by one route and ascend by another, creating an interesting and challenging loop trip. Poison Spring Draw is east of the old North Rim Ranger Station, near the east end of the North Rim Drive. Park at the **Kneeling Camel View** and walk east along the drive for 0.1 mile. Begin hiking north on the service road, shortly reaching the abandoned ranger station. Turn east (right) on the **Deadhorse Trail** (see Hike #9, page 180) and follow this old jeep track for 0.75 mile to a broad, sagebrush draw. This ravine is one of the few carrying a large spring runoff into the canyon, lasting into the early summer months. Throughout the remaining summer season, water continues to drip from the rocks. Turn southwest and head down the draw, following game trails at first, then bushwhack and scramble as difficulties present themselves. Large, overhanging rocks force you to carefully pick your route; and near the bottom are some house-sized boulders that appear to be impassable. Descend by carefully skirting along the extreme right side of the wall, make a traverse to the left wall, and then scramble down a few steps to an easy slope.

Upstream walking is limited; but a hiker can descend Poison Spring Draw, scramble a short ways downstream and return to the rim by way of **Slide Draw** (see Route # 31), or vice verso. Two large boulders seem to block this possibility; but one may carefully pass them at river level during low water periods, or climb over if the water level is high. The entire loop will take 6 to 8 hours.

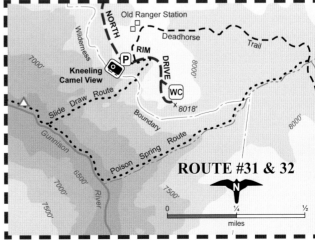

ROUTE #31 & 32

ROCK CLIMBING

With its remote circumstances, tick and poison ivy infested approaches, loose and unpredictable rock, challenging route finding, difficult and unprotected pegmatite bands, and long, committed routes of up to Grade VI, climbing in the Black Canyon of the Gunnison is not for novices or for climbers who are not fully competent in **free climbing** on big, remote walls. In fact, climbing at the Black Canyon — Colorado's version of Yosemite — is as much a form of mountaineering as it is pure rock climbing, dubbed "rockaneering" by Leonard Coyne, a pioneer of big routes at the canyon (see the *Rock and Ice* article by Coyne cited in *Additional Reading*, page 223.) The limited view of incoming weather or unforeseen problems on an otherwise "moderate" route can turn a pleasant day's outing into a nightmarish epic. Remember that every climber needs to be thinking "self rescue" in Black Canyon, as the gorge's remoteness and rugged terrain mean that your shouts for "help" are likely to be in vain. No helicopter will pluck you to safety and there is no rescue crew maintained at the Park. Still, for experienced, competent and committed climbers who can hack it, the fearsome "Black" offers some of North America's greatest rock climbing challenges in a wild and rugged setting.

A **standard rack** at the Black Canyon includes a full range of free climbing gear, — a couple sets of RPs and stoppers, two sets of cams, some off-width protection (such as *Big Bros* or larger *Tri-Cams* — plus a selection of hooks and pins for aid work.

The climbing season at Black Canyon runs from early April through the first of November. Spring can be wet, with possible wind, rain and snow. Summer can be pretty hot, especially on south-facing routes. Climbs on the shadier walls of the North Rim might be the ticket during August heat. Fall is the perfect time to climb at the Black Canyon; with dry, warm days and cool nights the norm (although, winter storms can come early at the canyon on occasion.)

All climbs (excepting bouldering at Marmot Rocks) are within the designated Wilderness Area of the Park's Inner-Canyon and you will need to obtain a free **backcountry permit** at either the North Rim Ranger Station or the South Rim Visitor Center. Both places have self-registration materials out front for after hours check in. (See page 106 for more information about obtaining permits for activities in the Inner-Canyon.) An extensive "climber's notebook" is kept at both the North Rim Ranger Station and the South Rim Visitor Center for reference. You can copy the descriptions and topos, but be wary of the accuracy of this stuff, as some of it is pretty ancient. There is now a **guidebook** for rock climbing in Black Canyon, available at the Visitor Center and at area retailers (consult the **Additional Reading** section on page 222.)

Don't underestimate the scope of undertaking a climb from the depths of the gorge. Unless your prepared for bivying on the wall and hauling pounds of equipment, the best strategy is to be prepared and competent enough to complete these long, arduous routes in a day. Besides a full complement of standard **big wall gear**, you'll need plenty of water (2-4 quarts per person per day), clothing to stay warm and dry in the event of bad weather, and emergency bivy gear. You should also have a second rope to facilitate retreat. Rescue is difficult-to-impossible in this terrain. Be prepared mentally and physically for anything.

Approaches range from descending draws on simple hiker's trails, to arduous, multi-raps down gullies choked with boulders, brush and ticks. Along the river are many bivy sites; but also, there's poison ivy in abundance. What follows are some suggestions for the major climbing walls; but the possibilities (including, for new routes) are endless. Consult the guidebook and the rangers for details about the routes, approaches and bivy sites.

Be aware that popular areas, like Painted Wall, can be **seasonally closed** to climbing to protect the nesting sites of peregrine falcons and other raptors. For exact dates (usually May to July) each year, contact the Park. Also, **power drills** are banned in the Park.

Bouldering

Marmot Rocks are a set of boulders with generally solid rock where climbers can tackle "problems" unroped at heights (usually no more than 20 feet off the ground) that aren't considered fatal in the case of a fall. To get there, park at the **Painted Wall Overlook** on the South Rim Drive and walk west along the road toward Cedar Point Overlook until it bends to the right. Look for a worn path to the left (south), leading in 100 feet or so to the collection of boulders.

Pick up a copy beforehand of the free **Marmot Rocks Bouldering Guide** at the South Rim Visitor Center, describing 19 boulder problems rated from "easy" (suitable for beginners) to "very difficult" (with moves equivalent to a *Yosemite rated* 5.11 or 5.12.) The easier routes tend to follow a crack system, while harder ones are usually up steep faces. The landing areas are generally level and clear.

North Rim Routes

Despite the fact that climbs on the south-facing cliffs and buttresses can be unbearably hot at times, the immense walls of the North Rim have traditionally captured climber's attention and offered the most routes at the Black Canyon. In summer, dark rock can be almost too hot to touch and it can be nearly impossible to bring enough water for a 25-pitch route — obvious from such route names as **High and Dry**, **Dry Hard** and **Swallow Wall**. Rock quality varies tremendously — from excellent to terrible — often on the same climb. Approach routes are generally fast and simple, and the walk-offs for many of the most popular routes are only minutes away from the access road and the North Rim Campground.

North Chasm View Wall has good access, reputedly the best rock in the canyon and has been a focus of climbing development for decades with dozens of established routes. The wall's east and south routes are approached by **Cruise Gully**; a very steep, boulder-filled draw that drops down the east face. Access it by walking east from the campground entrance on the North Rim Drive for about 50 yards, picking up a path south through the scrub oak. A pair of rappels is required to reach the bottom. Some of the more popular routes accessed from here include: **Leisure Climb** (II 5.9 R), one of the canyon's shorter climbs with good rock and adequate protection, but requires a confident lead on the crux pitch; **Musical Partners** (III 5.10 R), seven pitches following cracks and shallow grooves; **Journey Home** (IV 5.10-), one of the finest routes in the canyon that climbs a classic corner; **The Cruise** (V 5.10+), among Colorado's best free routes on a classic 15-pitch line; its equally worthy variant **The Scenic Cruise** (V 5.10+), the most popular climb in Black Canyon and one of the best 5.10s in the country; **Hallucinogen Wall** (VI 5.10 A3), one of the finest big walls in the canyon and sees lots of ascents each year; **Air Voyage** (V 5.12a), a modern testpiece, very airy with plenty of difficult crack climbing; **Stoned Oven** (V 5.11+), a very sustained and serious off-width crack climb; and **No Pig Left** (V 5.12 A1), a difficult, recent effort destined to be a classic.

Sitting just below the rim and accessed by scrambling east from near the base of Cruise Gully, **Checkerboard Wall** has a few very good lines on its small buttress, ranging from 4 to 8 pitches. The best is certainly **The Checkerboard Wall** (III 5.10 R), with a very exhilarating face climb.

S.O.B. Draw is a relatively easy way down to the river (see Inner-Canyon Route #29, page 200) and is popular with hikers, fisherman and climbers intent on some classic routes. Several good lines are part way down the gully, climbing obvious aretes or the slabby buttress on your left. The **Casual Route** (II 5.8) is one of the better introductory climbs in Black Canyon with 4 or 5 pitches. There are several variations to the route, including **Casually Off-Route** (II 5.9) which also offers a moderate route on fairly clean rock. **Comic Relief** (III 5.10) follows a very elegant and sustained hand crack, then an equally fine corner. **Lauren's Arete** (III 5.8) is a long knife-edge arete up the middle of the gully; while **The Russian Arete** (IV 5.9) is further down the draw and has several routes, including an old Layton Kor/Larry Dalke climb that is still very popular with moderate climbers.

Painted Wall has long been like an irresistible magnet for big wall climbers, intrigued about scaling Colorado's tallest rock wall, despite the fact that rock quality is not always the best. From the bottom of S.O.B. Draw, follow the river downstream for less than an hour to the base of the wall. There are flat, sandy, bivy sites along the riverbank. Of the numerous choices that draw climbers, the **Forest-Walker** (VI 5.10+ A2), the original route on the main face, is still popular, climbing a large corner system dubbed "Death Valley." **Stratosfear** (VI 5.11+ X), the longest free climb in Colorado at 30 pitches and considered a Black Canyon testpiece, has the same start, but veers off into a very bold and spectacular route, where protection is limited and the route finding murky. **The Southern Arete** (V 5.10) climbs a combination of cracks at the bottom, then ascends the headwall with the exciting crux near the top.

Long Draw (see Inner-Canyon Routes, page 202) offers a quick and easy approach to a couple of buttresses towering above this narrow gully. **Great White Wall** (IV 5.10) is on the left while descending the draw and features a prominent right-facing corner at the top. **Tourist Route** (IV 5.9) starts only a few yards further down the gully, climbing the same wall by a wandering route that is "hard" for such a moderate-rated climb. **Shattered Glass** (IV 5.11) is on the right of the gully, directly below Balanced Rock View. As the name implies, there is some very loose climbing on this difficult route.

South Rim Routes

The South Rim offers excellent climbs on the shady north-facing side of the canyon that can be a refuge from the summer heat. However, most routes on South Rim walls are much more difficult to reach than those on the North Rim.

Access to the popular climbs in and around **Chillumstone Gully** are via the deep, scree-filled ravine where the namesake chockstone forces a double-roped rappel. It is important to start the correct ravine, as all others cliff out. Drive to **Devils Overlook** on the South Rim Drive and walk 0.25 mile west along the road to the first main gully below the guardrail, where the road bends to the left. Once past the 160 foot rappel, several high-quality climbs present themselves on either side of the draw. **Cimarron Slabs** (III 5.8) is on the right, an enjoyable, moderate route for those comfortable with some runout. **Ground Control to Major Tom** (III 5.8) is nearby, joining Cimarron Slabs near the top; and likewise, it requires a leader competent with runout climbing. The excellent and sustained **Blackjack** (III 5.10-) is perhaps the most popular route in this area. It's on the left side after the rappel and follows the obvious, classic dihedral.

Huge **South Chasm View Wall** has several major routes, but none can be reached without major effort. Recently, the most common way to get down has been a multi-stage rappel through fixed anchors near the **Astro Dog** route, dubbed the *Astro Slog*. At times, climbers also have set up a tyrolean traverse across the river from S.O.B Draw. Speaking of the 14-pitch Astro Dog (V 5.11+), it is the acknowledged classic on South Chasm View Wall and one of the best free climbs in the canyon. **The Black Hole** (VI 5.12b) has great summer shade and offers quality crack-climbing, joining Astro Dog over its last few pitches. Another interesting route, **The South Rim Route** (V 5.11-), wanders up an arete on the western side of the wall.

Currently, only three outfitters have been approved by the Park Service to operate **guided rock climbs** in the Black Canyon (see page 228 for details.)

CONQUERING THE PAINTED WALL

The **San Juan Mountaineers** made the first serious attempts to climb the sheer walls of the Black Canyon, including the Curecanti Needle, in the 1930s. Their climbs, while important, did not cause a rush among climbers to the Black Canyon; but they did demonstrate the difficulty and dangers associated with climbing at the Black Canyon.

Early climbs tended to follow pronounced ribs extending from canyon floor to rim. San Juan Mountaineer, **Melvyn Griffiths**, described his experience climbing in the Black Canyon in 1932:

"…the climbs on the ribs are more inviting than the descents into the canyon. Perhaps this is due to the psychology born of the surroundings. On such a descent, one leaves a bright, sunny world behind and climbs down into a rocky, forbidding hole eighteen hundred feet below the warm, inviting soil above, a hole which is filled with the terrifying boom of the river and the gloomy, grotesque aspects of water-worn rock. One comes away with an overwhelming realization of the titanic forces of nature. Since the normal procedure is reversed, the ascent following the descent, one will do well to watch his time, remembering that it will take him longer to get back out than it took him to descend . . ."

Mel Griffiths noted the difficulty of the climb and stated that ". . . the surface has not been scratched as yet. This short treatment of a few climbs only hints at the exploration which remains to be made."

Explorations of routes continued but the greatest challenge, **Painted Wall**, Colorado's highest cliff, remained unclimbed. With the boom of climbing in the 1960s and 1970s, several important climbs took place, including several attempts on the Painted Wall. Bob LaGrange and **Layton Kor** pioneered a 1700-foot route up the cliffs of the South Rim. In 1963, Layton Kor returned to the Black Canyon, accompanied by Jim McCarthy and Ted Bossier, where they made a first attempt of a 1700-foot route at Chasm View. The route took three and a half days, with two bivouacs, and featured climbing through overhangs and a section of bad rock. One overhanging pitch took Kor eight hours to climb. The route is so difficult that it may not have been climbed since. Kor returned a year later with Larry Dalke and pioneered yet another route at Chasm View. He later wrote that it ". . . is one of the most difficult climbs in the area, comparable with the north face of Sentinel Rock via the Steck-Salathe route [in Yosemite]."

The first serious attempts to climb the Painted Wall on the north side of the Black Canyon began in the early 60s. In 1962, Kor climbed the northern arête with Jim Disney; and in 1967, climbed the southern arête accompanied by Larry Goss and Mike Covington. Each time Kor carefully studied the main face of the Painted Wall for a possible route. His attempt there came later in 1967, along with Bob Culp and Larry Dalke. Beginning at the center of the wall, rotten rock immediately presented the first of several difficulties. After a series of pitches, they met an overhang that ended the climb. Two more attempts were made on the Painted Wall in the late 1960s, and both failed again.

Attempts by some of the best climbers of the day failed; until finally, success was achieved in 1972. **Bill Forrest** and **Kris Walker** carefully studied a series of telephoto photographs carefully taken by Forrest from the South Rim. The climbers poured over the photographs for weeks hoping to define a route that would work with nuts and pitons, avoided the time-consuming and rock-damaging expansion bolts used on earlier attempts. The climb began on April 23, 1972. Camping at the base of the wall, the two climbers started up, requiring two days to arrive at a point just eight hundred feet up. A heavy storm moved in, and with snow falling, they decided to leave the ropes in place and descend. Two days later, after the storm's passing, the climbers returned, spending an additional day hauling equipment and food to the point achieved three days before.

The climb progressed without further incident until April 30, when Walker in the lead loosened a huge rock that, if it fell, would strike and probably kill Forrest. He tried to ease it out, since pushing it back into place proved impossible, and direct its fall into a crevice that would guide it away from Forrest. Walker warned Forrest that the rock was going to fall and let it go. The huge boulder missed the crevice, and instead, careened directly for Forrest. Believing this to be the end, both men waited. Thankfully, the rock just missed Forrest and broke into pieces far below. Terrified by the incident, Forrest could hardly continue; but after ascending three more pitches and some four hundred vertical feet, he came to grips with his fear and the climb continued.

On the next day, the climbers reached a point fifteen hundred feet up the face. There they entered a 500-foot high, steep crack system with a great deal of loose rock. The belayer had to be constantly alert to rock fall from the climber overhead. This dangerous area of the climb they dubbed "Death Valley." Now at 2000 feet and with only 500 feet more to go, Forrest and Walker bivouacked and planned the next day's climb.

Their bivouac lay directly under the summit; but they faced huge overhangs, with both men wondering if they could actually get through them. Retreat would be impossible because of all the loose rock they had passed through; and it would be unlikely a rescue team could reach them. On May 3, Forrest led the next pitch. He related his feelings and sense of the climb in a later interview, "This was probably the most difficult pitch I've ever done in my life. I got to a point where I couldn't go any higher. I thought if I tried to go down, all my pins would come out."

Forrest devised a way to complete the climb. A pendulum system would allow a traverse to be made to a climbable area. To affect the maneuver, he needed to get to a higher point. So he drilled a hole for a *skyhook*, making this the only bolt used in the entire climb. He then successfully pendulumed over to a crack. Walker soon followed. In two more pitches, the Painted Wall had been climbed for the first time; in all, taking eight days. Forrest's and Walker's achievement is one of the greatest in Colorado's climbing history. The difficulty of this route on Painted Wall has earned a Grade VI rating.

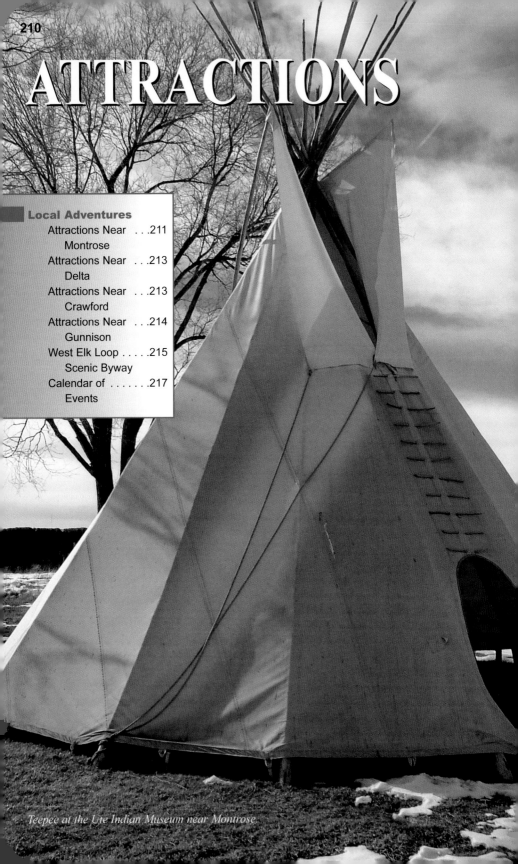

ATTRACTIONS

Teepee at the Ute Indian Museum near Montrose.

LOCAL ADVENTURES

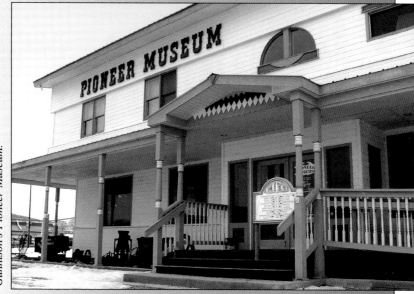

Gunnison's Pioneer Museum.

From cowboys to Indians, from cherished antiques to colorful aspen, a visit to some of the fascinating attractions in the Gunnison, Uncompahgre and North Fork Valleys can easily be combined with your trip to the Black Canyon of the Gunnison National Park to create a weekend, or much more, of fun Colorado adventures! Good sources of information on attractions in the area are the **Chambers of Commerce** in Gunnison, Montrose, Delta and Crawford (for contact info, see the **Local Facilities** section starting on page 116.)

We list some of the happenings in the area under a **Calendar of Events**. There are a number of special events, festivals, workshops, classes and other fun, interesting things to do in the area, especially during the warmer months. Most are annual events that have been held for years; others turn up on the calendar for the first time.

Attractions Near Montrose

History buffs and train enthusiasts will want to visit the historic Denver and Rio Grande Western Depot building that now houses the **Montrose County Historical Museum**. The building itself is wonderfully preserved with much of its original character intact, including the freight scales still in working order. The museum collection focuses on early pioneer life and railroad memorabilia; including an extensive collection of wagons and buggies, farm machinery and tools, household wares, period clothing and a completely furnished homesteader's cabin. Photographs and old newspapers from about 1880 to the

210 N. Rio Grande Avenue
Montrose, CO 81401
(970) 249-2085
web site: www.visitmontrose.net/museum

1940s are available for research. The museum is open mid-May through September, Monday through Saturday from 9 a.m. to 4:30 p.m., and on Sundays from 1-5 pm. There is a fee charged for admission.

You can continue your pursuit of local history by picking up a copy of a free map/brochure at the museum on an **historic walking tour** that explores interesting sites around town. Or if you prefer to own your own piece of history, ask for the map/brochure of the **Montrose Antique Trail** to an array of shops that offer everything from the vintage collectible to finely crafted furniture. There is actually an "antique row" of sorts with several shops grouped together a few miles south of town off the east side of CO-550.

Want to get the "big picture" of the Big Hole? Take advantage of small plane tours through the Black Canyon of the Gunnison run by **Samaritan Aviation**, an international outreach organization that meets the needs of people in remote areas of the world. For a donation ($25 minimum per person suggested), they'll take you up for a one hour scenic flight to view the spectacular gorge. Schedule your flight by contacting them at ☎ *(970) 249-4341.*

The **Ute Indian Museum** sits in the heart of traditional Ute wintering grounds in the Uncompahgre Valley on land once homesteaded by Chief Ouray. Located about three miles south of town on US-550, the museum commemorates the Utes, Chief Ouray and his wife Chipeta who is buried on the grounds. Recently expanded and remodeled, the center now includes the Chief Ouray Memorial Park, a native plants garden, a marker about the Dominquez-Escalante Expedition of 1776, a Visitor Information Center, gallery space, classrooms and a museum store. There are shady picnic areas, and teepees are often set up for visitors to explore. The **Montrose Visitor Information Center** is also located at the museum to give you info on other Montrose attractions. Parking and use of the picnic area and grounds are free, but the museum charges $3 (seniors $2.50 and children $1.50) for admission. It's open year-round, except for Christmas and New Year's Day. Summer hours (mid May to mid-October) are 9 a.m. to 4:30 p.m. on Monday through Saturday, and Sundays, 11 a.m. to 4:30 p.m. In winter, it's 9 a.m. to 4:30 p.m. Monday through Saturday only.

17253 Chipeta Road
Montrose, CO 81401
☎ *(970) 249-3098*
(970) 252-8741 FAX

There are beautiful metal sculptures on the side of the museum.

Attractions Near Delta

Delta is known as "the city of murals" for the **11 murals** (a twelfth is in the works) scattered throughout the city that showcase local artists. You can pick up a copy of the "Mural Tour Guide" at several locations in town. The huge works of art are easy to spot on the sides of downtown businesses along Main Street, depicting local connections, for instance *fruit labels*!

Speaking of fruit (or vegetables, for that matter), the Uncompahgre Valley and surrounding mesas are some of

Mural along Delta's Main Street.

the richest agricultural lands in Colorado, producing a cornucopia of food stuffs. You'll want to sample some of the famous local fare at the numerous **roadside stands** in Delta County. Try along CO-92 between Delta and Hotchkiss, and continue north along CO-133 to Paonia, from late June through October for cherries, apricots, plums, peaches, pears, apples, plus various vegetables. Olathe, just 11 miles south of Delta on US-50, is known for its delicious sweet corn.

Step back in time to the 1820s, when **Fort Uncompahgre**, near the confluence of the Gunnison and Uncompahgre Rivers at present day Delta, was a thriving fur-trading post, run by Antione Robidoux. You can experience that exciting time again through knowledgeable and authentically dressed interpreters that guide you through experiences such as trapping beaver, making buckskin, working the forge, and going twelve months between baths (just kidding about that last one!) Actually, this tour is educational, plus a fun family activity — like visiting the original post! The **Fort Uncompahgre Living History Museum** is open March through September, Tuesday through Saturday from 10 a.m. to 4 p.m. Admission is a very reasonable **$5** ($4 for kids and seniors).

205 Gunnison River Drive
Delta, CO 81416
(970) 874-8349

Attractions Near Crawford

The tranquil beauty of Crawford Country seems to attract artists and craftspeople, as there are an unusually large contingent of creative types in this small village working in pottery, glass, and other media. **K Dahl Art Studios** is one of the small studios offering tours of their hot glass shop,

202 Fir Avenue
Crawford, CO 81415
(970) 921-6160
email: info@kdahlglass.com

as well as their stained glass and sculpting studio. They don't blow 2100° F molten glass every day, so call ahead for the current schedule. They craft everything from lamps and lighting, to bowls and vases.

FEES (as of 2004)
▌ **$7** day-pass per vehicle
▌ or **$55** for an annual *Colorado State Parks Pass*, which may be purchased at the Park entrance. Colorado residents who are 62 years of age or older are eligible to purchase a **$27** *Aspen Leaf Annual Pass*
▌ Camping fee, **$12** per night or **$16** for electrical sites

Colorado has an extensive system of State Parks, known for excellent camping and recreational facilities. **Crawford State Park**, just a mile or two south of town on CO-92, is one of the nicest and is also very convenient as a base for exploring the North Rim area of the Black Canyon of the Gunnison. The Park is built around a reservoir, with two hiking trails on either side. The wide, gentle-sloped east side trail is excellent for wheelchair or disabled visitors. There is good fishing for perch (no limit), crappie, channel catfish, largemouth bass and northern pike; as well as boating, waterskiing and scuba diving. For more information, ☎ *(790) 921-5721* or you can email them at ✉ *crawford.park@state.co.us*.

Attractions Near Gunnison

102 S. Main Street
Gunnison, CO 81230
☎ *(970) 641-4029*
✉ *email: gcarts@gunnison.cc*

The **Gunnison Arts Center** invites you to experience the arts in the Gunnison Valley. The center's facilities include two exhibition galleries, a 75-seat theatre, a dance studio and classrooms. They have music concerts nearly weekly, as well as exhibits of local artists in various visual media.

Gunnison's past as an early railroad hub and pioneer settlement comes to life at the town's **Pioneer Museum**, located at the east end of town off US-50. You can't really miss it — there's an old Denver and Rio Grande Western railway locomotive parked out front! The museum itself is open from mid-May to mid-September, Monday through Saturday from 9 a.m. to 5 p.m. and Sundays from 1 p.m. to 5 p.m. They have a collection of stuff from the early days, including farm implements and clothing, as well as an interesting collection of arrowheads and minerals. Admission is **$7** (kids 6 to 12 pay $1). Of particular interest might be

At Gunnison's Pioneer Museum.

a tour of the famous **Aberdeen Quarry**, just a few miles outside of town, where granite was quarried for many important buildings, including the Colorado State Capitol. The museum folks run jeep tours out there in the summer. You can sign up at ☎ *(970) 641-4530*.

What the heck is a *lek?* Well, let's just say that it's kind of a dating scene for birds. And not just for any bird. We are talking a rare bird indeed — the **Gunnison sage grouse**, a candidate for designation as an endangered species. Birders may visit the **Waunita Lek** to observe the grouse's bizarre courtship display from late March to mid-May. Go east on US-50 for 19 miles from Gunnison, turn north on County Road 887, and stop in 0.6 miles at a small turn-off where you can view the birds with binoculars or spotting scopes. Arrive BEFORE sunrise and REMAIN IN your vehicle, so as not to disturb or stress the birds. For more info, contact the **Colorado Division of Wildlife** at ☎ *(970) 641-7063*.

West Elk Loop Scenic Byway

Curecanti NRA lies at the heart of a state-designated, scenic drive through some of western Colorado's most magnificent scenery, offering a slice of the state's rich history and varied lifestyles. The **West Elk Loop Scenic/Historic Byway**, one of 21 scenic byways in Colorado, circumnavigates the **West Elk Mountains** — traveling the length of beautiful Blue Mesa Reservoir, contouring the rim of Black Canyon, passing through the classic western ranchlands and fruit producing areas of the North Fork, climbing up through shimmering aspen forests to crest a mountain pass, and finishing with a tour through an historic mining district. The byway travels through a great variety of microclimates. The North Fork Valley's mild climate is perfect for growing bumper crops of delicious fruit; while the Gunnison Valley has some of the coldest winters on record in the state. The contrast between the dry, barren adobe hills south of Hotchkiss and the lush, flower-strewn meadows of 10,000-foot Kebler Pass is amazing.

The 160-mile loop described here is an all-day affair with many possible side trips and great photo opportunities along the way. It is over two-laned, paved and gravelled roads, suitable for all vehicles. With warm days, cool-crisp nights, and hillsides resplendent in fall colors, September to early October is a perfect time to experience the West Elk Loop. (Note that the road over Kebler Pass is closed in winter, usually from November through May.) What follows is a brief outline of attractions along the byway — for an enjoyable and detailed account of the entire scenic/historic byway, pick up a copy of *Elk Mountains Odyssey* by Paul Anderson and Ken Johnson, available in local bookstores.

Our tour begins and ends in the old railroad town of **Gunnison**. Travel west on US-50, entering Curecanti National Recreation Area in about 5.0 miles. The highway winds along the shoreline of Blue Mesa Reservoir, crossing it at scenic **Middle Bridge**. The quiet, summer-cottage community at **Sapinero** was once a rip-roaring railhead for the Denver and Rio Grande Western, first abandoned by the line in 1949, then relocated by the lake's rising waters in the 1960s.

Turn right onto CO-92 just after crossing the Lake Fork Arm and descend to impressive **Blue Mesa Dam**. CO-92 begins its serpentine climb along the rim of upper Black Canyon and then over Black Mesa into Crawford Country. Skirting the northern edge of Curecanti NRA, this is an exceedingly beautiful drive

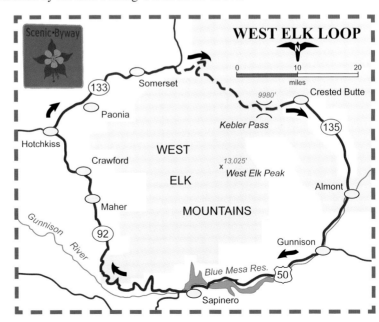

with several scenic overlooks that exploit striking views of the canyon and the high peaks of the San Juan Mountains. The highway roughly follows the route that early cattlemen took their herds over Black Mesa to the railhead at Sapinero, cresting the mesa at 9,000-foot **Morrow Point**, before beginning a winding descent into **Crawford Country**. The landscape changes from aspen and fir-covered slopes, to scrub and open rangeland. For an interesting side trip at Crawford, turn right on FSR-712 next to the post office, following it east for a few miles to view the local landmark, **Needle Rock**, a spectacular volcanic plug exposed by erosion.

Continuing north from Crawford, jackrabbits, prairie dogs and lots of contented cows dot the dry, adobe hills until the highway crosses the gently-flowing North Fork at **Hotchkiss**. Turn right onto CO-133, following it north into the fertile, fruit-growing region of the upper North Fork Valley. Roadside stands, bursting with offerings of newly ripened cherries, apples or peaches, entice with samples. The orchards and vineyards surrounding **Paonia** are some of the highest in the world, thriving in

Welcoming sign at Paonia.

a "banana-belt" of sorts in this sheltered valley beneath Lands End Peak.

The highway courses north into a narrowing valley, through the historic, coal-mining towns of Bowie and Somerset. Just below Paonia Reservoir, turn right onto gravelled **Kebler Pass Road** (Gunnison County Rd. 12) and begin the climb up into the cool forests of the West Elk Mountains. Rugged **Marcellina Mountain** is the showpiece up the valley, and Mount Gunnison and Beckwith Mountain, honoring early explorers of the region, are in view to the south of the road. The entire western slope of the range is clothed in a shimmering display of **quaking aspen**, believed to be "the largest continuous aspen forest in the world." The peak time to experience this drive is usually the second or third week in September, when the hillsides blaze with gold and red.

Marcellina Mountain.

The road crests among meadows filled with gorgeous summer wildflowers on **Kebler Pass**, before descending past relics from gold rush days into the lush valley around **Crested Butte**. For an interesting side trip, turn and follow the signs to **Lake Irwin**, to explore a high-country ghost town beneath the colorful Ruby Range. Mining once ruled Crested Butte; now a major ski resort, fueled by 300 inches of powder snow each winter. Go through town and turn south onto CO-135 for the 28-mile run down the valley, passing an eclectic blend of new trophy homes and century-old cattle ranches, through **Almont** where the East and Taylor Rrivers combine to form the Gunnison River, finishing the West Elk Loop back at the town of Gunnison.

Calendar of Events

FEBRUARY

Gunnison ▮

The annual **Winter Carnival** features a variety of activities on Main Street for all ages, from snow sculpture to a human polar bear dive. Will it be cold enough to keep the sculptures from melting? *You've just got to be kidding!* For exact dates this year, ☎ *(970) 641-1229.*

MARCH

Montrose ▮

It's a long way from Dublin, or Boston for that matter, to western Colorado. But that doesn't stop these cowboys from the wearing of the green. Come watch the marchers as Montrose conducts their annual **St. Patrick's Day Parade**. There almost certainly will be green beer somewhere. For information, call ☎ *(970) 240-1414.*

APRIL

Gunnison ▮

The annual **Kiwanis Club Blue Mesa Fishing Tournament** is a fund raiser for that club and lasts over a couple weekends in late April and early May. The ice will be long gone and the fish should be bitin'. Prizes are awarded for hauling in the lunkers. To pre-register, ☎ *(970) 641-8000.*

MAY

Hotchkiss ▮

Dog lovers will be thrilled to watch the amazing interplay between handler and man's best friend, as they compete in teams to herd their wooly friends at the **Sheep Camp Stock Dog Trails** this spring in Hotchkiss. For more information, ☎ *(970) 872-3226.*

JUNE

Crawford ▮

Every June, Crawford celebrates its rich heritage as a western ranching community with **Pioneer Days**, a three-day weekend of festivities including a parade with Pioneer Day's Queen and King, a melodrama, a pancake breakfast, baking contests, arts and crafts booths featuring many local artists, barbeques and a spectacular fireworks finale at Crawford State Park at dusk. *Whew!* You'll see lots of western characters and perhaps step in a couple cow pies, but it's all good family fun. For more information on the exact dates this year, ☎ *(970) 921-4000* or visit 🖱️ *www.crawfordcountry.org/chamber_events.htm.*

Calendar of Events

▌ Montrose

The annual, 6 or 7 day **Ride the Rockies** bicycle event in mid to late June follows a different route into the Rocky Mountains each year, but the route for the 2,000 cyclists included a stop in Montrose on several different occasions from 1991-2002. See if the odds are in your favor this June by visiting ⊟✓ *www.ridetherockies.com* or ☎ *(303) 820-1338.*

▌ Delta

Late June come to the Delta for the **Deltarado Days**, the county's oldest festival. Generally the fun is kicked off on a Friday night and runs through the weekend with a parade, rodeos and lots of family activities, like a horseshoe tournament and square dancing — there's excitement everywhere you turn! ☎ *(866) 289-2765* for dates and more details.

J ULY

▌ Gunnison

Succulent smells and sweet sounds come together at the **Chuck Wagon Cookoff and Writing the West Contest** featuring an old-fashioned cookoff with wagons from all over the United States, followed by a Western music concert. Call for dates at ☎ *(970) 641-1501* or email them at ⊟✓ *info@gunnisonchamber.com.*

July is also **Cattlemen's Days**, a nearly week long celebration of stock raising with a parade, horse and stock shows, cowboy poetry readings, barrel racing, roping, and, what's billed as, the oldest rodeo in the West (102nd anniversary in 2004). There's something going on every day and plenty for the family to enjoy. Call for dates at ☎ *(970) 641-1501* or email them at ⊟✓ *info@gunnisonchamber.com.*

A UGUST

▌ Olathe

While an admittedly corny affair, the **Olathe Sweet Corn Festival** is also a lot of fun for the family. Each year, the crowd of about 20,000 manages to consume about 70,000 ears of the "best sweet corn on the planet;" apparently taking advantage of all-you-can-eat. There's more than corn; including agricultural exhibits and live entertainment each night. Admission is **$8** per day, or $25 for an all-events, all-weekend pass. For more info and exact dates, ☎ *(970) 874-8616.*

▌ Montrose

The last week of July and into the first part of August is the traditional time for the **Montrose County Fair**, one of the largest in the area. For more information and the exact dates this year, contact the Montrose Visitors and Convention Bureau at ☎ *(970) 240-1414* or go to their website at ⊟✓ *www.visitmontrose.net.*

Calendar of Events

SEPTEMBER

Crawford ▌

Render the Rock is an annual invitation to artists worldwide to capture the majesty of Needle Rock, a local volcanic monolith and symbol of Crawford Country. The weekend event culminates with an auction of the artists' works with the proceeds going to various community improvements. Artists have from dawn to dusk to create their masterpieces. Contact the event's organizers at ☎ *(970) 921-4000* or visit ✉ *www.crawfordcountry.org/chamber_events.htm.*

Delta ▌

Feel your heart pound to the beat of Indian drums at the **Annual Council Tree Pow Wow and Cultural Festiva**l, a three-day, not-to-be-missed experience that celebrates the Ute tribes and the City of Delta. The name commemorates a 200-year old cottonwood tree that had long been a meeting place between Chief Ouray and the Utes and white settlers in the area. The colorful event features traditional dancing, drums and vendors; as well as other cultural activities. For the exact dates, contact ☎ *(970) 921-4000,* or email ✉ *counciltree@doci.net.*

Gunnison ▌

Gunnison County is where the whole mountain biking craze started way back in the 1970s and it's still a big thing today with the locals. That's why the competition is sure to be stiff in the **24 Hours In The Sage Race**, a mountain bike trial at nearby Hartman Rocks. For info and to register, call ☎ *(970) 641-0285.*

NOVEMBER

Crawford ▌

Don't miss the **Crawford Town Lighting and Parade of Lights** over a three-day weekend at the end of this month. Crawford becomes a village of lights with an exciting parade, special entertainment, extended shop hours, wagon rides and a craft fair. For exact dates, ☎ *(970) 921-4000* or visit ✉ *www.crawfordcountry.org/chamber_events.htm.*

Montrose ▌

What can match the sight of two dozen, spectacularly colored, hot air balloons rising above Columbine Field against a backdrop of Black Canyon and the Rocky Mountains? The annual **Black Canyon Balloon Classic** is scheduled for the end of November with balloonists from Colorado and all over the country. Call for details, ☎ *(970) 240-1414.*

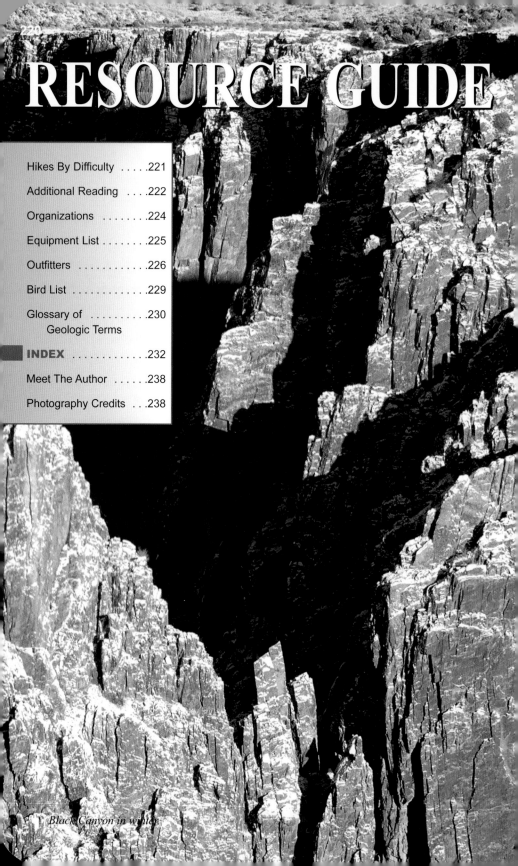

RESOURCE GUIDE

Black Canyon in winter

Checking the map.

HIKES BY DIFFICULTY
(Mileages are "round-trip")

Difficulty	Name of Trail/Route	Starting Location	Mileage	Km	Feet	Meters	Duration
Easy	Rim Rock Trail	South Rim Campground	1.0	1.7	200	61.0	1 Hour
Easy	Oak Flat Loop Trail	South Rim Visitor Center	2.0	3.2	350	106.7	2 Hours
Easy	Uplands Trail	South Rim Visitor Center	1.0	1.7	100	30.5	1 Hour
Easy	Cedar Point Nature Trail	Cedar Point Parking Area	0.6	1.0	40	12.2	1 Hour
Easy	Warner Point Nature Trail	High Point Parking Area	1.5	2.4	200	61.0	2 Hours
Easy	Chasm View Nature Trail	North Rim Campground	0.3	0.5	40	12.2	1 Hour
Easy	Neversink Trail	Never Sink Picnic Area	1.5	2.4	40	12.2	1 Hour
Easy	Cooper Ranch Trail	Cooper Ranch Picnic Area	0.5	0.8	50	15.2	1 Hour
Easy	Pine Creek Trail	Pine Creek Parking Area	2.0	3.2	200	61.0	2 Hours
Easy	Mesa Creek Trail	Morrow Point Dam Overlook	1.5	2.4	100	30.5	2 Hours
Moderate	North Vista Tr. to Exclamation Pt.	North Rim Ranger Station	3.0	5.0	120	36.6	3 Hours
Moderate	North Vista Tr. to Green Mtn.	North Rim Ranger Station	7.0	11.2	900	274.4	Half Day
Moderate	Deadhorse Trail	Kneeling Camel View Parking Area	5.0	8.3	300	91.5	Half Day
Moderate	Dillon Pinnacles Trail	Dillon Pinnacles Picnic Area	4.0	6.7	300	91.5	3 Hours
Moderate	Curecanti Creek Trail	Pioneer Point Overlook Parking Area	4.0	6.7	900	274.4	Half Day
Moderate	Crystal Creek Overlook Trail	Crystal Creek Picnic Area	5.0	8.3	300	91.5	Half Day
Moderate	Chukar Trail	Chukar Trail Parking Area	2.2	3.7	560	170.7	3 Hours
Moderate	Bobcat Trail	Bobcat Trail Parking Area	3.0	5.0	800	244.0	Half Day
Moderate	Duncan Trail	Duncan Trail Parking Area	3.0	5.0	900	274.4	Half Day
Moderate	Ute Trail	Ute Trail Parking Area	9.0	14.4	1,200	365.8	Full Day
Moderate	N. Fork to Smith Fork Trail	Gunnison Forks Day Use Area	4.0	6.4	200	61.0	Half Day
Difficult	Hermits Rest Trail	Hermits Rest Parking Area	6.0	10.0	1,800	548.8	Full Day
Difficult	Black Ridge Trail	Ute Trail Parking Area	20.0	33.3	3,900	1189.0	Full Day
V. Difficult	Gunnison Route	South Rim Visitor Center	2.0	3.2	1,800	548.8	Full Day
V. Difficult	Echo Canyon Route	Rock Point Overlook Parking Area	1.5	2.4	1,600	487.8	Full Day
V. Difficult	Tomichi Route	South Rim Campground	2.0	3.2	1,960	597.6	Full Day
V. Difficult	Warner Route	High Point Parking Area	5.4	9.0	2,660	811.0	Two Days
V. Difficult	East Portal Route	East Portal Campground	4.0	6.7	300	91.5	Full Day
V. Difficult	S.O.B. Draw Route	North Rim Campground	3.6	6.0	1,800	548.8	Full Day
V. Difficult	Long Draw Route	Balanced Rock Overlook Parking Area	2.0	3.2	1,800	548.8	Full Day
V. Difficult	Slide Draw Route	Kneeling Camel View Parking Area	2.0	3.2	1,620	494.0	Full Day
V. Difficult	Poison Spring Route	Kneeling Camel View Parking Area	2.9	4.8	1,600	487.8	Full Day

ADDITIONAL READING

NATURAL HISTORY

Black Canyon of the Gunnison National Park.
Web site: http://www.nps.gov/blca.

Black Canyon Video, The. Great Divide Pictures L.L.C., 1998.

Colorado Division of Wildlife. Web site: http://wildlife.state.co.us/view.

Curecanti National Recreation Area.
Web site: http://www.nps.gov/cure/home.

Gunnison Gorge National Recreation Area.
Web site: http://www.co.blm.gov/ubra/gorgenca.htm

Hansen, Wallace R. *The Black Canyon of the Gunnison: Today And Yesterday.* (Geological Survey Bulletin 1191.) U.S. Government Printing Office, Washington D.C., 1965.

Houk, Rose. *Curecanti National Recreation Area.* Southwest Parks and Monuments Association, Tucson, Arizona, 1991.

Honk, Rose. *Black Canyon of the Gunnison.* Southwest Parks and Monuments Association, Tucson, Arizona, 1991.

Magley, Robb. *Deep Black: An Adventure Through the Black Canyon.* Western Reflections Printing Company, Montrose, Colorado, 2002.

Parker, Trocy Scott. *South Rim Driving Tour Guide.* Southwest Parks and Monuments Association, Tucson, Arizona, 1993.

Peterson, Roger Tory. *A Field Guide to Western Birds.* Houghton Mifflin Company, Boston, Mass., 1961.

Skelton, Renee, *A Kids Guide to Exploring Black Canyon of the Gunnison National Park.* Western National Parks Association, 2003.

Zaenger, Paul L. *Beyond the Brink of Time: A Walking Guide for the Chasm View Nature Trail.* National Park Service with the Southwest Parks and Monument Association, Tucson, Arizona, 2000.

Zaenger, Paul L. *A Walk with Mark Warner: A Walking Guide for the Warner Point Nature Trail.* National Park Service with the Southwest Parks and Monument Association, Tucson, Arizona, 1996.

CULTURAL HISTORY

Andersen, Paul and Ken Johnson, *Elk Mountains Odyssey.* Redstone Press, Carbondale, Colorado, 1998.

Bueler, William M. *Roof of the Rockies: A History of Colorado Mountaineering.* Colorado Mountain Club Press, Golden, Colorado, 2000.

Colorado Railroad Historical Foundation. *Narrow Gauge Transcontinental.* Colorado Railroad Historical Foundation, Golden, Colorado, 1991.

Colorado Railroad Historical Foundation. *Scenic Line of the World.* Colorado Railroad Historical Foundation, Golden, Colorado, 1977.

Pettit, Jan. *Utes, The Mountain People.* Johnson Books, Boulder, Colorado, 1990.

Smith, David P. *Ouray, Chief of the Utes.* Wayfinder Press, Ridgway, Colorado, 1990.

HIKING

Blomquist, Geraldine Molettiere and Paul B. Blomquiat. *Hiking the Gunnison River Basin.* Wayfinder Press, Ridgway, Colorado, 2001.

Hirschfeld, Cindy. *Canine Colorado.* Fulcrum Publishing, Golden, Colorado, 2001.

Jacobs, Randy, Robert M. Ormes. *Guide to the Colorado Mountains.* Colorado Mountain Club Press, Golden, Colorado, 2000.

Pearson, Mark, Fielder, John. *Colorado's Canyon Country.* Westcliffe Publishing, Englewood, Colorado, 2001.

Walter, Claire. *Snowshoeing Colorado.* Fulcrum Press, Golden, Colorado, 1998.

Warren, Scott. *100 Classic Hikes in Colorado.* The Mountaineers Books, Seattle, Washington, 2001.

ROCK CLIMBING

Coyne, Leonard. "The Black Canyon," *Rock & Ice Magazine - No. 20.* Eldorado Publishing Company, Boulder, Colorado, July/August 1987.

Green, Stewart M. *Rock Climbing Colorado.* Falcon Publishing, Inc., Helena, Montana 1995.

Lazar, Scott. "The Black Canyon," *Rock & Ice Magazine - No. 81.* Eldorado Publishing Company, Boulder, Colorado, October 1997.

Williams, Robbie. *Black Canyon Rock Climbs.* Sharp End Publishing, 2002.

MOUNTAIN BIKING

Alley, Sarah Bennett. *Bicycling America's National Parks: Utah and Colorado.* Countryman Press, 2000.

MAPS

Black Canyon of the Gunnison National Park #245. National Geographic/Trails Illustrated, Evergreen, Colorado, 2000.

ORGANIZATIONS

American Alpine Club
710 10th Street #100
Golden, CO 80401
(303) 384-0110
(303) 384-0111 Fax
www.americanalpineclub.org
A climbers' organization devoted to exploration of high mountain elevations, dissemination of information about mountaineering, conservation and preservation of mountain regions.

American Hiking Society
1422 Fenwick Lane
Silver Spring, MD 20910
(301) 565-6704
(301) 565-6714 Fax
www.americanhiking.org
A national organization dedicated to promoting hiking and to establishing, protecting and maintaining foot trails throughout the United States.

The Colorado Fourteeners Initiative
710 Tenth Street, Suite 220
Golden, Colorado 80401
(303) 278-7525
(303) 279-9690 Fax
www.coloradofourteeners.org
An organization to protect and preserve the natural integrity of Colorado's Fourteeners and the quality of the recreational opportunities they provide.

Colorado Mountain Club
710 10th Street #200
Golden, CO 80401
(303) 279-3080
(303) 279-9690 Fax
www.cmc.org
The largest hiking/climbing club in the Rocky Mountain Region. The club organizes over 2,000 hikes, ski trips, backpacking trips, and other outdoor activities annually; and offers numerous classes in mountain-related activities. The CMC has a chapter based in Montrose (called the *Sneffels Group*) which sponsors trips and outings to the Black Canyon.

Colorado Outward Bound School
910 Jackson Street
Golden, CO 80401
(720) 497-2400
(720) 497-2401 Fax
www.cobs.org
An educational institution dedicated to teaching wilderness-oriented skills and leadership, including backpacking and mountaineering courses.

Black Canyon Audubon Society
P. O. Box 1371
Paonia, CO 81428-1371
(970) 835-8867
www.western.edu/audubon/
A chapter of the national organization, based around the Black Canyon of the Gunnison, offering local field trips, events and programs open and free to the public.

Leave No Trace, Inc.
P.O. Box 997
Boulder, CO 80306
(800) 332-4100
(303) 442-8217 Fax
www.lnt.org
An organization whose mission is to promote and inspire responsible outdoor recreation through education and partnerships.

The Mountaineers
300 Third Ave West
Seattle, Wa 98119
(206) 284-6310
(206) 284-4977 Fax
www.mountaineers.org
The largest outdoor recreation and conservation club in the Puget Sound region with an extensive outing and outdoor education program.

National Outdoor Leadership School
284 Lincoln Street
Lander, WY 82520-2848
(307) 332-5300
(307) 332-1220 Fax
www.nols.edu
An educational institution dedicated to teaching wilderness-oriented skills and leadership, including backpacking and mountaineering courses.

EQUIPMENT LIST

THE 10 ESSENTIALS
Food
Water
Emergency shelter
Extra clothing
First aid kit
Flashlight
Map and compass
Matches/fire starter
Pocket knife
Sunglasses/sunscreen

When preparing for a hike, always start with the *Ten Essentials* as your foundation. Boots should be light but sturdy (no tennis shoes). Backpackers will want heavier, stiffer boots for good support. For clothing, modern synthetics, like polypropylene and pile, are light, insulate well and dry quickly. But traditional wool clothing is still effective, even when damp. Avoid cotton entirely, as it loses all insulating ability when wet. Effective, good-quality clothing and other gear will often determine the difference between a safe, enjoyable day in the canyon and an unpleasant, or even potentially disastrous, experience.

FOR DAY HIKING

- [ ] Day-pack:1500 to 3000 cubic inches
- [ ] Insulating layer: poly tops and bottoms
- [ ] Shirt or sweater: poly or wool
- [ ] Pants: poly or wool
- [ ] Parka shell: waterproof, windproof
- [ ] Pants shell: waterproof, windproof
- [ ] Hat
- [ ] Gloves: poly or wool
- [ ] Extra socks

Add for Winter Trips:
Cold-rated insulated clothing
Double boots or insulated foot wear
Face mask
Hand warmers
Snowshoes or skis, plus repair kit
Ski poles

FOR BACKPACKING

- [ ] Backpack: 3500 cubic in. or more
- [ ] Pack cover: waterproof
- [ ] Sleeping bag
- [ ] Sleeping pad
- [ ] Extra clothing
- [ ] Stove and fuel
- [ ] Cooking gear
- [ ] Eating utensils
- [ ] Food and food bags
- [ ] Tent or bivy sack
- [ ] Groundcloth: waterproof
- [ ] Personal toiletries
- [ ] Camp shoes
- [ ] Headlamp
- [ ] Repair kit and sewing kit

- [ ] Water filter and/or iodine tablets
- [ ] Plastic trowel: for catholes
- [ ] Plastic bags: for garbage
- [ ] Rope or cord

Optional Gear:
Pillow
Camera gear and film
Reading material and/or journal
Fishing gear
Binoculars
Camp chair
Radio and cell phone
Walking stick(s) or pole(s)

OUTFITTERS

Outfitters in Gunnison Gorge NCA

The following outfitters are the ONLY ones permitted by the BLM for commercial rafting, fishing, horse pack-ins and shuttle service within the **Gunnison Gorge National Conservation Area**. Check this list when booking trips in the NCA, or call the BLM ☎ *(970) 240-5300.*

RAFTING AND FLOATFISHING OUTFITTERS

GUNNISON RIVER EXPEDITIONS
Hank Hotz
P.O. Box 315
Montrose, CO 81402
(970) 249-4441 or (800)-297-4441
FAX: (970) 249-4441
Email: hhotze@gwe.net
http://www.cimarroncreek.com/
    FLYFISHING/FF_GRE.html

RIVER RATS
Bob Harris
P.O. Box 5929
Snowmass, CO 81615
(970) 923-4544
FAX: (970) 923-4994
Email: blazing@ros.net
http://www.blazingadventures.com

TELLURIDE OUTSIDE
Todd Herrick
POB 685
Telluride, CO 81435
(970) 728-3895 or (800)-831-6230
FAX: (970) 728-2062
Email: fun@tellurideoutside.com
http://www.tellurideoutside.com

DVORAK'S EXPEDITIONS
Bill Dvorak
17921 US Highway 285
Nathrop, CO 81236
(719) 539-6851 or (800)-824-3795
FAX: (719) 539-3378
Email: dvorakex@rmi.com
http://www.dvorakexpeditions.com
    /welcome.htm

WILDERNESS AWARE
Joe and Sue Greiner
P.O. Box 1550
Buena Vista, CO 81211
(719) 395-2112

FAX: (719) 395-6716
Email: rapids@inaraft.com
http://www.vtinet.com/inaraft/

ECHO CANYON RIVER EXPEDITIONS
Dave Burch
45000 US Highway 50 W
Canon City, Co 81212
(719) 2753154
FAX: (719) 275-5809
Email: echocanyon@worldnet.att.net

ADRIFT ADVENTURES
Pat Tierney
POB 192
Jensen, UT 84035
(800) 824-0150 or (800) 824-0150
FAX: (801) 781-1953
Email: info@adrift.com
http://www.adrift.com/welcome.htm

PEREGRINE RIVER OUTFITTERS
Tom Klema
64 Ptarmigan Lane
Durango, CO 81301
(970) 385-7600
FAX: (970) 259-7600
Email: whiteh2o@peregrineriver.com
http://www.peregrineriver.com/

**OUTDOOR LEADERSHIP
TRAINING SEMINARS**
Arkansas River Tours
Rick Medrick
POB 20281Denver, CO 80220
(303) 333-7831 or (800) 331-7238

GUNNISON RIVER PLEASURE PARK
Leroy Jagodinski
POB 32
Lazear, CO 81420
(970) 872-2525
Cjago270@cs.com
http://www.troutfisherman.net/

(Outfitters In Gunnison Gorge NCA con't.)

UPLAND FISHING OUTFITTERS

COLORADO CUTTHROAT ADVENTURES
Roger Cesario
P.O. Box 1116
Crested Butte, CO 81224
(970) 349-1228
FAX: (970) 349-0737
Email: flyrodmc@crestedbutte.net

TELLURIDE OUTSIDE
Todd Herrick
POB 685
Telluride, CO 81435
(970) 728-3895 or (800) 831-6230
FAX: (970) 728-2062
Email: fun@tellurideoutside.com
http://www.tellurideoutside.com

GUNNISON RIVER EXPEDITIONS
Hank Hotze
P.O. Box 315
Montrose, CO 81402
(970) 249-4441 or (800) 297-4441
FAX: (970) 249-4441
Email: hhotze@gwe.net
http://www.cimarroncreek.com
          /FLYFISHING/FF_GRE.html

GUNNISON RIVER PLEASURE PARK
Leroy Jagodinsk
POB 32
Lazear, CO 81420
(970) 872-2525
Cjago270@cs.com
http://www.troutfisherman.net/

HORSE OUTFITTER

J & RAY GUIDES & OUTFITTERS
Larry Franks
8310 6400 Road
Montrose, CO 81401
(970) 323-0115
Email: WbarX@aol.com
http://www.sportsmansdream.com/jray/

SHUTTLE SERVICE

GUNNISON RIVER PLEASURE PARK
Leroy Jagodinski
POB 32
Lazear, CO 81420
(970) 872-2525
Cjago270@cs.com
http://www.troutfisherman.net/

Pet Boarding

The following kennels are located in the Montrose and Gunnison areas. Read about **Hiking With Your Dog** on page 181.

ALTA VISTA VETERINARY CLINIC
1845 E. Main Street
Montrose, CO 81401
(970) 249-8185

DOUBLE DIAMOND KENNELS
23661 Horsefly Rd.
Montrose, CO 81401
(970) 249-3067

MONTROSE VETERINARY CLINIC
2260 S. Townsend
Montrose, CO 81401
(970) 249-5469

REDCLIFFE KENNELS
16793 Chipeta Rd.
Montrose, CO 81401
(970) 249-6395

SAN JUAN VETERINARY CLINIC
822 Spring Creek Blvd.
Montrose, CO 81401
(970) 249-4490

CRITTER SITTERS & OUTFITTERS
98 County Road 17
Gunnison, CO 81230
(970) 641-0460

TOMICHI PET CARE CENTER
106 S. 11th Street
Gunnison, CO 81230
(970) 641-2460

TOWN & COUNTRY ANIMAL HOSP.
525 Hwy 135
Gunnison, CO 81230
(970) 641-2215

Outfitters in Curecanti NRA

The following commercial outfitters are permitted by the National Park Service to operate within the **Curecanti National Recreation Area**.

GUIDED FISHING

CUTTHROAT ADVENTURES
P.O. Box 1116
Crested Butte, CO 81224
(970) 349-1228

FERRO'S BLUE MESA OUTFITTERS
P.O. Box 853
Gunnison, CO 81230
(970) 641-4671

GUNNISON FISH AND RAFT
P.O. Box 7122
Gunnison, CO 81230
(970) 641-6928

HIGH MOUNTAIN DRIFTERS
115 S. Wisconsin
Gunnison, CO 81230
(970) 641-4243

THREE RIVERS OUTFITTING
P.O. Box 339
Almont, CO 81210
(970) 641-1303

TROUTFITTER SPORTS CO.
313 Elk Ave.
Crested Butte, CO 81224
(970) 349-1323

KAYAKING

GUNNISON VALLEY ADVENTURES
P.O. Box 1845
Gunnison, CO 81230
(970) 641-5541

THE ROCK AT UTE TRAIL RANCH
1329 Hwy. 149
Powderhorn, CO 81243
(970) 641-0717

THREE RIVERS OUTFITTING
P.O. Box 339
Almont, CO 81210
(970) 641-1303

SCENIC RIVER TOURS
703 W. Tomichi
Gunnison, CO 81230
(970) 641-3131

RAFTING

CUTTHROAT ADVENTURES
P.O. Box 1116
Crested Butte, CO 81224
(970) 349-1228

SCENIC RIVER TOURS
703 W. Tomichi
Gunnison, CO 81230
(970) 641-3131

THREE RIVERS OUTFITTING
P.O. Box 339
Almont, CO 81210
(970) 641-1303

ROCK CLIMBING

GUNNISON VALLEY ADVENTURES
P.O. Box 1845
Gunnison, CO 81230
(970) 641-5541

HIKING & CAMPING

ADAPTIVE SPORTS CENTER
P.O. Box 1639
Crested Butte, CO 81224
(970) 349-5075

THE ROCK AT UTE TRAIL RANCH
1329 Hwy. 149
Powderhorn, CO 81243
(970) 641-0717

Outfitters in the NP

The following commercial outfitters have been approved by the National Park Service for guided rock climbs in **Black Canyon of the Gunnison National Park**.

GUNNISON VALLEY ADVENTURES
P. O. Box 1845
Gunnison, CO 81230
(970) 641-5541

SKYWARD MOUNTAINEERING
P. O. Box 323
Ridgway, CO 81432
(970) 209-2985

SAN JUAN MOUNTAIN GUIDES
P. O. Box 895
Ouray, CO 81427
(970) 325-4925

BIRD LIST

The following bird species have been sighted in Black Canyon of the Gunnison National Park. Of these, 23% are permanent residents and the rest are seasonal residents or species that migrate through the area. The Park requests that you turn in your sightings so that they may update their records.

- Mallard
- Canada Goose
- Common Merganser
- California Condor
- Turkey Vulture
- Red-tailed Hawk
- Northern Goshawk
- Cooper's Hawk
- Sharp-shinned Hawk
- Northern Harrier
- Golden Eagle
- Bald Eagle
- American Kestrel
- Prairie Falcon
- Peregrine Falcon
- Blue Grouse
- Sage Grouse
- Chukar
- Ring-necked Pheasant
- Turkey
- Great Blue Heron
- Killdeer
- Spotted Sandpiper
- Mourning Dove
- Rock Dove
- Band-tailed Pigeon
- White-throated Swift
- Black Swift
- Hammond's Flycatcher
- Dusky Flycatcher
- Gray Flycatcher
- Western Flycatcher
- Olive-sided Flycatcher
- Western Wood-Peewee
- Say's Phoebe
- Violet-green swallow
- Tree Swallow
- Barn swallow
- Saw Whet Owl
- Long-eared Owl
- Great Horned Owl

- Common Nighthawk
- Common Poor-will
- House Wren
- Canyon Wren
- Rock Wren
- Sage Thrasher
- American Robin
- Mountain Bluebird
- Hermit Thrush
- Townsend's Solitare
- Ruby-crowned Ringlet
- Golden-crowned Ringlet
- Blue-gray Gnatcatcher
- Loggerhead Shrike
- European Starling
- Solitary Vireo
- Warbling Vireo
- Gray Vireo
- Broad-tailed Hummingbird
- Black-chinned Hummingbird
- Rufous Hummingbird
- Belted Kingfisher
- Northern Flicker
- Hairy Woodpecker
- Downy Woodpecker
- Yellow-bellied Sapsucker
- Williamson's Sapsucker
- Lewis' Woodpecker
- Western Kingbird
- Ash-throated Flycatcher
- Gray Jay
- Scrub Jay
- Pinyon Jay
- Steller's Jay
- Black-billed Magpie
- Clark's Nutcracker
- Common Raven
- Mountain Chickadee
- Black-capped Chickadee
- Plain Titmouse
- Bushtit

- White-breasted Nuthatch
- Red-breasted Nuthatch
- Brown Creeper
- American Dipper
- Orange-crowned Warbler
- Tennessee Warbler
- Virginia's warbler
- Yellow-rumped Warbler
- Yellow Warbler
- Townsend's Warbler
- Black-throated Gray Warbler
- MacGillivray's Warbler
- Wilson's Warbler
- Red-winged Blackbird
- Brown-headed Cowbird
- Western Meadowlark
- Northern Oriole
- Brewer's Blackbird
- Western Tanager
- Gray Catbird
- Black-headed Grosbeak
- Evening Grosbeak
- Pine Grosbeak
- Northern Mockingbird
- Sage Thrasher
- Cassin's Finch
- House Finch
- Lazuli Bunting
- Pine Siskin
- American Goldfinch
- Red Crossbill
- Green-tailed Towhee
- Rufous-sided Towhee
- Gray-headed Junco
- Black-throated Sparrow
- Brewer's Sparrow
- Chipping Sparrow
- White-crowned Sparrow
- Vesper Sparrow
- Song Sparrow
- Lark Sparrow

GLOSSARY OF GEOLOGIC TERMS

Adobe Hills (or badlands): An area of intricate erosion, producing steep slopes, sharp ridge lines and a maze of ravines. The Mancos shale deposits of the western portion of Gunnison Gorge NCA have eroded into adobe hills.

Amphibolite: a metamorphic rock of medium to coarse grain composed of amphibole (generally hornblende) and plagioclase feldspar.

Basement Rock: the oldest rocks in a given area; the complex of igneous and metamorphic rocks that underlie all the sedimentary formations in the Black Canyon area.

Breccia: a volcanic rock of consolidated, large angular fragments. This rock is common along the rims of Curecanti NRA and in the surrounding West Elk and San Juan Mountains.

Caldera: a large, circular depression in volcanic terrain, typically originating from a collapse or explosion. The explosion of the La Garita Caldera, largest in the world, in the San Juan Mountains formed tuffs widely over the region.

Conglomerate: a sedimentary rock composed of rounded pebbles and small boulders; the rock equivalent of gravel.

Country Rock: the rock into which an igneous rock intrudes.

Crystal: a form of matter in which atoms or molecules are arranged regularly in all directions to form a regular, repeated network. Individual crystals, such as those that have formed in pegmatite bodies in the Black Canyon of the Gunnison, can be formed up to several yards across.

Dike: a body of igneous rock that has intruded while molten into fissures of the surrounding country rock. Dikes of pegmatite and diabase are very abundant in and around the Black Canyon of the Gunnison.

Fault: a fracture in the earth's crust along which there is relative displacement.

Gneiss: a coarse-grained metamorphic rock that shows banding and parallel alignment of unlike minerals. One of the most common rocks in the Inner-Canyon of the National Park.

Granite: a coarse-grained, intrusive igneous rock composed of quartz, orthoclase feldspar, sodium-rich plagioclase feldspar and mica.

Igneous Rocks: a rock formed by the solidification of magma, either at depth (intrusive) or on the earth's surface (extrusive.)

Joint: a fracture in a rock across which there is no relative displacement of the two sides. Erosion along joints in Inner-Canyon of the Black Canyon of the Gunnison have produced isolated islands or monoliths.

Laramide Orogeny: the mountain building episode that uplifted the Rocky Mountains.

Limestone: a sedimentary rock composed mostly of calcium carbonate, usually as the mineral calcite.

Metamorphic Rocks: a rock whose original composition has been changed due to the effects of temperature, pressure, or the gain or loss of chemical components.. The most common class of rocks in the Black Canyon of the Gunnison by volume.

Migmatite: a rock of both igneous and metamorphic characteristics that show large crystals and laminar flow structures, probably formed metamorphically in the presence of water and without melting.

Mineral: a naturally occurring, solid, inorganic element or compound with a definite composition, and usually possessing a regular internal crystalline structure.

Mudstone: a very fine-grained sedimentary rock, originating from mud and similar to shale but more massive.

Orogeny: a tectonic process where large areas are uplifted and folded in which mountain ranges are formed.

Pegmatite: an igneous rock with very large grains, usually a granite. In the Black Canyon of the Gunnison, pegmatite has intruded into fissures in older Precambrian rock.

Quartz monzonite: a granite-like igneous rock with more than 5% quartz and nearly equal amounts pf alkalic and soda-lime feldspars. A prevalent rock in the Inner-Canyon of the National Park and in upper Black Canyon of the Gunnison in Curecanti NRA.

Rock: a naturally formed aggregate of grains of one or more minerals, constituting most of the earth's crust.

Sandstone: a rock composed of cemented sand grains. A common rock in the top tier of the Gunnison Gorge's double canyon system.

Schist: a metamorphic rock characterized by strong foliation or parallel arrangement of sheet or prisms of minerals, oriented so that it tends to split in layers.

Sedimentary Rocks: a rock formed by the accumulation and cementation of mineral grains transported by wind, water or ice. The top tier of the Gunnison Gorge's double canyon system is overwhelmingly this class of rocks.

Shale: a very fine-grained sedimentary rock formed from consolidated mud or clays that splits along bedding planes.

Syncline: a large trough-like fold.

Talus: Coarse grained rock fragments, usually fist-size and larger, that have accumulated at the base of and derived from a cliff. Talus covered slopes are very common at the bottom of the Black Canyon of the Gunnison. **Scree** is considered to be rock fragments smaller than fist-size.

Tuff: a consolidated rock of small fragments and volcanic ash. If is is melted together by its own heat, it is a "welded tuff." This rock is common along the rims of Curecanti NRA and in the surrounding West Elk and San Juan Mountains.

Unconformity: a surface that separates two strata, representing an interval of time in which deposition stopped, erosion removed some sediments and rock, and deposition, resumed. There are several good examples on the rims of the Black Canyon of the Gunnison.

Volcano: any opening in the crust that has allowed magma to reach the surface, including the deposits immediately surrounding the vent. Massive amounts of volcanic activity took place in the West Elk and San Juan Mountains, north and south of the Black Canyon of the Gunnison.

Weathering: the process of decay and break up of bedrock by a combination of physical fracturing or chemical decomposition.

INDEX

MEET THE AUTHOR
and
PHOTOGRAPHY CREDITS

MEET THE AUTHOR

John Jenkins is a fourth generation Coloradan who grew up hearing stories of those who took part in the state's history, including early mining days, ranching, farming, and business. The author graduated with a history degree at Western State College in Gunnison. While there, the author became familiar with the Black Canyon and the Western Slope, with its colorful history. The author wrote the history of an important mining town in Gunnison County, White Pine, north of Sargents. Later, as a seasonal employee at the National Park Service, several historic works were completed, including an historic site survey at Yellowstone National Park, a mining study at Denali and Wrangell-St. Elias National Parks in Alaska, and several National Register Nominations. While an interpreter at Bent's Old Fort near La Junta, Colorado, the author filled the role of the "post trader," learning a great deal about Western and Colorado history.

A book written by Jenkins about avalanches that have occurred in Colorado since the Gold Rush was published in 2000. The author's outdoor pursuits include ultra-marathon running, telemark ski instructor, and backcountry skier and guide.

PHOTO AND ARTWORK CREDITS

All photography by **John Jenkins**, *except* as noted below. All copyrights are the property of the individual:

Courtesy, The **Colorado Mountain Club**: pages 63 (top), 72 (fourth from top), 155 (upper two), 204, 221, 239

Courtesy, the **National Park Service:** page 67 (fourth and fifth from top)

Courtesy, **Denver Public Library**, Western History Collection: pages 85 (DPL call #Z-1467), 87 (DPL call #X-30561), 88 (DPL call #OP-7933), 90 (DPL call #X-9364) , 91 (DPL call #Z-2969), 95 (DPL call #Z-1351)

Courtesy, **Colorado Historical Society**: page 83 (CHS call #X-3047)

Allen Russell/Index Stock Imagery: page 100

Charlie & Diane Winger: pages 63 (second, third and fourth from top), 149, 175

David Gaskill: pages 74

Joyce Gellhorn: pages 166 (third from top), 178 (lower)

Mike Endres: cover (inset), title page, 129

Terry Root: pages 51, 63 (fifth from top), 64 (fourth from top), 67 (first, second and third from top), 68 (all), 72 (first, second and third from top), 76, 89, 112, 113, 116, 117, 118, 119, 120, 122, 124, 126, 127, 138, 140, 147, 154, 163, 164, 166 (first and second from top), 168, 170, 181, 185, 186, 191, 192, 210, 211, 212, 213, 214, 216

Todd Caudle and *Skyline Press*: pages 3, 4-5, 16-17, 18 (background), 20, 21, 32, 38, 40, 52, 53, 54-55, 56-57, 59, 61, 96, 151, 153, 159, 162, 169, 220

Artwork: *Blackie, the Peregrine Falcon* by **Lisa Gardiner**

ABOUT THE COLORADO MOUNTAIN CLUB

The Colorado Mountain Club is a non-profit outdoor recreation, education and conservation organization founded in 1912. Today with over 10,000 members, 14 branches in-state, and one branch for out-of-state members, the CMC is the largest organization of its kind in the Rocky Mountains. *Membership opens the door to:*

Outdoor Recreation: *Over 3100 trips and outings led annually.* Hike, ski, climb, backpack, snowshoe, bicycle, ice skate, travel the world and build friendships that will last a lifetime.

Conservation: *Supporting a mission which treasures our natural environment.* Committed to environmental education, a strong voice on public lands management, trail building and rehabilitation projects.

Outdoor Education: *Schools, seminars, and courses that teach outdoor skills through hands-on activities.* Wilderness trekking, rock climbing, high altitude mountaineering, telemark skiing, backpacking and much more — plus the Mountain Discovery Program designed to inspire lifelong stewardship in children and young adults.

Publications: *A wide range of outdoor publications to benefit and inform members.* Trail and Timberline Magazine, twice-a-year Activity Schedule, monthly group newsletters, and 20% discount on titles from CMC Press.

The American Mountaineering Center: *A world-class facility in Golden, Colorado.* Featuring the largest mountaineering library in the western hemisphere, a mountaineering museum, a 300-seat, state-of-the-art auditorium, a conference center, free monthly program nights and a technical climbing wall.

Visit us at the beautiful American Mountaineering Center!

JOINING IS EASY!

Membership opens the door to:
ADVENTURE!

The Colorado Mountain Club
710 10th St. #200 Golden, CO 80401
(303) 279-3080 1(800) 633-4417
FAX (303) 279-9690
Email: cmcoffice@cmc.org
Website: www.cmc.org

ALSO AVAILABLE!

THE ESSENTIAL GUIDE TO GREAT SAND DUNES NATIONAL PARK & PRESERVE, *by Charlie & Diane Winger.* This complete recreational guide to our nation's newest National Park includes all the information you need on hiking, climbing, backpacking, camping, sand skiing/snowboarding and the history of this fascinating part of Colorado, plus full color maps and photos!

Celebrating Colorado's National Parks and Monuments

More Colorado titles for you to enjoy from the Colorado Mountain Club Press:

GUIDE TO THE COLORADO MOUNTAINS, 10th Edition, *edited by Randy Jacobs.* The complete guide to Colorado's peaks, passes, lakes and trails is more complete than ever with over 1500 hiking and climbing destinations and a ranked listing of the state's 200 highest summits. The best-selling Colorado book of all time, with nearly 1/4 million in print.

THE COLORADO TRAIL: THE OFFICIAL GUIDEBOOK, 6th Edition, *by The Colorado Trail Foundation..* Written for both through hikers or those doing a section at a time, this comprehensive guide has everything you need: detailed descriptions of every mile, resupply information, natural history, color maps and elevation profiles, and over 90 full-color photos. New features include over 800 GPS locations, plus *Gudy's Tips!*

THE COLORADO TRAIL: THE TRAILSIDE DATABOOK, 2nd Edition, *by The Colorado Trail Foundation..* Now there's a new resource for enjoying the spectacular 471-mile trail, perfect for backpackers or anyone interested in going light. Weighing only ounces but packed with an amazing amount of info, including campsites, watersources, distances, color maps and much more.

ROOF OF THE ROCKIES: A HISTORY OF COLORADO MOUNTAINEERING, 3rd Edition, *by William M. Bueler.* This revised edition of a mountaineering classic captures exciting tales of 200 years of Colorado climbing adventures, complete with archival photographs.

THE ANNUAL OFFICIAL COLORADO MOUNTAIN CLUB SCENIC CALENDAR: THE FOURTEENERS. This large, full-color wall calendar captures gorgeous images of the CMC's favorite peaks from CMC members and award-winning photographer Todd Caudle — *an annual favorite!*

COLORADO!
It's Your Place

Explore it with books from the experts in the Rockies
The Colorado Mountain Club Press   *Golden, Colorado*

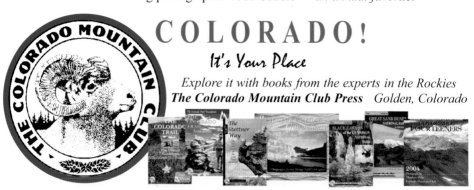